THE CALL

FINDING AND FULFILLING THE CENTRAL PURPOSE OF YOUR LIFE

Os Guinness

WORD PUBLISHING
Nashville · London · Vancouver · Melbourne

Unless otherwise indicated, Scripture references are from the Holy Bible, New International Version (NIV). Copyright © 1973, 1978, 1984, International Bible Society. Used by permission of Zondervan Bible Publishers.

The author expresses appreciation for permission to reprint from these sources:

Amadeus by Peter Schaffer. Copyright © 1980, 1981 by Peter Schaffer. Published by HarperCollins.

"The Memorial" from *Pensées* by Blaise Pascal, translated by A.J. Krailsheimer. Published by Penguin Classics.

"Who Am I?" by Dietrich Bonhoeffer from *Letters and Papers from Prison, The Enlarged Edition* © 1971 by SCM Press and by HarperCollins Publishers, Ltd.

Sonnet No. 285 from *The Poetry of Michelangelo*, translated by James M. Saslow. Published by Yale University Press.

Library of Congress Cataloging-in-Publication Data

Guinness, Os.
  The call : finding and fulfilling the central purpose of your life / Os Guinness.
    p. cm.
  ISBN 0-8499-1291-1
  1. Vocations—Christianity—Meditations. 2. Devotional calendars. I. Title.
BV4740.G85 1998
248.4—dc21   97–52654
                                                                   CIP

Printed in the United States of America
0 1 2 3 4 5 BVG 15 14 13 12 11 10

D.O.M.

and to C. J.

with love and gratitude.

Contents

Note: These chapters have been written as a series of individual meditations, to be read one day at a time.

1

THE ULTIMATE WHY

As you know, I have been very fortunate in my career and I've made a lot of money—far more than I ever dreamed of, far more than I could ever spend, far more than my family needs." The speaker was a prominent businessman at a conference near Oxford University. The strength of his determination and character showed in his face, but a moment's hesitation betrayed deeper emotions hidden behind the outward intensity. A single tear rolled slowly down his well-tanned cheek.

"To be honest, one of my motives for making so much money was simple—to have the money to hire people to do what I don't like doing. But there's one thing I've never been able to hire anyone to do for me: find my own sense of purpose and fulfillment. I'd give anything to discover that."

In more than thirty years of public speaking and in countless conversations around the world, I have heard that issue come up more than any other. At some point every one of us confronts the question: How do I find and fulfill the central purpose of my life? Other questions may be logically prior to and lie even deeper than this one—for example, Who am I? What is the meaning of life itself? But few questions are raised more loudly and more insistently today than the first. As modern people we are all on a search for significance. We desire to make a difference. We long to leave a legacy. We yearn, as Ralph Waldo Emerson put it, "to leave the world a bit better." Our passion is to know that we are fulfilling the purpose for which we are here on earth.

1

All other standards of success—wealth, power, position, knowledge, friendships—grow tinny and hollow if we do not satisfy this deeper longing. For some people the hollowness leads to what Henry Thoreau described "as lives of quiet desperation"; for others the emptiness and aimlessness deepen into a stronger despair. In an early draft of Fyodor Dostoevsky's *The Brothers Karamazov*, the Inquisitor gives a terrifying account of what happens to the human soul when it doubts its purpose: "For the secret of man's being is not only to live . . . but to live for something definite. Without a firm notion of what he is living for, man will not accept life and will rather destroy himself than remain on earth. . . ."

Call it the greatest good (*summum bonum*), the ultimate end, the meaning of life, or whatever you choose. But finding and fulfilling the purpose of our lives comes up in myriad ways and in all the seasons of our lives:

Teenagers feel it as the world of freedom beyond home and secondary school beckons with a dizzying range of choices.

Graduate students confront it when the excitement of "the world is my oyster" is chilled by the thought that opening up one choice means closing down others.

Those in their early thirties know it when their daily work assumes its own brute reality beyond their earlier considerations of the wishes of their parents, the fashions of their peers, and the allure of salary and career prospects.

People in midlife face it when a mismatch between their gifts and their work reminds them daily that they are square pegs in round holes. Can they see themselves "doing that for the rest of their lives"?

Mothers feel it when their children grow up, and they wonder which high purpose will fill the void in the next stage of their lives.

People in their forties and fifties with enormous success suddenly come up against it when their accomplishments raise questions concerning the social responsibility of their success and, deeper still, the purpose of their lives.

People confront it in all the varying transitions of life—from moving homes to switching jobs to breakdowns in marriage to crises of health. Negotiating the changes feels longer and worse than the changes themselves because transition challenges our sense of personal meaning.

Those in their later years often face it again. What does life add up to? Were their successes real, and were they worth the trade-offs? Having gained a whole world, however huge or tiny, have we sold our souls cheaply and missed the point of it all? As Walker Percy wrote, "You can get all A's and still flunk life."

This issue, the question of his own life-purpose, is what drove the Danish thinker Søren Kierkegaard in the nineteenth century. As he realized well, personal purpose is not a matter of philosophy or theory. It is not purely objective, and it is not inherited like a legacy. Many a scientist has an encyclopedic knowledge of the world, many a philosopher can survey vast systems of thought, many a theologian can unpack the profundities of religion, and many a journalist can seemingly speak on any topic raised. But all that is theory and, without a sense of personal purpose, vanity.

Deep in our hearts, we all want to find and fulfill a purpose bigger than ourselves. Only such a larger purpose can inspire us to heights we know we could never reach on our own. For each of us the real purpose is personal and passionate: to know what we are here to do, and why. Kierkegaard wrote in his *Journal*: "The thing is to understand myself, to see what God really wants *me* to do; the thing is to find a truth which is true *for me*, to find the *idea for which I can live and die*."

In our own day this question is urgent in the highly modern parts of the world, and there is a simple reason why. Three factors have converged to fuel a search for significance without precedent in human history. First, the search for the purpose of life is one of the deepest issues of our experiences as human beings. Second, the expectation that we can all live purposeful lives has been given a gigantic boost by modern society's offer of the maximum opportunity for choice and change in all we do. Third, fulfillment of the search for purpose is thwarted by a stunning fact: Out of more than a score of great civilizations in human history, modern Western civilization is the very first to have no agreed-on answer to the question of the purpose of life. Thus more ignorance, confusion—and longing—surround this topic now than at almost any time in history. The trouble is that, as modern people, we have too much to live with and too little to live for. Some feel they have time but not enough money; others feel they have money but not enough time. But for most of us, in the midst of material plenty, we have spiritual poverty.

This book is for all who long to find and fulfill the purpose of their lives. It argues that this purpose can be found only when we discover the specific purpose for which we were created and to which we are called. Answering the call of our Creator is "the ultimate why" for living, the highest source of purpose in human existence. Apart from such a calling, all hope of discovering purpose (as in the current talk of shifting "from success to significance") will end in disappointment. To be sure, calling is not what it is commonly thought to be. It has to be dug out from under the rubble of ignorance and confusion. And, uncomfortably, it often flies directly in the face of our human inclinations. But nothing short of God's call can ground and fulfill the truest human desire for purpose.

The inadequacy of other answers is growing clearer by the day. Capitalism, for all its creativity and fruitfulness, falls short when challenged to answer the question "Why?" By itself it is literally meaning-less, in that it is only a mechanism, not a source of meaning. So too are politics, science, psychology, management, self-help techniques, and a host of other modern theories. What Tolstoy wrote of science applies to all of them: "Science is meaningless because it gives no answer to our question, the only question important to us, 'what shall we do and how shall we live?'" There is no answer outside a quest for purpose and no answer to the quest is deeper and more satisfying than answering the call.

What do I mean by "calling"? For the moment let me say simply that *calling is the truth that God calls us to himself so decisively that everything we are, everything we do, and everything we have is invested with a special devotion and dynamism lived out as a response to his summons and service.*

This truth—calling—has been a driving force in many of the

4

greatest "leaps forward" in world history—the constitution of the Jewish nation at Mount Sinai, the birth of the Christian movement in Galilee, and the sixteenth-century Reformation and its incalculable impetus to the rise of the modern world, to name a few. Little wonder that the rediscovery of calling should be critical today, not least in satisfying the passion for purpose of millions of questing modern people.

For whom is this book written? For all who seek such purpose. For all, whether believers or seekers, who are open to the call of the most influential person in history—Jesus of Nazareth. In particular, this book is written for those who know that their source of purpose must rise above the highest of self-help humanist hopes and who long for their faith to have integrity and effectiveness in the face of all the challenges of the modern world.

Let me speak personally. I've written several books during the last twenty-five years, but no book has burned within me longer or more fiercely than this one. The truth of calling has been as important to me in my journey of faith as any truth of the gospel of Jesus. In my early days of following Jesus, I was nearly swayed by others to head toward spheres of work they believed were worthier for everyone and right for me. If I was truly dedicated, they said, I should train to be a minister or a missionary. (We will examine this fallacy of "full-time religious service" in chapter 4.) Coming to understand calling liberated me from their well-meaning but false teaching and set my feet on the path that has been God's way for me.

I did not know it then, but the start of my search (and the genesis of this book) lay in a chance conversation in the 1960s, in the days before self-service gas stations. I had just had my car filled up with gas and enjoyed a marvelously rich conversation with the pump attendant. As I turned the key and the engine of the forty-year-old Austin Seven roared to life, a thought suddenly hit me with the force of an avalanche: This man was the first person I had spoken to in a week who was not a church member. I was in danger of being drawn into a religious ghetto.

Urged on all sides to see that, because I had come to faith, my future must lie in the ministry, I had volunteered to work in a well-known church for nine months—and was miserable. To be fair, I admired the pastor and the people and enjoyed much of the work. *But it just wasn't me.* My passion was to relate my faith to the exciting and exploding secular world of early 1960s Europe, but there was little or no scope for that in the ministry. Ten minutes of conversation with a friendly gas pump attendant on a beautiful spring evening in Southampton, England, and I knew once and for all that I was not cut out to be a minister.

Needless to say, recognizing who we aren't is only the first step toward knowing who we are. Escape from a false sense of life-purpose is only liberating if it leads to a true one. Journalist Ambrose Bierce reached only halfway. "When I was in my twenties," he wrote, "I concluded one day that I was not a poet. It was the bitterest moment of my life."

Looking back on the years since my conversation at the gas station, I can see that calling was positive for me, not negative. Released from what was "not me," my discovery of my calling enabled me to find what I was. Having wrestled with the stirring saga of calling in history and having taken up the challenge of God's individual call to me, I have been mastered by this truth. God's call has become a sure beacon ahead of me and a blazing fire within me as I have tried to figure out my way and negotiate the challenges of the extraordinary times in which we live. The chapters that follow are not academic or theoretical; they have been hammered out on the anvil of my own experience.

Do you long to discover your own sense of purpose and fulfillment? Let me be plain. You will not find here a "one-page executive summary," a "how-to manual," a "twelve-step program," or a ready-made "game plan" for figuring out the rest of your life. What you will find may point you toward one of the most powerful and truly awesome truths that has ever arrested the human heart.

"In Ages of Faith," Alexis de Tocqueville observed, "the final aim of life is placed beyond life." That is what calling does. "Follow me," Jesus said two thousand years ago, and he changed the course of history. That is why calling provides the Archimedean point by which faith moves the world. That is why calling is the most comprehensive reorientation and the most profound motivation in human experience—the ultimate Why for living in all history. Calling begins and ends such ages, and lives, of faith by placing the final aim of life beyond the world where it was meant to be. Answering the call is the way to find and fulfill the central purpose of your life.

Do you have a reason for being, a focused sense of purpose in your life? Or is your life the product of shifting resolutions and the myriad pulls of forces outside yourself? Do you want to go beyond success to significance? Have you come to realize that self-reliance always falls short and that world-denying solutions provide no answer in the end? Listen to Jesus of Nazareth; answer his call.

2

SEEKERS SOUGHT

He was only sixty-four years old, but battered by the vagaries of life, he was taken to be in his seventies. Nearing the end of his life far from his sunlit Italy, burdened by the irreparable disintegration of his greatest masterpiece, and brooding on his life's grand failures, he was submerged in melancholy. Almost doodling perhaps, he took a sheet and drew a series of little rectangles. Each one stood for one of his life's great endeavors, the dreams and aspirations that had inspired his adult days as the greatest artist of his generation and probably the most versatile and creative inventor of all time.

First he sketched the little rectangles upright. But then, as if he'd pushed them, he drew them toppling one on top of another like collapsing dominoes. Underneath he wrote, "One pushes down the other. By these little blocks are meant the life and the efforts of men."

Who, knowing his story, could blame Leonardo da Vinci? Strong, handsome, gifted, self-reliant, and ambitious, he had set out in life with extraordinary assurance but refreshing modesty. When he was young and living in Florence, he had even copied into his notebook the verse:

> Let him who cannot do the thing he would
> Will to do that he can. To will is foolish
> Where there's no power to do. That man is wise
> Who, if he cannot, does not wish he could.

But da Vinci soon left such cautious modesty behind. Throughout his adult life, whether in Florence, Milan, Rome, or France, he was bent on stretching the limits of his powers. Some would say he merely exemplified the hard lot of artists amid the rivalries, jealousies, and favoritisms of the world of Renaissance art and its patrons. As Giorgio Vasari, the Renaissance artist and historian, wrote, "Florence treats its artists as time its creatures: it creates them and then slowly destroys and consumes them."

Others, both then and later, said that da Vinci would have been wiser to concentrate on a few gifts rather than the many that comprised his genius. This lack of focus, they said, was why he "procrastinated" while others, like Michelangelo, "produced." "Alas," Pope Leo X exclaimed dismissively of da Vinci, "this man will never get anything done, for he is thinking about the end before he begins." Vasari himself regretted that da Vinci had not kept to painting rather than pursuing his myriad inventions that were years, sometimes centuries, before their time.

But the real problem lay elsewhere. The creator of such peerless masterpieces as the *Last Supper* and the *Mona Lisa* was a passionate seeker with a voracious hunger for knowledge and a pressing sense of the fleeting nature of time. But da Vinci's creative gifts, his ardent pursuit of knowledge, and his awareness of the brevity of life all clashed to create a crushing sense that the pursuit of perfection was a tragic impossibility. It was always, "So little time. So much left undone." He could never accomplish more than a tiny part of all that his extraordinary mind had seen.

Only months before da Vinci died in 1519, he returned to the church of Santa Maria delle Grazie in Milan to discover that damp was already breaking through his fresco of the *Last Supper*. The maestro's greatest masterpieces were unfinished, destroyed, or decaying in his own lifetime. He could only conclude with sadness that all his vast knowledge and extraordinary inventions were unused, and his voluminous writings unpublished and inaccessible. One day, not long before he died at the royal palace of Cloux in the Loire Valley, he wrote in his notebook in unusually small script (as if, one writer commented, he were a little ashamed): "We should not desire the impossible."

Much of the greatness of the human spirit can be seen in our passionate pursuit of knowledge, truth, justice, beauty, perfection, and love. At the same time, few things are so haunting as the stories of the very greatest seekers falling short. Leonardo da Vinci's magnificent failures point to a very personal entry point to the wonder of calling—*when something more than human seeking is needed if seeking is to be satisfied, then calling means that seekers themselves are sought.*

A TALE OF TWO LOVES

The term *seeker* is in vogue today. This trend is unfortunate because its use in a shallow way obscures its real importance. Too often *seeker* is used to describe the spiritually unattached of the Western world. Seekers, in this loose sense, are those who do *not* identify themselves as Christian, Jew, Muslim, atheist, and so forth and who do *not* attend or belong to any church, synagogue, mosque, or meeting place.

Such seekers are rarely looking for anything in particular. Often they are drifters, not seekers, little different from the "hoppers and shoppers" who surf the media and cruise the malls of the postmodern world. Uncommitted, restless, and ever-open, they have been well described as "conversion prone" and therefore congenitally ready to be converted and reconverted *ad nauseam*—without the conviction that would stop the dizzying spin and allow them to be at home somewhere. Simone Weil, the Jewish philosopher and follower of Christ, disliked the casual arrogance of the term *seeker.* "I may say," she wrote in understandable reaction, "that never at any moment in my life have I 'sought for God.' For this reason, which is probably too subjective, I do not like this expression, and it strikes me as false."

True seekers are different. On meeting them you feel their purpose, their energy, their integrity, their idealism, and their desire to close in on an answer. Something in life has awakened questions, has made them aware of a sense of need, has forced them to consider where they are in life. They have become seekers because something has spurred their quest for meaning, and they have to find an answer.

True seekers are looking for something. They are people for whom life, or a part of life, has suddenly become a point of wonder, a question, a problem, or a crisis. This happens so intensely that they are stirred to look for an answer beyond their present answers and to clarify their position in life. However the need arises, and whatever it calls for, the sense of need consumes the searchers and launches them on their quest.

Notice that "a sense of need" does not justify people's believing. People do not come to believe in the answers they seek *because* of need—that would be irrational and make the believer vulnerable to the accusation that faith is a crutch. Rather, seekers *dis*believe in what they believed in before because of new questions their previous beliefs could not answer. The question of what and why they then come to believe is answered at a later stage. As Malcolm Muggeridge's biographer wrote of the conversion of the great English journalist, "He knew what he disbelieved long before he knew what he believed."

Notice, too, that seeking itself can be pursued from quite different perspectives and that these differences crucially affect the outcome of the search. Over the years I have talked with many seekers and have observed four major perspectives that structure their seeking. For most people two are less satisfactory, and two are worth considering more deeply, but only one is finally satisfying.

One less-satisfactory perspective is the attitude common to well-educated, more liberal people that the search is everything and discovery matters little. Often expressed in such phrases as "The search is its own reward" or "Better to travel hopefully than to arrive," such attitudes fit in well with modern skepticism about final answers and the modern prizing of tolerance, open-mindedness, ambiguity, and ambivalence.

For the serious seeker this view quickly proves unsatisfactory. An "open mind" can be an "empty head," and "tolerance" can be indistinguishable from believing nothing. These are no help in finding honest answers to honest and important questions. To think that it is "better to travel hopefully than to arrive" is to forget that hopeful travel is travel that hopes to reach a goal or destination. Self-condemned to travel with no prospect of arriving anywhere is the modern thinker's equivalent of the curse of the "flying Dutchman," condemned to perpetual wandering.

The other less-satisfactory perspective is the ancient South Asian view that desire itself is the problem. This view perceives desire not as a good thing that can go wrong but as essentially evil. Desires keep us bound to the world of suffering and illusion. The solution, therefore, is not to fulfill desire but to stop it, finally transcending it altogether in the state of "extinguishedness" called *nirvana*. Though it appears sophisticated, consistent, and practical within its own circle of assumptions, this Eastern view is radically world-denying. As such its appeal to a culture as world-affirming as ours is inevitably limited.

Thus, whether or not they realize it, most serious seekers turn from these unsatisfactory approaches and pursue their search from one of the two contrasting views of love that have shaped Western searching for the past three thousand years.

One view of love is the way of *eros*. It sees the search as "the great ascent" of humans toward their desired goal. For the Greeks in particular and the ancient world generally, *eros* was love as desire, yearning, or appetite aroused by the attractive qualities of the object of its desire—whether honor, recognition, truth, justice, beauty, love, or God. To seek is therefore to long to love and so to direct one's desire and love to an object through which, in possessing it, one expects to be made happy. From this perspective, seeking is loving that becomes desiring that becomes possessing that becomes happiness. For experience shows that "we all want to be happy," as Cicero said in *Hortensius*, and reasonable thought would indicate that the greatest happiness comes in possessing the greatest good.

The rival view of love is the way of *agape*, which sees the secret of the search as "the great descent." Love seeks out the seeker—not because the seeker is worthy of love but simply because love's nature is to love regardless of the worthiness or merit of the one loved. This view agrees with both the Eastern and the Greek views that desire is at the very core of human existence. But it agrees with the Greek view and differs from the Eastern in believing that desire itself is (or can be) good, not evil. The legitimacy of the desire depends on the legitimacy of the object desired. All human beings are alike in seeking happiness. Where they differ is in the objects from which they seek it and the strength they have to reach the objects they desire.

The way of *agape* is the way introduced by Jesus. It parts company with the way of *eros* at two points: the goals and the means of the search. First, the way of *agape* says, "By all means love, by all means desire, but think carefully about *what* you love and *what* you desire." Those who follow *eros* are not wrong to desire happiness but wrong to think that happiness is to be found where they seek it. The very fact that we humans experience desire is proof that we are creatures. Incomplete in ourselves, we desire whatever we think is beckoning to complete us.

God alone needs nothing outside himself, because he himself is the highest and the only lasting good. So all objects we desire short of God are as finite and incomplete as we ourselves are and, therefore, disappointing if we make them the objects of ultimate desire.

Our human desire can go wrong in two ways: when we stop desiring anything outside ourselves and fall for the pathetic illusion that we are sufficient in ourselves, or when we desire such things as fame, riches, beauty, wisdom, and human love that are as finite as we are and thus unworthy of our absolute devotion.

The way of *agape* insists that, because true satisfaction and real rest can only be found in the highest and most lasting good, all seeking short of the pursuit of God brings only restlessness. This is what Augustine meant in his famous saying in Book One of *Confessions*: "You have made us for yourself, and our hearts are restless until they find their rest in you."

Second, the way of *agape* parts company with the way of *eros* over the means of the search. Considering the distance between the creature and the Creator, can any da Vinci-like seeker—however dedicated, brilliant, virtuous, tireless, and however much a genius by human standards—hope to bridge the chasm? The answer, realistically, is no. We cannot find God without God. We cannot reach God without God. We cannot satisfy God without God—which is another way of saying that our seeking will always fall short unless God's grace initiates the search and unless God's call draws us to him and completes the search.

If the chasm is to be bridged, God must bridge it. If we are to desire the highest good, the highest good must come down and draw us so that it may become a reality we desire. From this perspective there is no merit in either seeking or finding. All is grace. The secret of seeking is not in our human ascent to God, but in God's descent to us. We start out searching, but we end up being discovered. We think we are looking for something; we realize we are found by Someone. As in Francis Thompson's famous picture, "the hound of heaven" has tracked us down. What brings us home is not our discovery of the way home but the call of the Father who has been waiting there for us all along, whose presence there makes home *home*.

THE MOUSE'S SEARCH FOR THE CAT?

The old story of "the seeker sought" is illustrated clearly in the journey to faith of C. S. Lewis, the Oxford philosopher and literary scholar who became the most respected and widely read religious author of the twentieth century. Later calling himself a "lapsed atheist," Lewis described the movements that shifted him from atheism to faith in Christ.

A critical phase in the first movement centered on Lewis's experiences of being "surprised by joy," described in his autobiography by the same name. Suddenly, without warning, ordinary everyday experiences triggered in him what he gropes to call a "memory," a "sensation," a "desire," a "longing" for something inexpressible and indefinable. Such experiences, he said, were of "an unsatisfied desire which is itself more desirable than any other satisfaction"—so much so that he cannot call it happiness or pleasure, which are too dependent on circumstances or the five senses; he must call it "joy."

Later, in his famous essay "The Weight of Glory," Lewis described these intimations as a "desire for our own far-off country . . . the scent of a flower we have not found, the echo of a tune we have not heard, news from a country we have never yet visited."

The jolt of these experiences moved Lewis out of atheism and made him a seeker. Each instance of being "surprised by joy" was simultaneously a contradiction and a yearning. The experiences were a contradiction of what he originally believed, his atheism, because they punctured and pointed beyond his secular, naturalistic worldview. They were also a yearning for something new because they pointed toward something transcendent without which he could not make sense of these yearnings he could equally not deny.

It was later, in the summer of 1929, that C. S. Lewis's search came to its climax. Strikingly, even though he had pursued his search with an intense engagement, he still spoke of this stage as the time when "God closed in on me." To his surprise, and even terror, he said, things suddenly lost their abstract, theoretical, arm's-length character:

> As the dry bones shook and came together in that dreadful Valley of Ezekiel's, so now a philosophical theorem, cerebrally entertained, began to stir and heave and throw off its graveclothes, and stood upright and became a living presence. I was to be allowed to play at philosophy no longer. It might, as I say, still be true that my "Spirit" differed in some way from the God of popular religion. My Adversary waived the point. It sank into utter unimportance. He would not argue about it. He only said, "I am the Lord"; "I am that I am"; "I am."
>
> People who are naturally religious find difficulty in understanding the horror of such a revelation. Amiable agnostics will talk cheerfully about "man's search for God." To me, as I then was, they might as well have talked about the mouse's search for the cat.

Looking back at the way his search suddenly culminated in the shock of his own arrest, Lewis remarked wryly: "Really, a young atheist cannot guard his faith too carefully."

Today the term *seeker* is often used promiscuously. Fortunately, experiences that require its true use are also on the rise. With

unbelief challenged as sharply as belief, and recent modern orthodoxies as much under fire as ancient traditional orthodoxies, an extraordinary new day for true seekers and true searching has begun. But
for those drawn to lives like da Vinci's, yet sobered by the tragic
impossibilities of finite, unaided human searching, the truth of calling holds out comfort and promise. We not only have Jesus' explicit
promise that seekers will find ("seek and you will find"), but we also
have his direct example to show that seekers themselves are sought.
Indeed, from the seeking wise men onward, Jesus is the greatest mag-
net for seekers in all history. The words given in Mark's Gospel to
Bartimaeus, the blind beggar who desperately sought healing from
Jesus, are God's encouragement to all who truly seek: "Take heart.
He is calling you."

*Do you long to know the One you have sought, knowingly or
unknowingly, as your heart's true home and one true desire?
Listen to Jesus of Nazareth; answer his call.*

3

THE HAUNTING
QUESTION

All who witnessed the stirring events of 1989 and the collapse of the Soviet Empire will have their own indelible memories of what was called "the year of the century"—the exultant dismantling of the Berlin wall, the flowers jauntily thrusting out of the gun barrels of Soviet tanks, and the toppling of the statues of Marx, Lenin, and Stalin. My favorite memories are accounts and images from the "Velvet revolution" in Czechoslovakia and in particular from the gigantic rallies in Wenceslas Square, Prague, in November 1989, with the spontaneous crowd responses and the mesmerizing speeches of a slim, boyish, mustachioed figure on the office balcony—Václav Havel.

Václav Havel became the internationally famous president of the free Czech Republic. But to his own people he was already well known as a playwright, a writer who spoke truth to the power of Soviet totalitarianism, and a dissident and founding spokesman for the Charter 77 Movement.

This last stance led Havel to two prison sentences—one, after a travesty of a trial, to four and a half years of hard labor in a "First Category Correctional Institution" in 1979. While there, Havel wrote *Letters to Olga*, a series of reflections on life in the guise of weekly letters to his wife. Self-published almost instantly in the Russian *samizdat* style, *Letters to Olga* has joined Dietrich Bonhoeffer's World War II *Letters and Papers from Prison* and Boethius's sixth-century *Consolation of Philosophy* as the three classic prison letters of the West.

Havel's weekly letters, always strictly censored and never certain to be delivered, were the only writing he was allowed to do. Soon they came to give meaning to his stay in prison. "The letters," he wrote later, "gave me a chance to develop a new way of looking at myself and examining my attitudes to the fundamental things in life. I became more and more wrapped up in them, I depended on them to the point where almost nothing else mattered."

In the letters Havel sets out like a classical hero on a quest. He is resolved to withstand all the tests fate and prison life put in his way. But soon he discovers that although he has mastered the physical difficulties of prison, he is faced with the far harder struggle of the meaning of life. In following this more perilous quest, Havel touches on many themes—such as the nature of faith and fanaticism, and the dehumanizing tendencies of the modern world. But one theme recurs repeatedly and swells to become central in the 144 letters—responsibility as the key to human identity.

For each of us our own identity matters supremely. Whatever other people think, whatever current philosophies say, whatever the ups and downs of life may suggest, we intuitively act and think as if we have supreme value. Simone Weil speaks for us all when she writes, "We possess nothing in this world other than the power to say I." But why? Considering how many millions of others are alive at the same time as we are, let alone the countless billions before us and after us, how can we explain this intuition against all odds?

Havel's mounting conviction is that "the secret of man is the secret of his responsibility." None of us arrives in this world complete, and none of us has the wisdom and strength to create ourselves by ourselves. Instead we grow and mature as we respond to what is outside us. But we do not just respond to other people or society, let alone to internal things like a conscience or our genes. Such responses are relatively trivial. At our highest and most human, we are responding to whatever is behind the world and life itself.

It is only by responding and growing responsible, Havel argues, that one "stands on one's own two feet." He then asserts what all his thinking has led him to: "I would say that responsibility for oneself is a knife we use to carve our own inimitable features in the panorama of Being; it is the pen with which we write into the history of Being that story of the fresh creation of the world that each new human existence always is."

A knife to carve our portraits on reality? A pen with which to write our stories on the scroll of history? Havel's images of the power of responsibility are vivid, and he goes on to describe this responsible view of human life as a conversation between the "I" and the "eye"—the "I" as we each see ourselves, and the "eye" behind everything to which we are responding. Elsewhere he uses the metaphor of a "voice" calling us. But he realizes he is begging the question. "Human responsibility, as the word itself suggests, is responsibility to something. But to what? What is this omnipresent, omnipotent and undeceivable instance of authority, and where in fact does it reside?"

Here Havel agonizes. If so much hangs on responsibility, then it matters infinitely to what or to whom we are responding. Clearly this "eye" or "voice" is higher than conscience and more urgent than close friends and public authorities. Indeed he gropes and insists it is from "someone eternal, who through himself makes me eternal as well . . . someone to whom I relate entirely and for whom, ultimately, I would do everything. At the same time, the 'someone' addresses me directly and personally."

"But who is it? God?" Havel cannot quite bring himself to that conclusion. But he admits that "for the first time in my life I stood— if I may be allowed such a comparison—directly in the study of the Lord God himself." Unfortunately for the letters but fortunately for him, Václav Havel did not stay in prison much longer, so the letters are a conversation cut off abruptly at his release and contain few tidy conclusions. But his wrestling reveals a deep contradiction and yearning in contemporary thinking.

On the one hand, each human identity assumes and requires responsibility. As Havel says, "Responsibility does establish identity, but we are not responsible because of our identity; instead we have an identity because we are responsible." On the other hand, the notion of responsibility and talk of "callings" remain bafflingly hollow unless there is something or Someone to whom we are responsible, or response-able, to whom we are able to respond. There is no calling unless there is a Caller.

THE BIOGRAPHY QUESTION

Václav Havel is rare among political leaders in today's world. But his passionate questionings parallel similar dilemmas at simpler levels. Together these wrestlings highlight another deeply personal entry point to seeing the importance of the truth of calling: *The notion of calling, or vocation, is vital to each of us because it touches on the modern search for a basis for individual identity and an understanding of humanness itself.*

Part of our contemporary crisis of identity can be summed up by saying that modern people are haunted by an inescapable question of biography: Who am I? From magazine covers to psychiatrists' couches to popular seminars, we are awash with self-styled answers to this question. But many people are dissatisfied with the answers peddled because they have a terrible deficiency: They don't explain what to each of us is the heart of our yearning—to know why we are each unique, utterly exceptional, and therefore significant as human beings.

Some years ago I came out of a friend's apartment on the Upper East Side of Manhattan to find an intense-looking man in his twenties standing outside what turned out to be his psychiatrist's office. He was pounding the slim telephone table in the hall and cursing vehemently. "Every time I go to that man I come out skewered to his categories like a butterfly pinned to a specimen board."

With feelings like that, I thought, he could have spent his money more wisely. But his point was unarguable. Many of the categories people offer to explain or heal us today are too general. In the case of my hallway acquaintance, the categories were also entirely negative. Thus Marxists interpret us by categories of class, Freudians by childhood neuroses, feminists by gender, and pop-commentators of all sorts by generational profiles—such as the "silent generation," the "baby boomers," the "Generations Xers." And so it goes.

In each case the perspectives may be relatively true or false, helpful or unhelpful, but they do not address the deepest questions: Who am I? Why am I alive? Being general, the categories never address us as individuals. At best our individuality is lost in the generality. At worst, it is contradicted and denied. Such categories force us to lie on their Procrustean bed, and anything about us that doesn't fit they lop off. They trim the picture of our personalities to fit their mass-produced frames.

All attempts to explain human individuality in general terms can be summed up as varieties of being "constrained to be." Their inadequacy is obvious. We become "prisoners" of our category, be it gender, class, race, generation, or ancestry. Our individuality is ignored.

A second and opposite position has equally obvious weaknesses—varieties of "the courage to be." As this view sees it, we all have the freedom—some see it as the terrible freedom—to be whatever we want to be. All it takes is courage and willpower. We can actually, we are told, "invent ourselves." A classical version of this position is William Shakespeare's Coriolanus who stood "as if a man were Author of himself, and knew no other kin." Similarly, John Keats later remarked, "That which is creative must create itself."

This position beckons to us in countless ways today. In a high society version, a French perfume maker currently sells its fragrance to the English-speaking market under the byline "*La vie est plus belle quand on l'écrit soi-même*" (Life is best played by your own script). Not so long ago, in more intellectual French circles, grand existentialist terms were used to portray the courage-to-be as a heroic stand of "authenticity" against "bad faith" and final absurdity. Closer to home this position often comes across as "be all you can be" (courtesy, for instance, of the United States Army), or more simply "just do it," "just be," "follow your dream," or "if you believe in yourself, you can accomplish anything."

Unquestionably, the most dangerous but alluring version of "the courage to be" comes from Friedrich Nietzche and his disciples. "God is dead," they assert, so meaning is not revealed. Nor can we read it off the pages of the universe, as advocates of the "fiction" of natural law believe. Instead, we start from the abyss of a world without meaning and, by sheer will power, create our own meaning out of nothing. Hence, the courage to be of the Superman.

According to Nietzche, we have only two choices—obey ourselves or be commanded—which leaves no choice to the heroes who wish to climb beyond the level of the herd to the highest mountains. They must summon their courage, take action on their own behalf, and become the individuals they are. To do so requires self mastery and will power. Their goal is to be able to say with Nietzche, "I have willed it thus."

In Western society at a more suburban level, "identity" has become our most important private project, and devotees of the grand pursuit of "identity construction" focus first and foremost on the body. Hence the enduring fascination with cookbooks, fitness manuals and diet programs, and the mind-boggling fortunes made through health foods, drugs, plastic surgery, body-care products, exercise gadgets, and "teach yourself" books of every kind.

Such self-construction is ceaseless and expensive. And, as the passion for public hygiene and safety, and the virulence of antismoking campaigns show, even politics becomes a form of body care by other means. After all, in the secular view the body is all we have and all we are. As one of the best-selling "bibles of macrobiotics" put it, "The kitchen is the studio where life is created . . . only you are the artist who draws the painting of your life."

The absurdity of this position is obvious for all but the rich, the strong, the wealthy, the young, and the fanatical. For one thing, even if we can do what we want, the question remains: What do we want? The near-omnipotence of our means of freedom doubles back to join hands with the near-emptiness of our ends. We do not have a purpose to match our technique. So, ironically, we have the greatest capacity when we have the least clue what it is for. Which makes us vulnerable to all the "expert services" whose "self-help" methods promise us everything we crave, but end in delivering to us new forms of constraint—and charging us for them.

For another thing, reality reminds us that all the will in the world may not make us what we want to become. When it comes to will power, will is common but power is rare. True identity is always socially bestowed more than self-constructed, so we cannot achieve it with do-it-yourself methods. In short, it takes more than "courage to be." If being "constrained to be" is unhelpful to us as individuals, being told that our individuality is all a matter of "the courage to be" is unrealistic. Little wonder that a third position is growing popular.

This third perspective views individuality as a matter of being "constituted to be." From our very birth, we are told, we bear the seeds of our eventual character; we carry the script of our life stories. Often described as the "acorn theory" and developed in the direction of New Age thinking, this view sees each of us as having not only a soul but also a soul-companion. This guardian-spirit, or "daemon," directs us even in the choice of our bodies and our parents. So the secret of life is to "read" our life stories and glimpse the guardian-spirit in action and give it free rein. Only so will the acorn become the oak and each of us grow to be the people we are constituted to be—by our personal destiny, or fate. "Everyone's nature," as Pablo Picasso expressed it, "is determined in advance." By starting from who we are as individuals, this position at least takes individuality seriously. But the words *fate* and *determined in advance* betray the failings of this third perspective.

Each of the three positions contains a grain of truth. To some extent we are all "constrained to be." An understanding of the many forces shaping us is invaluable. To that very extent we must also have the "courage to be"—if we are truly to be ourselves and not prisoners of our past and victims of our circumstances. And to a certain extent the "courage to be" will lie along the trajectory of what we are "constituted to be." But anyone who appreciates the significance of these three approaches and their shortcomings—and especially anyone who feels the force of his or her own passionate uniqueness—can truly see the wonder of the truth of calling.

Where each of these perspectives falls short or heads in the wrong direction, calling comes into its own. Instead of being "constrained to be," we are "called to be." The Caller sees and addresses us as individuals—as unique, exceptional, precious, significant, and free to respond. He who calls us is personal as well as infinite and personal in himself, not just to us. So we who are called are addressed as individuals and invited into a relationship ("I have called you by name," God said). We are known with an intimacy that is a source of gratitude and soul-shivering wonder ("Such knowledge," the psalmist wrote, "is too wonderful for me"). The notion of life as *karma,* or the belief that your future is unchangeably "written," is as far from the truth of calling as you can get.

Humanness is a response to God's calling. This is far deeper than the exhortation to write your own script for life. Responding to the call requires courage, but we are not purely on our own. The challenge is not solely up to us. A bootstraps rise is unnecessary as well as unrealistic. Responding to the call means rising to the challenge, but in conversation and in partnership—and in an intimate relationship between the called and the Caller.

In contrast to "constituted to be" and its sense that life is fated and predetermined, "calling to be" stresses freedom and the future. "Who am I?" is not simply a matter of "reading back" early recollections that intimate and announce our later destiny. God leads forward as we respond to his call. Following his call, we become what we are constituted to be by creation. We also become what we are not yet, and can only become by re-creation as called people.

After all, as Václav Havel wrote in his concluding letter on responsibility, "one's identity is never in one's possession as something given, completed, and unquestionable." Rather than a place to sit or a pillow on which to rest, human identity is neither fixed nor final in this life. It is incomplete. As such we may refuse the call and remain stunted—unresponsive and irresponsible. Or we may respond to the call and rise to become the magnificent creatures only one Caller can call us to be.

Is this a recipe for a faceless personality and a cramped life? On the contrary. As C. S. Lewis pointed out, "The more we get what we now call 'ourselves' out of the way and let Him take us over, the more truly ourselves we become." The alternative is the real disaster. "The more I resist Him and try to live on my own, the more I become dominated by my own heredity and upbringing and surroundings and natural desires. In fact what I so proudly call 'Myself' becomes merely the meeting place for trains of events which I never started and which I cannot stop."

Only when we respond to Christ and follow his call do we become our real selves and come to have personalities of our own. So when it comes to identity, modern people have things completely back to front: Professing to be unsure of God, they pretend to be sure of themselves. Followers of Christ put things the other way around: Unsure of ourselves, we are sure of God. No one has captured this tension more movingly than Dietrich Bonhoeffer from his cell in Berlin as the last days of his life and the last days of World War II ran out together.

Who Am I?

Who am I? They often tell me
I would step from my cell's confinement
calmly, cheerfully, firmly,
Like a squire from his country-house.

Who am I? They often tell me
I would talk to my warders
freely and friendly and clearly,
as though it were mine to command.

Who am I? They also tell me
I would bear the days of misfortune
equably, smilingly, proudly,
Like one accustomed to win.

Am I then really all that which other men tell of?
Or am I only what I know of myself,
restless and longing and sick, like a bird in a cage,

struggling for breath, as though hands were
    compressing my throat,
hungry for colours, for flowers, for the voices of birds,
thirsty for words of kindness, for neighbourliness,
trembling with anger at despotisms and
    petty humiliation,
caught up in expectation of great events,
powerlessly grieving for friends at an infinite distance,
weary and empty at praying, at thinking, at making,
faint, and ready to lay farewell to it all?

Who am I? This or the other?
Am I one person today, and tomorrow another?
Am I both at once? A hypocrite before others,
and before myself a contemptibly woebegone weakling?
Or is something within me still like a beaten army,
fleeing in disorder from victory already achieved?

Who am I? They mock me, these lonely questions
    of mine.
Whoever I am, thou knowest, O God, I am thine.

Do you want to know the secret of the mystery of your very being and rise to become what you were born to be? Listen to Jesus of Nazareth; answer his call.

4

EVERYONE, EVERYWHERE, EVERYTHING

One evening in 1787 a young English M.P. pored over papers by candlelight in his home beside the Houses of Parliament. Wilberforce had been asked to propose the Abolition of the Slave Trade although almost all Englishmen thought the Trade necessary, if nasty, and that economic ruin would follow if it stopped. Only a very few thought the Slave Trade wrong, evil."

So opened a fascinating lecture on William Wilberforce given by his biographer John Pollock at the National Portrait Gallery in London in 1996.

Wilberforce's research pressed him to excruciatingly clear conclusions. "So enormous, so dreadful," he told the House of Commons later, "so irremediable did the Trade's wickedness appear that my own mind was completely made up for Abolition. Let the consequences be what they would, I from this time determined that I would never rest until I had effected its abolition."

"That was a key moment in British and world history," Pollock told his audience. "For a few months later, on Sunday, October 28, 1787, he wrote in his Journal the words that have become famous: 'God Almighty has set before me two great objects, the suppression of the Slave Trade and the Reformation of Manners'—in modern terms, 'habits, attitudes, morals.'"

Amazingly, no great reformer in Western history is so little known as William Wilberforce. His success in the first of the "two great objects" was described by Pollock as "the greatest moral achievement of the British people" and by historian G. M. Trevelyan as "one of the turning events in the history of the world." His success in the second was credited by another historian with saving England from the French Revolution and demonstrating the character that was to be the foundation of the Victorian age. An Italian diplomat who saw Wilberforce in Parliament in his later years recorded that "everyone contemplates this little old man . . . as the Washington of humanity."

Equally amazingly, Wilberforce's momentous accomplishments were achieved in the face of immense odds. As regards the man himself, Wilberforce was by all accounts an ugly little man with too long a nose, a relatively weak constitution, and a despised faith—"evangelicalism" or "enthusiasm." As regards the task, the practice of slavery was almost universally accepted and the slave trade was as important to the economy of the British Empire as the defense industry is to the United States today. As regards his opposition, it included powerful mercantile and colonial vested interests, such national heroes as Admiral Lord Nelson, and most of the royal family. And as regards his perseverance, Wilberforce kept on tirelessly for nearly fifty years before he accomplished his goal.

Constantly vilified, Wilberforce was twice even waylaid and physically assaulted. A friend once wrote to him cheerfully: "I shall expect to read of you carbonadoed by West Indian planters, barbecued by African merchants and eaten by Guinea captains, but do not be daunted, for—I will write your epitaph!"

Perhaps most amazingly of all, William Wilberforce came within a hair's breadth of missing his grand calling altogether. His faith in Jesus Christ animated his lifelong passion for reform. At one stage he led or actively participated in sixty-nine different initiatives, several of world-shaping significance. But when Wilberforce came to faith through the "Great Change" that was his experience of conversion in 1785 at the age of twenty-five, his first reaction was to throw over politics for the ministry. He thought, as millions have thought before and since, that "spiritual" affairs are far more important than "secular" affairs.

Fortunately, a minister—John Newton, the converted slave trader who wrote "Amazing Grace"—persuaded Wilberforce that God wanted him to stay in politics rather than enter the ministry. "It's hoped and believed," Newton wrote, "that the Lord has raised you up for the good of the nation." After much prayer and thought, Wilberforce concluded that Newton was right. God was calling him to champion the liberty of the oppressed—as a Parliamentarian. "My walk," he wrote in his journal in 1788, "is a public one. My business is in the world; and I must mix in the assemblies of men, or quit the post which Providence seems to have assigned me."

CALLING—THE CORE

Sadly, for every follower of Christ who, like William Wilberforce, chooses not to elevate the spiritual at the expense of the secular, countless others fall for the temptation. Wilberforce's celebrated "near miss" therefore leads us to the heart of understanding the character of calling and the first of two grand distortions that cripple it. Earlier, I defined the notion of calling this way: *Calling is the truth that God calls us to himself so decisively that everything we are, everything we do, and everything we have is invested with a special devotion, dynamism, and direction lived out as a response to his summons and service.*

Now it is time to unpack that truth further, beginning with four essential strands in the biblical notion of calling that we must always hold.

First, calling has a simple and straightforward meaning. In the Old Testament the Hebrew word that has been translated as "call" usually has the same everyday meaning as our English word. Human beings call to each other, to God, and to animals. Animals too can call. (The psalmist, for example, wrote that God "provides food for the cattle and for the young ravens when they call.") Under the pressure of theology and history, the term *call* has traveled a long way from this simple beginning, but this straightforward sense and its obvious relational setting should never be lost. When you "call" on the phone, for example, you catch someone's ear for a season.

Second, calling has another important meaning in the Old Testament. To call means to name, and to name means to call into being or to make. Thus in the first chapter of Genesis, "God called the light 'day' and the darkness he called 'night.'" "This type of calling is far more than labeling, hanging a nametag on something to identify it. Such decisive, creative naming is a form of making. Thus when God called Israel, he named and thereby constituted and created Israel his people. Calling is not only a matter of being and doing what we are but also of becoming what we are not yet but are called by God to be. Thus "naming-calling," a very different thing from name-calling, is the fusion of being and becoming.

Third, calling gains a further characteristic meaning in the New Testament. It is almost a synonym for salvation. In this context, calling is overwhelmingly God's calling people to himself as followers of Christ. Just as God called Israel to him as his people, so Jesus called his disciples. The body of Jesus' followers as a whole is the community of the "called-out ones" (the origin of *ecclesia*, the Greek word for church). This decisive calling by God is salvation. Those who are called by God are first chosen and later justified and glorified. But calling is the most prominent and accessible of these four initiatives of God. Not surprisingly it often stands for salvation itself, and the common description of disciples of Jesus is not "Christian" but "followers of the Way."

Fourth, calling has a vital, extended meaning in the New Testament that flowers more fully in the later history of the church. God calls people to himself, but this call is no casual suggestion. He is so awe inspiring and his summons so commanding that only one response is appropriate—a response as total and universal as the authority of the Caller. Thus in the New Testament, as Jesus calls his followers to himself, he also calls them to other things and tasks: to peace, to fellowship, to eternal life, to suffering, and to service. But deeper even than these particular things, discipleship, which implies "everyone, everywhere, and in everything," is the natural and rightful response to the lordship of Christ. As Paul wrote the followers of Christ in the little town of Colosse, "Whatever you do, work at it with all your heart, as working for the Lord, not for men."

In short, calling in the Bible is a central and dynamic theme that becomes a metaphor for the life of faith itself. To limit the word, as some insist, to a few texts and to a particular stage in salvation is to miss the forest for the trees. To be a disciple of Jesus is to be a "called one" and so to become "a follower of the Way."

The third and fourth strands of the meaning of calling are the basis for the vital distinction elaborated later in history—between primary and secondary calling. *Our primary calling as followers of Christ is by him, to him, and for him.* First and foremost we are called to Someone (God), not to something (such as motherhood, politics, or teaching) or to somewhere (such as the inner city or Outer Mongolia).

Our secondary calling, considering who God is as sovereign, is that everyone, everywhere, and in everything should think, speak, live, and act entirely for him. We can therefore properly say as a matter of secondary calling that we are called to homemaking or to the practice of law or to art history. But these and other things are always the secondary, never the primary calling. They are "callings" rather than the "calling." They are our personal answer to God's address, our response to God's summons. Secondary callings matter, but only because the primary calling matters most.

This vital distinction between primary and secondary calling carries with it two challenges—first, to hold the two together and, second, to ensure that they are kept in the right order. In other words, if we understand calling, we must make sure that first things remain first and the primary calling always comes before the secondary calling. But we must also make sure that the primary calling leads without fail to the secondary calling. The church's failure to meet these challenges has led to the two grand distortions that have crippled the truth of calling. We may call them the "Catholic distortion" and the "Protestant distortion."

THE "CATHOLIC DISTORTION"

The truth of calling means that for followers of Christ, "everyone, everywhere, and in everything" lives the whole of life as a response to God's call. Yet this holistic character of calling has often been distorted to become a form of dualism that elevates the spiritual at the expense of the secular. This distortion may be called the "Catholic distortion" because it rose in the Catholic era and is the majority position in the Catholic tradition.

Protestants, however, cannot afford to be smug. For one thing, countless Protestants have succumbed to the Catholic distortion as Wilberforce nearly did. Ponder, for example, the fallacy of the contemporary Protestant term *full-time Christian service*—as if those not working for churches or Christian organizations are only part-time in the service of Christ. For another thing, Protestant confusion about calling—which we will examine in the next chapter—has led to a "Protestant distortion" that is even worse. This is a form of dualism in a secular direction that not only elevates the secular at the expense of the spiritual but also cuts it off from the spiritual altogether.

The earliest clear example of the Catholic distortion is in *Demonstration of the Gospel* by Eusebius, bishop of Caesarea. A prolific but rather unpolished writer, Eusebius is the principal historian of the early church from the apostolic age down to his own day and an invaluable witness to the church's state of mind just before the "conversion" of Constantine in A.D. 312 and the Roman Empire.

Eusebius argues that Christ gave "two ways of life" to his church. One is the "perfect life"; the other is "permitted." The perfect life is spiritual, dedicated to contemplation and reserved for priests, monks, and nuns; the permitted life is secular, dedicated to action and open to such tasks as soldiering, governing, farming, trading, and raising families. Whereas those following the perfect life "appear to die to the life of mortals, to bear with them nothing earthly but their body, and in mind and spirit to have passed to heaven," those following the "more humble, more human" permitted life have "a kind of secondary grade of piety."

Higher vs. lower, sacred vs. secular, perfect vs. permitted, contemplation vs. action . . . the dualism and elitism in this view need no underscoring. Sadly this "two-tier" or "double-life" view of calling flagrantly perverted biblical teaching by narrowing the sphere of calling and excluding most Christians from its scope. It also dominated later Christian thinking. For example, both Augustine and Thomas Aquinas praised the work of farmers, craftsmen, and merchants but always elevated the contemplative life (*vita contemplativa*) over the active life (*vita activa*). The active life was depicted as second class, a matter of necessity; the contemplative life as first class, a matter of freedom. In short, Aquinas wrote, the life of contemplation was "simply better than the life of action." Even today, when one can find examples of Catholics recovering a more holistic view of calling, "answering the call" is commonly the jargon for becoming a priest or nun.

The Catholic distortion created a double standard in faith that in turn produced an important irony. Monasticism began with a *reforming mission*—it sought to remind an increasingly secularized church that it was still possible to follow the radical way of life required by the gospel. But it finished with a *relaxing effect*—the double standard reserved the radical way for the specialists (the aristocrats of the soul) and let everyone else off the hook. Thus the irony: Monasticism reinforced the secularization it originally set out to resist. In the end the monasteries themselves succumbed to the secularization and became a central carrier of elitism, power, arrogance, and corruption.

It goes without saying that there were exceptions to this distortion even in the Middle Ages. The strongest, strikingly, were the mystics Meister Eckehart and Johann Tauler who condemned "all those who would stop at contemplation, but scorn action." But for most people in Christendom in medieval times, the term *calling* was reserved for priests, monks, and nuns. Everyone else just had "work."

Into that long-established, rigidly hierarchical, and spiritually aristocratic world, Martin Luther's *The Babylonian Captivity of the Church* exploded like a thunderclap in 1520. Writing as an Augustinian monk himself, Luther recommended the abolition of all orders and abstention from all vows. Why? Because the contemplative life has no warrant in the Scriptures; it reinforces hypocrisy and arrogance; and it engenders "conceit and a contempt of the common Christian life."

But even these radical-sounding proposals pale beside the next paragraph Luther wrote: "The works of monks and priests, however holy and arduous they be, do not differ one whit in the sight of God from the works of the rustic laborer in the field or the woman going about her household tasks, but that all works are measured before God by faith alone. . . . Indeed, the menial housework of a manservant or maidservant is often more acceptable to God than all the fastings and other works of a monk or priest, because the monk or priest lacks faith."

If all that a believer does grows out of faith and is done for the glory of God, then all dualistic distinctions are demolished. There is no higher/lower, sacred/secular, perfect/permitted, contemplative/active, or first class/second class. Calling is the premise of Christian existence itself. Calling means that everyone, everywhere, and in everything fulfills his or her (secondary) callings in response to God's (primary) calling. For Luther, the peasant and the merchant—for us, the business person, the teacher, the factory worker, and the television anchor—can do God's work (or fail to do it) just as much as the minister and the missionary.

For Martin Luther and subsequent reformers, the recovery of the holistic understanding of calling was dramatic. Writing about the "Estate of Marriage" in 1522, Luther declared that God and the angels smile when a man changes a diaper. William Tyndale wrote that, if our desire is to please God, pouring water, washing dishes, cobbling shoes, and preaching the Word "is all one." William Perkins claimed polishing shoes was a sanctified and holy act. John Milton wrote in *Paradise Lost:*

> To know
> That which before us lies in daily life
> Is the prime wisdom.

Bishop Thomas Becon wrote, "Our Saviour Christ was a carpenter. His apostles were fishermen. St. Paul was a tent-maker."

Perkins's *A Treatise of the Vocations or Callings of Men* provides a typical Reformation summary: "The action of a shepherd in keeping sheep, performed as I have said in his kind, is as good a work before God as is the action of a judge in giving sentence, or of a magistrate in ruling, or a minister in preaching."

Little wonder that the cultural implications of recovering true calling were explosive. Calling gave to everyday work a dignity and spiritual significance under God that dethroned the primacy of leisure and contemplation. Calling gave to humble people and ordinary tasks an investment of equality that shattered hierarchies and was a vital impulse toward democracy. Calling gave to such practical things as work, thrift, and long-term planning a reinforcement that made them powerfully influential in the rise of modern capitalism. Calling gave to the endeavor to make Christ Lord of every part of life a fresh force that transformed not only the churches but also the worldviews and cultures of the Reformation countries. Calling gave to the idea of "talents" a new meaning, so that they were no longer seen purely as spiritual gifts and graces but as natural and a matter of giftedness in the modern sense of the term.

In short, the recovery of a holistic view of calling was powerful in culture as well as in the church, and calling was a vital element in the transition from the traditional to the modern world. It demanded and inspired the transforming vision of the lordship of Christ expressed in the famous saying of the great Dutch prime minister, Abraham Kuyper: "There is not one square inch of the entire creation about which Jesus Christ does not cry out, 'This is mine! This belongs to me!'"

Do you want to accept a challenge that will be the integrating dynamic of your whole life? One that will engage your loftiest

*thoughts, your most dedicated exertions, your deepest emotions,
all your abilities and resources, to the last step you take and
the last breath you breathe? Listen to Jesus of Nazareth;
answer his call.*

5

By Him, to Him, for Him

Jobs are not big enough for people. It's not just the assembly line worker whose job is too small for his spirit, you know. A job like mine, if you really put your spirit into it, you would sabotage immediately. You don't dare. So you absent your spirit from it. My mind has been so divorced from my job, except as a source of income, it's really absurd."

The speaker, Norah Watson, was a twenty-eight-year-old Pennsylvania writer who worked for an institution that published health-care literature. She was being interviewed by Studs Terkel for his book *Working*, a series of interviews with ordinary people who "talk about what they do all day and how they feel about what they do."

Terkel realized, as he set out in his interviews, that working is about the search for daily meaning in the struggle for daily bread. Most people, he found, live somewhere between a grudging acceptance of their job and an active dislike of it. But a recurring theme in the interviews is a yearning for a sense of meaning that comes when calling precedes and overarches work and career.

Norah Watson's frustration was not fueled simply by her job. It came as much from the contrast between her experience and her father's, as a pastor in a small mountain town in Western Pennsylvania. "My father was a preacher," she explained. "I didn't like what he was doing, but it was his vocation. That was the good part of it. It was not just: go to work in the morning and punch a time clock. It was a profession of himself. I expected work to be like that."

Watson had started out idealistically—going to work early, staying late, going the extra mile on each assignment, and then asking for more. But, she says, "I found out I was wrecking the curve, I was out of line. The people, just as capable as I and just as ready to produce, had realized it was pointless, and had cut back."

Eventually Watson followed suit and was surprised to discover: "The amazing, absurd thing was that once I decided to stop doing a good job, people recognized a kind of authority in me. Now I'm just moving ahead like blazes."

But Watson knew she couldn't be satisfied with success at such a cynical price. Her conscience was whispering in one ear: "It's simply that I know I'm vegetating and being paid to do exactly that." And her heart was whispering in the other: "For all that was bad about my father's vocation," she sighed, "he showed me it was possible to fuse your life to your work. . . . There's nothing I would enjoy more than a job that was so meaningful that I brought it home."

Norah Watson's pained candor about her work would not speak for those at the bottom of the totem pole or for those at the top. To the former such analysis would be an unaffordable luxury. They work to put bread on the table. To the latter it would be redundant; their work is often as satisfying and handsomely remunerated as work can get. But Norah Watson speaks for countless people in modern society who face the Catch-22 of modern work. Neither work nor career can be fully satisfying without a deeper sense of calling—but "calling" itself is empty and indistinguishable from work unless there is Someone who calls.

The same dilemma is equally striking at the theoretical level. For example, one contemporary bestseller argues—admirably—that we need to "make a life, not just a living," and that to do this we need to inject "values and vocation" back into the world of work. With such a "new paradigm," the book claims, work can become "a vehicle for transformation," personally and socially.

On what basis? The author dusts off the word *calling* to give a sense of meaning and high purpose to work. But what is calling for those, like her, who believe that there is no personal God to call? Her answer is to redefine vocation as "the call, the summons of that which needs doing."

What sort of answer is this? Modern work lacks meaning. Meaning comes with a sense of calling. But calling is only the summons of what needs doing. So the answer to meaningless work is the requirement to do what needs doing—often more meaningless work. Tell that to the paper pusher in the government office or the widget maker on the factory assembly line. Work that feels meaningless is transformed, she says, by being made into work "which needs doing." Stripped of the semantic magic of the word *calling,* the solution is circular. It solves nothing and leaves us where we started.

The hollowness of the argument comes out most clearly in the author's laudable attempt to propose an answer to "workaholism." "The workaholic," she writes, "like an alcoholic, is indiscriminate in his compulsion. He attempts to find meaning by working. The individual with vocation, on the other hand, finds meaningful work."

But again notice the sleight of hand. True vocation, when there is a Caller to call, is truly different from workaholism. But the difference between the workaholic who wants to "find meaning by work" and the worker whose "vocation" is to do "that which needs doing" is too slight for comfort. A better and more honest solution is needed.

THE "PROTESTANT DISTORTION"

Such contortions in the modern effort to reinvest work with dignity pinpoint the second of the two grand distortions that cripple calling—the "Protestant distortion." Indeed, these contortions are a direct result of the Protestant distortion. Whereas the Catholic distortion is a spiritual form of dualism, elevating the spiritual at the expense of the secular, the Protestant distortion is a secular form of dualism, elevating the secular at the expense of the spiritual.

Under the pressure of the modern world, the Protestant distortion is more extreme. It severs the secular from the spiritual altogether and reduces vocation to an alternative word for work. In so doing, it completely betrays the purpose of calling and, ironically, activates a counterreaction that swings back to the Catholic distortion again. Better, it would seem, the dualism of making calling purely spiritual than the dualism of making calling purely secular.

The seeds of the Protestant distortion can be traced right back to the Puritans themselves. Overall, the Puritans were magnificent champions of calling. Like the earlier reformers, the best and clearest thinking of them never split the primary call ("by God, to God, for God") from the secondary call ("everyone, everywhere, in everything").

John Calvin, it is true, does come close to speaking of a calling as equated with work. For Martin Luther, believers answer the call when through faith they serve God in their work, but Calvin sometimes speaks more boldly in equating calling and work. For both reformers, there were some occupations that could not be from God and, therefore, could never really be viewed as vocations. But Calvin in his tract "Against the Libertines" refers even to these illegitimate occupations as vocations—although sarcastically. "Let a brothel keeper . . . ply his trade . . . let a thief steal boldly, for each is pursuing his vocation."

But what may have been a latent imbalance earlier grows steadily in the Puritan era into a full-grown distortion. Slowly such words as *work, trade, employment,* and *occupation* came to be used interchangeably with *calling* and *vocation*. As this happened, the guidelines for callings shifted; instead of being directed by the commands of God, they were seen as directed by duties and roles in society. Eventually the day came when faith and calling were separated completely. The original demand that each Christian should have a calling was boiled down to the demand that each citizen should have a job.

Finally, the wheel came full circle. Callings had become jobs and jobs had become corrupt, so the radical seventeenth-century Protestant group, the Diggers, called for the abolition of callings altogether. Gerrard Winstanley, in a 1650 tract in England, wrote: "The judges and law officers buy and sell justice for money, and wipe their mouth like Solomon's whore and say 'It is my calling,' and are never troubled at it." Thus, ironically, whereas the reformers had set out the rediscovery of "calling" as a consequence of true faith, some of their spiritual descendants called for the "abolition of callings"—also as a consequence of true faith.

To be sure, the tight logic of the Diggers was too radical for most people. In the broad mainstream of European and American life, the steady secularization of calling continued apace. Slowly but surely secondary callings swallowed up the primary calling. By the high noon of the Industrial Revolution, the results were complete and devastating.

On the one hand, the triumph of secondary callings over the primary calling meant that work was made sacred. Whereas the Bible is realistic about work, seeing it after the fall as both creative and cursed, the late nineteenth and early twentieth centuries lost the balance. Work was not only entirely good, but it also was virtually made holy in a crescendo of enthusiasm that was later termed "the Protestant ethic." "The man who builds a factory builds a temple," President Coolidge declared. "The man who works there worships there." "Work," Henry Ford proclaimed, "is the salvation of the human race, morally, physically, socially."

On the other hand, the same triumph meant that calling was made secular. Like a booster rocket discarded when burned out, the dynamic of "calling" had launched the good ship "work" into space and had fallen away. *Vocation* could now be saved as a genteel word for lesser paid but sacrificial workers (such as nurses), for the religious (such as missionaries), and for the more practically oriented. Students attended the new "vocational colleges" and received "vocational training" because they were not up to the standard of the liberal arts colleges and universities.

The condescension of such attitudes is as bad as the distortion of vocation on which it is based. Whereas the Protestant reformers had regarded "worldly calling," in Dietrich Bonhoeffer's words, as "the final, radical protest against the world," the Protestant deformers made it the religious sanction of worldliness. Thus "costly grace was turned into cheap grace without discipleship."

Is there a way back from the disaster of the Protestant distortion? At least two things are required: the debunking of the notion of calling without a Caller and the restoring of the primacy of the primary calling.

First, we must resolutely refuse to play the word games that pretend calling means anything without a Caller—and we must not allow people to play such games on us. A hundred years ago Friedrich Nietzsche rightly scorned those who said, "God is dead" and went on living exactly the same as before. One of those in his sights was novelist George Eliot who wrote, "God is 'inconceivable' and immortality 'unbelievable,' but duty is nonetheless 'peremptory and absolute.'"

Nietzsche derided such people as "odious windbags of progressive optimism" who think it possible to have Christian morality without Christian faith. "They are rid of the Christian God," he wrote in *Twilight of the Idols*, "and now believe all the more firmly that they must cling to the Christian morality. . . . When one gives up the Christian faith, one pulls the right to Christian morality out from under one's feet."

What is true of morality is true of calling too. In C. S. Lewis's homespun picture, those who still conjure meaning out of calling when they do not believe there is a Caller are as silly as "the woman in the first war who said that if there were a bread shortage it would not bother her house because they always ate toast." If there is no Caller, there are no callings—only work.

Second, and more positively, we must restore the primary calling to its primary place by restoring the worship that is its setting and the dedication to Jesus that is its heart. There is no surer guide here than the devotional writer Oswald Chambers. "Beware of anything that competes with loyalty to Jesus Christ," he wrote. "The greatest competitor of devotion to Jesus is service for Him. . . . The one aim of the call of God is the satisfaction of God, not a call to do something for Him."

Do we enjoy our work, love our work, virtually worship our work so that our devotion to Jesus is off-center? Do we put our emphasis on service, or usefulness, or being productive in working for God— at his expense? Do we strive to prove our own significance? To make a difference in the world? To carve our names in marble on the monuments of time?

The call of God blocks the path of all such deeply human tendencies. We are not primarily called to do something or go somewhere; we are called to Someone. We are not called first to special work but to God. The key to answering the call is to be devoted to no one and to nothing above God himself. As Chambers said, "The men and women Our Lord sends out on His enterprises are the ordinary human stuff, plus dominating devotion to Himself wrought by the Holy Spirit." The most frequent phrase in his writings: "Be absolutely His."

In sum, we must avoid the two distortions by keeping the two callings together, stressing the primary calling to counter the Protestant distortion and secondary callings to counter the Catholic distortion. Whereas dualism cripples calling, a holistic understanding releases its power—the passion to be God's concentrates the energy of all who answer the call.

Do you want to be his, entirely his, at all costs his, and forever his so that secondary things remain so and first things are always first? Listen to Jesus of Nazareth; answer his call.

6

DO WHAT
YOU ARE

Yehudi Menuhin, the renowned maestro and violinist, has held audiences all over the world spellbound with his conducting and virtuoso playing. Like many great musicians, his gifts were precocious. He made his violin debut in San Francisco at the age of seven and launched his worldwide career at the age of twelve with a historic concert at Carnegie Hall. In his memoirs, *Unfinished Journey*, Menuhin tells the story of how he began his long love affair with the violin.

From the time he was three years old, Menuhin's parents frequently took him to concerts in New York where he heard the concertmaster and first violinist Louis Persinger. When Persinger broke into solo passages, little Yehudi, sitting with his parents up in the gallery, was enchanted.

"During one such performance," Menuhin wrote, "I asked my parents if I might have a violin for my fourth birthday and Louis Persinger to teach me to play it."

Apparently his wish was granted. A family friend gave the little boy a violin, but it was a toy one, made of metal with metal strings. Yehudi Menuhin was only four. He could hardly have had the arms and fingers to do justice to a full-sized violin, but he was furious.

"I burst into sobs, threw it on the ground and would have nothing to do with it." Reflecting years later, Menuhin said he realized he wanted nothing less than the real thing because "I did know instinctively that to play was to be."

Stories like that are common in the lives of creative artists. Artie Shaw, a famous clarinetist in the old Big Band days, shared his heart with an interviewer. "Maybe twice in my life I reached what I wanted to. Once we were playing 'These Foolish Things' and at the end the band stops and I play a little cadenza. That cadenza—*no one* can do it better. Let's say it's five bars. That's a very good thing to have done in a lifetime. An artist should be judged by his best, just as an athlete. Pick out my one or two best things and say, 'That's what we did: all the rest was rehearsal.'"

John Coltrane, the saxophonist who played for Dizzie Gillespie and Miles Davis, said something very similar. In the early 1950s "Trane" nearly died of a drug overdose in San Francisco, and when he recovered he quit drugs and drinking and came to put his faith in God. Some of his best jazz came after that, including "A Love Supreme," an ardent thirty-two minute outpouring to thank God for his blessing and offer him Coltrane's very soul.

After one utterly extraordinary rendition of "A Love Supreme," Coltrane stepped off the stage, put down his saxophone, and said simply, "*Nunc dimittis.*" (These are the opening Latin words for the ancient prayer of Simeon, sung traditionally at evening prayers: "Lord, now lettest thou thy servant depart in peace, for mine eyes have seen thy salvation.") Coltrane felt he could never play the piece more perfectly. If his whole life had been lived for that passionate thirty-two minute jazz prayer, it would have been worth it. He was ready to go.

WHAT DO YOU HAVE THAT
WAS NOT GIVEN YOU?

"To play was to be," said Yehudi Menuhin. "All the rest was rehearsal," said Artie Shaw. "*Nunc dimittis,*" said John Coltrane. Somehow we human beings are never happier than when we are expressing the deepest gifts that are truly us. And often we get a revealing glimpse of these gifts early in life. Graham Greene wrote in *The Power and the Glory,* "There is always one moment in childhood when the door opens and lets the future in." Countless examples could be added to these stories, but they all point to another crucial aspect of calling—*God normally calls us along the line of our giftedness, but the purpose of giftedness is stewardship and service, not selfishness.*

Giftedness does not stand alone in helping us discern our callings. It lines up in response to God's call alongside other factors, such as family heritage, our own life opportunities, God's guidance, and our unquestioning readiness to do what he shows. But to focus on giftedness as a central way to discern calling reverses the way most people think. Usually when we meet someone for the first time, it isn't long before we ask, "What do you do?" And the answer comes, "I'm a lawyer," "I'm a truck driver," "I'm a teacher," or whatever.

Far more than a name or a place of birth, a job helps us place a person on the map in our minds. After all, work, for most of us, determines a great part of our opportunity for significance and the amount of good we are able to produce in a lifetime. Besides, work takes up so many of our waking hours that our jobs come to define us and give us our identities. We become what we do.

Calling reverses such thinking. A sense of calling should precede a choice of job and career, and the main way to discover calling is along the line of what we are each created and gifted to be. Instead of, "You are what you do," calling says: "Do what you are." As the great Christian poet Gerard Manley Hopkins wrote in his poem about kingfishers and dragonflies, "What I do is me: for that I came." Albert Einstein, even as a teenager, had theoretical physics and mathematics in his sights. He wrote in a homework essay in Aarau, Switzerland, "That is quite natural; one always likes to do the things for which one has ability."

There is, to be fair, a growing trend toward fitting jobs to people. "Suit yourself—the secret of career satisfaction" one book promises. But many of these approaches are inadequate compared to calling. First, the more secular approaches tend to use very general "personality types" in their testing. So the results are too broad to be specific for individuals, and they are more about general personality traits than about the specific gifts of individuals.

Second, even the more clearly Christian approaches often suffer from weaknesses. Some use testing that concentrates on spiritual gifts and ignores natural gifts. This allows the testers, usually large churches, to use the results to direct people to employ their discovered gifts in their churches—thus diverting them from their callings in secular life and deepening the Catholic distortion further.

Others broaden the testing to discover both spiritual and natural gifts, but they divorce the discovery of giftedness from the worship and listening that is essential to calling—thus deepening the Protestant distortion further. The result is a heightened awareness of giftedness, but the emphasis on giftedness leads toward selfishness rather than stewardship. Archbishop William Temple underscored this danger sternly. To make the choice of career or profession on selfish grounds, without a true sense of calling, is "probably the greatest single sin any young person can commit, for it is the deliberate withdrawal from allegiance to God of the greatest part of time and strength."

In the biblical understanding of giftedness, gifts are never really ours or for ourselves. We have nothing that was not given us. Our gifts are ultimately God's, and we are only "stewards"—responsible for the prudent management of property that is not our own. This is why our gifts are always "ours for others," whether in the community of Christ or the broader society outside, especially the neighbor in need.

This is also why it is wrong to treat God as a grand employment agency, a celestial executive searcher to find perfect fits for our perfect gifts. The truth is not that God is finding us a place for our gifts but that God has created us and our gifts for a place of his choosing—and we will only be ourselves when we are finally there.

This theme of the wider purpose of gifts is unambiguous to the Puritans. John Cotton, for example, was an eminent seventeenth-century minister and the architect of New England congregationalism. Educated at Trinity and Emmanuel Colleges, Cambridge, he preached the famous farewell sermon "God's Promise to His Plantation" at the sailing of the Arbella in 1630. Three years later, he came to the New World himself. His sermon "Christian Calling" is a stirring seven-point exposition on the subject.

Cotton gives three criteria for choosing a job. The top criterion is that "it be a warrantable calling, wherein we may not only aim at our own, but at the public good." The other criteria are that we are gifted for the job and guided toward it by God—criteria that would surely supersede Cotton's first one on most people's list today. All who seek to follow Christ and to answer his call should pursue the key link between their giftedness and their calling, and use the best Christian books and tests on the subject. There is joy in fulfilling a calling that fits who we are and, like the pillar of cloud and fire, goes ahead of our lives to lead us.

But who are we? And what is our destiny? Calling insists that the answer lies in God's knowledge of what he has created us to be and where he is calling us to go. Our gifts and destiny do not lie expressly in our parents' wishes, our boss's plans, our peer group's pressures, our generation's prospects, or our society's demands. Rather, we each need to know our own unique design, which is God's design for us.

OURS FOR OTHERS

Not surprisingly, the focus on giftedness can be dangerous as well as wonderful. The encouragement to "do what we are" can be taken as a blank check for self-indulgence. But the strongest temptations always come along the line of the noblest truths, and that is the case here: The principle is tempting because it is true.

God does call us to "be ourselves" and "do what we are." But we are only truly "ourselves" and can only truly "do what we are" when we follow God's call. Giftedness that is "ours for others" is therefore not selfishness but service that is perfect freedom.

The danger, however, remains. So it is worth noting some distinctions made throughout history regarding calling, which help us balance giftedness and stewardship. In each case the temptation is to remember only the giftedness and forget the stewardship. But by keeping both in mind, we can steer surely by the principles of calling and avoid the pitfalls.

In all the discussion, the terms *calling* and *vocation* should be synonymous. One word simply comes from an Anglo-Saxon root and the other from a Latin root. Beware of those who make "vocation" different from "calling." If "vocation" is ever distinguished from "calling" and used to refer to the clergy, it is a sure sign of the Catholic distortion; if "vocation" is distinguished from "calling" and used to refer to employment and occupation, it betrays the presence of the Protestant distortion.

First, we must remember the distinction between *the individual (or particular) calling* and *the corporate (or general) calling*. Selfishness prefers the first, but stewardship respects both. The individual calling is that part of our life-response to God that we make as unique individuals. As we have seen, our individual callings are unique simply because each of us is unique. The corporate calling, on the other hand, is that part of our life-response to God that we undertake in common with all other followers of Christ. For example, all followers of Christ are called to be holy and to be peacemakers—simply by virtue of being followers of Christ.

Our corporate calling, which will be examined in a later chapter, is vital because it prevents calling from developing into an excessive individualism. Individual callings should complement, not contradict, the corporate calling. If there is any disagreement, the corporate calling as set out in Scripture should take precedence. Anyone citing his or her individual calling as grounds for rejecting the church's corporate calling is self-deluded.

Characteristically, the Puritans thought about corporate calling as much as individual calling. William Perkins, the dean of Puritan writers on vocation, counseled that "every calling must be fitted to the man and every man fitted to his calling." Both halves of the rule are necessary, he said, "for when men are out of their proper callings in any society it is as much as if a joint were out of place in the body."

Second, we must remember the distinction between *a later, special calling* and *our original, ordinary calling*. Again, selfishness prefers the first, but stewardship respects both. A special calling refers to those tasks and missions laid on individuals through a direct, specific, supernatural communication from God. Ordinary calling, on the other hand, is the believer's sense of life-purpose and life-task in response to God's primary call, "follow me," even when there is no direct, specific, supernatural communication from God about a secondary calling. In other words, ordinary calling can be seen in our responsibility to exercise a high degree of "capitalist-style" enterprise about how we live our lives. For example, the servants in Jesus' parable of the talents and pounds were assessed according to how they "got on with it" when the master was away. In this sense no follower of Christ is without a calling, for we all have an original calling even if we do not all have a later, special calling. And, of course, some people have both.

This distinction has practical consequences. Many Christians make the mistake of elevating a special calling or of talking as if everyone needed a special call for every task. ("Were you called to this job?") Some use the word *calling* piously regarding all their decisions, thinking it is the word to use, when in fact they have not had any special call. To the surprise of both groups, there is not a single instance in the New Testament of God's special call to anyone into a paid occupation or into the role of a religious professional. Others feel that, without a special call, they have had no call at all. So they wait around for guidance and become passive, excusing themselves by saying they have had "no call." But all they are doing is confusing the two types of call and burying their real talent in the napkin in the ground.

Needless to say, the very notion of a special call by God often betrays the fact that something is awry in understanding the original call. This tension is sharpest in the prophet—the prophet is specially called to critique and challenge the people of God when they have forgotten or betrayed their original calling.

Thus Moses confronted the people of God over the golden calf, Elijah over the prophets of Baal, Jesus over legalism and hypocrisy, Martin Luther over the distortion of faith, and Karl Barth and Dietrich Bonhoeffer over the idolatry of nationalism. Such prophetic critiques were often delivered with outrage, but they were not denials of the chosenness of those attacked. On the contrary, the purpose of prophetic critique is restoration, not dismissal. The prophets were specially called and their prophetic messages were special calls to bring God's people back to the original calling from which they had fallen away.

Third, we must remember the distinction between something being *central* to our calling and something being *peripheral.* Again, selfishness prefers the first, but stewardship regards both. Many people use the word *calling* only for the core of our giftedness. They speak as if we should all be able to specify our callings as a single task expressed in a single sentence. But both people and life are richer than that, and calling is comprehensive, not partial. We need to remember that calling has multiple dimensions and includes our relationships. Martin Luther, for example, was among other things husband to his wife, father to his daughter, pastor to his congregation, professor to his students, and subject to his prince.

This distinction is important because it is easy to become spoiled if we concentrate on the core of our giftedness—as if the universe existed only to fulfill our gifts. But it is also easy to become discouraged by making the same mistake. We live in a fallen world, and the core of our gifts may not be fulfilled in our lives on earth. If there had been no Fall, all our work would have naturally and fully expressed who we are and exercised the gifts we have been given. But after the Fall this is not so. Work is now partly creative and partly cursed.

Thus to find work now that perfectly fits our callings is not a right, but a blessing. Those in modern societies who are middle class or higher can probably find such a fulfilling match between calling and work. But for many others today, and probably for most people in most societies, there is no happy match between work and calling. Work is a necessity for survival. Even the almost universally recognized artistic genius like Michelangelo once complained: "having seen, as I said, that the times are contrary to my art, I do not know if I have any hope of further salary."

This tension created by the Fall lies behind the notion of "tentmaking." Needless to say, there was no advertised job that was perfect for Paul's calling: "Apostle to the Gentiles: $50,000 per annum." So Paul, not wishing to depend on wealthy Corinthian patrons, earned money by making tents. Doubtless he made his tents well because they too were made to the glory of God. But tentmaking was never the *heart* of Paul's calling, it was only a *part,* as all of life is. As a part of our calling such "tentmaking" at worst is work that *frustrates* us because it takes time we wish to spend on things more central. But at best it is work that *frees* us to get to that which is central. By contrast, whatever is the heart of our calling is work that *fulfills* us because it employs our deepest gifts.

The difference is impossible to mistake. George Foreman, flamboyant heavyweight champion of the world and a Baptist preacher says, "Preaching is my calling. Boxing for me is only moonlighting in the same way Paul made tents."

Fourth, we must remember the distinction between the *clarity* of calling and the *mystery* of calling. Again selfishness prefers the first, but stewardship regards both. To the extent that through worship, listening to God, and discovering our giftedness we grasp what God is calling us to be and do, there will be a proper clarity in our sense of calling. But to the extent that we blithely rush to be explicit, we betray our modern arrogance and forget the place of mystery in God's dealing with us. Oswald Chambers even said, writing of a special call:

> If you can tell where you got the call of God and all about it, I
> question whether you have ever had a call. The call of God does
> not come like that, it is much more supernatural. The realization
> of it in a man's life may come with a sudden thunder-clap or with
> a gradual dawning, but in whatever way it comes it comes with
> the undercurrent of the supernatural, something that cannot be
> put into words.

Can you state your identity in a single sentence? No more should you necessarily be able to state your calling in a single sentence. At best you can only specify a part of it. And even that clarity may have to be qualified. In many cases a clear sense of calling comes only through a time of searching, including trial and error. And what may be clear to us in our twenties may be far more mysterious in our fifties because God's complete designs for us are never fully understood, let alone fulfilled, in this life.

William Wilberforce's 1787 journal entry, setting down his "two great objects," is perhaps the simplest and most stunning personal mission statement in history. But it would be wrong to hold it up as a model for all. Wilberforce was young, his sense of calling was clear, and he pursued that calling for the rest of his life almost as if he were running in a straight line.

Aleksandr Solzhenitsyn, a living legend in the twentieth century as a one-man resistance movement to totalitarianism, represents a very different way. When he was fifty-five and near the climax of his titanic struggle with the Soviets, with twenty more years of his writing projects still to be achieved, his sense of calling was passionate.

> The one worrying thing was that I might not be given time to carry out the whole scheme. I felt as though I was about to fill a space in the world that was meant for me and had long awaited me, a mold, as it were, made for me alone, but discerned by me only this very moment. I was a molten substance, impatient, unendurably impatient, to pour into my mold, to fill it full, without air bubbles or cracks, before I cooled and stiffened.

But Solzhenitsyn's sense of calling had not always been so clear and passionate. Originally it had not been there at all because he did not know his Caller and barely knew his gift. "I drifted into literature unthinkingly," he said, ". . . and hate to think what sort of writer I would have become." But his sense of calling grew in his experiences of the Gulag, his deadly struggle to write, the miracle of his cure from cancer, his conversion through a Jewish follower of Jesus, and his deepening burden to put "the dying wish of the millions" on record.

Solzhenitsyn therefore exemplifies Søren Kierkegaard's observation that life is lived forward but understood backward. "Later," he wrote in *The Oak and the Calf,* "the true significance of what happened would inevitably become clear to me, and I would be numb with surprise. I have done many things in my life that conflicted with the great aims I had set myself—and something has always set me on the true path again."

Solzhenitsyn's conclusion, quoting another Russian writer, is a bracing reminder to all who yearn for calling to be always simple and clear. "Many lives have a mystical sense, but not everyone reads it aright. More often than not it is given to us in cryptic form, and when we fail to decipher it, we despair because our lives seem meaningless. The secret of a great life is often a man's success in deciphering the mysterious symbols vouchsafed to him, understanding them and so learning to walk in the true path."

Do you want the best and most wonderful gifts God has given you to decay, spent on your own self? Or do you want them to be set free to come into their own as you link your profoundest abilities with your neighbor's need and the glory of God? Listen to Jesus of Nazareth; answer his call.

7

A Time to Stand

There are times when our hearts stir before heroism like fine crystal resonating to the sound of a violin. So it was for me when, only twelve, I first heard my headmaster and classics teacher tell the story of one of the most courageous stands in human history: Thermopylae. Years later I can see him still. Tall and powerful, with strong expressive hands, he was a sporting hero for England. But he became most animated when he summoned up the glories of ancient Greece and Rome. In lesson after lesson the twentieth century faded into unreality as he reawakened the past.

The year was 480 B.C. The East was on the move against the West. A colossal and terrible army, the greatest the world had ever seen, had poured across the Hellespont from Asia into Europe. Led by the all-powerful Persian King Xerxes, the vast host included fish-scale armored Persians, camel-riding Arabs, chariot-driving Libyans, turbaned Cissians, balloon-trousered Scythians, high-heel booted Sarangians, and scores of other tribes and nationalities. Eighty thousand men rode on horseback or in chariots; around them marched foot soldiers and archers beyond counting.

When this Grand Army marched, it was said, the ground trembled. When they ate, it was as if locusts had devoured everything in their path. When they drank, it seemed that whole pools were dried up and entire rivers reduced to a trickle. The imperial Persian war machine was like nothing anyone had seen before. Simply to pass by the king in review took a full week.

The Persian mission was revenge. Xerxes, the thirty-eight-year-old

55

"King of Kings," had set out from Susa, after four years of prepara-tion, to avenge the defeat of his father Darius. In the process he intended to subdue Greece, nip the budding menace of Athens and Sparta, and expand the far-flung empire of Persia. Athens, of course, was not yet the shining city of Pericles, Phidias, Aeschylus, and Sophocles. The marble wonder of the Parthenon and the golden age of science, philosophy, democracy, and theater lay in the future. Athens was merely a fractious little city. If anything, Sparta appeared to have greater military potential. But speculation on the future would have seemed absurd during those sweltering days in mid-August. Even if they united, the Greek city-states would have been no match for Xerxes' awesome force. But they were divided as well as unpre-pared. The quarrelsome Greeks were as much at war with each other as with the Persians.

So it was that the Persian super-army of perhaps a quarter of a million soldiers (Herodotus said three million) was opposed by a hastily assembled, ragtag force of seven thousand Greeks from five city-states. But at their core were three hundred Spartans, trained to stand or die. ("Come back *with* your shield or *on* it," a Spartan mother told her son.) They were led by a fifty-five-year-old Spartan prince, Leonidas. And they took their stand in a narrow pass, twenty yards wide, bounded by the sea on one side and the five thousand-foot cliffs of Mt. Kallidromos on the other. Hot sulfurous springs, which the Greeks called Thermopylae, or Hot Gates, bubbled out of these cliffs at the narrowest place.

For the Persians the whole encounter must have looked at first like a simple mopping-up operation, a tiny dust-storm scuffle. But for two days the unstoppables were stopped. Late on the second day, Xerxes, fearing a calamitous panic, sent in his crack division, "the Immortals"—who were repulsed too at tremendous cost. For two long days the Persian horde had attacked and the heroic handful of Greeks had held firm.

Then, disastrously, the Greeks were betrayed. By night a traitor led the Persians over the cliffs so that at daybreak Leonidas and his men were surrounded. The pass had been sold. The game was up.

Death was coming as surely as the dawn. Dismissing most of his army, Leonidas led his own three hundred Spartans and a few others to a little mound from which they could make their last desperate stand and hold back the oncoming avalanche. There the little band fought to the last man and died. When their swords were gone, according to Herodotus, they fought on with their hands and teeth. But before they died, they sent home the stirring message that has become their epitaph: "Stranger, tell the Spartans that we behaved as they would wish us to, and are buried here."

Brief, laconic, and to the point, these last words came from a little band of Greeks who had no idea what was to come. They could not see how their example would trigger a surge of pride and inspire their fellow countrymen to decisive victories at Salamis and Platae, that never again would the Persians seriously menace Greece, and that in thirty short years the city of Athens would rise to become the most influential city the world has ever known.

Dedicated and courageous, they did their duty. They stood firm in the line of history, and today all free people enjoy a freedom that flows partly from their stand. As the French philosopher Montaigne said of Thermopylae two thousand years later, "there are triumphant defeats that rival victories."

THE GREATEST CHALLENGE EVER FACED

Will it be said of followers of Jesus Christ across the world, "Passerby, tell our Lord that we have behaved as he would wish us to behave, and are buried here"? For at the threshold of the third millennium of its existence, the church of Jesus Christ confronts the greatest challenge it has ever faced. This challenge touches on behavior every bit as much as belief, yet it requires belief to inspire and stiffen that behavior.

What is the challenge? From one side, followers of Jesus Christ confront in the modern world the most powerful culture in human history so far as well as the world's first truly global culture. This culture has unprecedented power to shape behavior, and its damage to faith has already proved far greater than the malice and destruction of all the Christ-hating persecutors in history, from Nero to Mao Tse Tung. From the other side, followers of Jesus Christ confront a "global Mount Carmel" as the followers of new gods and newly awakened old gods openly compete with followers of Christ to direct and guide the course of the modern world.

For some years this challenge was remote to me. With the collapse of the Soviet Union, it was argued that the modern world had shifted from the era of "ideology" to the era of "civilization." Thus, many of the faultlines in our world today are faultlines between different civilizations: Western (Jewish and Christian), Marxist, Japanese, Islamic, Confucian, Slavic Orthodox, Hindu, African, Latin American, and so on. World War III, it has even been claimed, will be a war between civilizations.

But the full force of the challenge hit me squarely a few years ago when my son and I were in Singapore, Southeast Asia's vibrant "intelligence island." An economist from the University of Singapore was outlining his vision of the post-Cold War era world from the perspective of the Pacific Rim. His argument was unambiguous.

"What we in Singapore want," he said, "is the modern world, not the West. We want the Asian way, not the American way. We want to follow Confucius, not Christ." Continuing, he explained, "Having given rise to the modern world, the Jewish and Christian faiths have now been reduced to ruins by the modern world." Asian countries, he concluded, should take a different path. They should pursue the best opportunities of modern capitalism, industrialized technology, and telecommunication within the setting of their own beliefs and cultures.

Too often descriptions of this growing competition-cum-clash between different civilizations and religions are wrong. For example, some people speak of "the West versus the rest" as if the West were Christian and the rest non-Christian—when in fact the church of Christ is truly universal, found on all continents, and is often stronger outside the West than within it. Others speak of this competition with relish as a sort of "international culture war" or even a "jihad"—forgetting that the heart of the good news of Jesus is reconciliation.

In the current situation, the church's deepest challenge is neither political nor ideological, and certainly it is not military. It is spiritual and theological and comes to a head where behavior expresses belief and deeds express words. As Francis of Assisi said well, "Preach the gospel constantly and, if necessary, use words." As each great civilization, guided and inspired by a different religion, competes to demonstrate its vision of the best way forward for humankind, it is plain that we cannot afford fuzzy thinking and half-hearted living. In today's world, differences can be seen to make a difference. Beliefs have consequences. What begin as theoretically different views of God, the world, humanness, justice, freedom, community, money, and a hundred other issues, end in radically divergent societies and radically divergent ways of living and dying.

Is the church of Christ ready to meet the challenge? Are followers of Jesus sufficiently gripped by the gospel to "behave as he would wish us to behave"? Do we know in reality the great living truths of the faith that have a proven capacity to affect history and transform cultures as well as radically alter individual lives? Calling, as we shall see in a score of ways, is indispensable to the integrity and effectiveness of the church in this momentous hour.

Mention of "momentous hour," "cultures," and "culture-changing capacities" is deliberate, though I know such words leave many people cold. Some Christians prefer to keep their faith to the level of the personal, the relational, the spiritual, and the simple. I believe that such a view of faith is misguided. Calling is certainly a truth that touches our personal lives intimately, but it also touches cultural life potently. Calling is more than purely cultural, but it is also more than purely personal. Discover the meaning of calling and you discover the heart of the gospel itself.

My challenge is therefore deliberate. Many followers of Jesus today have not begun to wrestle with the full dimensions of the truth of calling because they have not been stretched by the real challenges of today's world and by the momentousness of the present hour. "A time to stand" is a time to behave as our Lord would wish us to behave. A time to behave is a time to believe as he has taught us to believe. A time to believe is a time to move from small, cozy formulations of faith to knowing what it is to be called by him as the deepest, most stirring, and most consuming passion of our lives.

The truth of calling is more than personal. It is one of the strongest grounds for an unshakable confidence that the good news of Jesus will prevail. My own critiques of the Western world and the Western church are as comprehensive and critical as anyone's, but at the end of the day, I am not the slightest bit discouraged, gloomy, or judgmental.

I am often asked how one can be radical in analyzing what is wrong, yet hopeful about the prospects for the church. Part of the answer is that the very crises themselves are opportunities— some people in both the church and wider society must surely blush to think of the things in which they trusted so recently. But the deeper answer is the character of the gospel itself. The gospel is a constellation of truths that simply cannot and will not be worsted.

Put differently, in the decades I have followed Jesus, second only to the joy of knowing him has been a sorrow at the condition of those of us today who name ourselves his followers. If so many of us profess to live by the gospel yet are so pathetically marginal to the life of our societies and so nondescript and inconsequential in our individual lives, is there something wrong with the gospel, or does the problem lie with us?

Years ago that question prompted me to a search through other times and places to look for instances in which the truths of the gospel were neither platitudinous nor impotent but fresh, compelling, explosive, and consequential. Along with the truth of the cross of Christ, the truth of calling has been as influential on individuals and societies as any truth in history—and will be again, when rediscovered.

Do you want to know a truth that in the momentous challenges of our modern world will be at once a quest to inspire you, an anchor to hold you fast, a rich fare to nourish you, and a relationship you will prize above all others? Listen to Jesus of Nazareth; answer his call.

8

Let God
Be God

George Steiner's *The Portage to San Christobal of A. H.* is one of the most controversial novels of the twentieth century. Little more than a hundred pages long, it is a small book with a huge claim. Scholarly in style, it is mind-blowing in its implications. But its real scandal lies in a third feature: Written by a Jew, it dares to think the unthinkable by arguing that "there had to be a solution, a *final* solution."

The story line is fascinatingly simple. Adolf Hitler—the "A. H." of the title—did not die in the fiery ruins of the Berlin chancery in May 1945. Instead he escaped to Latin America where for decades he hid in the jungle. But now he has been tracked down by dedicated Jewish Nazi-hunters and captured in San Christobal. Soon, like Adolf Eichmann, he will be flown to Israel and tried for his monstrous crimes against humanity.

From the very beginning the Jews' exhilaration at Hitler's arrest is troubled by the dark specters lining the route of the respective hunters and their families, reaching back to hell-holes like Auschwitz-Birkenau. But the captors also wrestle with the chasm between the terrible monster of their imaginations and the innocuous, elderly, reserved, almost senile old man in their hands.

Through much of the story, Hitler says little. But in the very last chapter, just as the deafening roar of the helicopters descends into the quiet of the jungle clearing, the accused speaks and the novel concludes in a fireball of claims and arguments.

"*Erster punkt.* Article one," the accused says. It was not he, Hitler, who dreamed up the master race. He had learned it and its terrible lessons from Jacob Grill, the son of a Polish rabbi, in 1910. "My racism was a parody of yours, a hungry imitation. . . . Judge me and you must judge yourselves. *Ubermenschen* [supermen], chosen ones!"

"What my client means," began the appointed Jewish lawyer for the defense. But he is brushed aside. Hitler has started to speak, and he will not be stopped.

"*Punkt* II. There had to be a solution, a *final* solution. For what is the Jew if not a long cancer of unrest? Gentlemen, I beg your attention, I demand it. Was there ever a crueler invention, a contrivance more calculated to harm human existence than that of an omnipotent, all-seeing, yet invisible, impalpable, inconceivable God?"

Here Hitler in his own defense waxes theological with a fiendishness that strikes close to the truth. The pagan earth before Sinai was crowded with small deities—man-made idols, portable, pliable, and accommodating gods. But in the fire and smoke of Sinai, "The Jew emptied the world by setting his God apart, immeasurably apart from man's senses. No image. No concrete embodiment. No imagining even. A blank emptier than the desert. Yet with a terrifying nearness. Spying on our every misdeed, searching out the heart of our heart for motive." You call me a tyrant? Hitler asks. What tyranny has been more total than that of the Jewish "God makers" who "invented conscience"? If the gods were finite and flawed, they could be charged with our failures. But if there is one God, absolute and good, all flaws and failures are ours.

But that, Hitler argues, was only stage one of the Jewish blackmail. Stage two was "the white-faced Nazarene" and his grand cunning. "Demand of human beings more than they can give, demand that they give up their stained, selfish humanity in the name of a higher ideal, and you will make of them cripples, hypocrites, mendicants for salvation. . . . Ask of man more than he is, hold before his tired eyes an image of altruism, of compassion, of self-denial which only the saint or madman can touch, and you stretch him on the rack. Till his soul bursts. What can be crueler than the Jew's addiction to the ideal?"

Hitler sees a third act after the "all-demanding God of Sinai" and "the terrible sweetness of Christ"—the secularized messianism of "Rabbi Marx" in which "the kingdom of justice comes here and now, next Monday morning." But whether Jewish, Christian, or Marxist, there is a common theme—the "blackmail of transcendence," the "bacillus of perfection," "the virus of utopia." Thus, Hitler says, the Jew is not the human conscience, only the bad conscience. "And we shall vomit you so we may live and have peace. A final solution. How could there be any other?"

Hitler concludes his defense with "*Punkt* III": He was only a man of his time. He then rises to his conclusion: "Gentlemen of the tribunal: I took my doctrines from you. I fought the blackmail of the ideal with which you have hounded mankind. My crimes were matched by those of others. The *Reich* begat Israel. These are my last words. The last words of a dying man against the last words of those who suffered; and in the midst of incertitude must matters be left till the great revelation of all secrets."

A DEVIL'S-EYE WITNESS TO TRUTH

Are these ideas only the crazed rationalizations of a monster unworthy of our attention? Does Steiner, the devout Jew, transgress moral boundaries even in framing this monstrous argument, as certain critics claimed? It is important to say that Steiner did not weave these ideas out of the air. He dug deep into the mind and writings of the young Austrian painter and fanatic who penned *Mein Kampf.* The dread warning, "There is no Why here," must always bar the door to the last chamber of the mystery behind the evil of the Final Solution. But no one has pressed deeper than Steiner. Below all the more obvious historical, economic, social, and psychological forces, he has captured a gleam of the essentially theological evil of Nazism.

Hitler's (or Steiner's) conclusion may be morally perverse, but it comes far closer to the core of the truth of calling than countless, cozy Christian formulations. As such we may take it as a devil's-eye witness to the truth and a challenge to all versions of calling that fall short.

"Calling?" you say. "Why calling? There is no mention of calling in Steiner's story. Covenant, perhaps. The character of God, perhaps. The Ten Commandments, certainly. But why calling?" Yet calling is absolutely central to the story of Sinai in a way that goes beyond the obvious use of the word in either Steiner's novel or in Exodus itself.

The straightforward use of "call" in the story is plain. On the one hand, the Lord called Moses. Intrigued by the burning bush that was not burned up, Moses stopped: "When the Lord saw that he had gone over to look, God called to him from within the bush, 'Moses! Moses!'" On the other hand, the Lord through Moses called the whole people of Israel, as the Old Testament says repeatedly. The prophet Hosea, for instance, conveyed God's lament that "the more I called Israel, the further they went from me." But this sadness only grows from God's original call: "When Israel was a child, I loved him, and out of Egypt I called my son."

But Steiner, although he never uses the word, points to an even deeper aspect of calling at the very center of Sinai. Why is the revelation of God at Sinai so new that it smashes all categories and idols? What exactly is so brain hammering and conscience wracking? Is it the fire, the smoke, and the thunder? These are but pyrotechnics, the merest fringe sideshow, compared with the nuclear sunburst of the truth revealed—"*I am who I am.*"

We may tidily label God's revelation to Moses "radical monotheism." We may knowledgeably pronounce it "unique" in the history of world ideas. We may even repeat "I am who I am" as if it were the theological equivalent of a familiar television jingle. But if we do, we do so at our peril. For at the heart of Sinai is a heart-stopping mystery before which we should remove our shoes. As Moses reminded the people of Israel in Deuteronomy, "You came near and stood at the foot of the mountain while it blazed with fire to the very heavens, with black clouds and deep darkness. Then the Lord spoke to you out of the fire. *You heard the sound of words but saw no form; there was only a voice* [emphasis added]."

No form, only a voice. . . . Why does God call? Why does he not show himself and defer to the eye, which Leonardo da Vinci called "the prince of the senses" and the "window of the soul"? Why does he not give us a picture that would be worth a thousand words? Why does he use words that are so fragile and disputable, words that so notoriously evaporate with our breath? Apparently the God of Sinai prohibits not only idols to rival him but also images to represent him. He does not allow imagining. God's attributes, as Arnold Schoenberg groped to express them in his opera *Moses and Aaron,* are

> inconceivable because invisible;
> because immeasurable;
> because everlasting;
> because eternal;
> because omnipresent;
> because omnipotent.

With the brief, merciful, and marvelous exception of his Word in human form, God speaks to us in words, and our responsibility as his creatures is to listen, to trust, and to obey those words. But the reverse side of this truth leads us to a fundamental aspect of calling: *Words are the deepest, fullest expression in which God now discloses himself to us, beginning with his calling us. So it is in listening to him, trusting him, and obeying him when he calls that we "let God be God" in all of his awe and majesty.*

God's primary call, his address to us, always has two dimensions: summons and invitation, law and grace, demand and offer. Unquestionably the former comes first, yet that side is missing among many followers of Christ today. The result is a casualness in faith and a slackness in behavior that show no sign of having listened to any call from either Sinai or Galilee, let alone Calvary.

Again and again when God calls people before the time of Jesus, they fall flat on their faces, prostrate in awe. "I fell face down," the prophet Ezekiel reported of his call, "and I heard the voice of one speaking." Those who meet God must hide their eyes from the holy one, but they cannot stop their ears.

The whole wonder of the gospel lies in the distance between Sinai and Galilee. But George Steiner is right to allow no divorce. The same summons rings loud and clear in the "terrible sweetness" of Jesus. The call issued by Jesus was terse and commanding: "Follow me." The Gospel of Mark records of Simon and Andrew, "At once they left their nets and followed him." A few verses later it says of James and John, "Without delay he called them, and they left their father Zebedee in the boat with the hired men and followed him." Clearly Christ's was a call that brooked no refusal. They left their father both in the boat and in the lurch.

All too often our familiarity with the Gospels breeds inattention. As Dietrich Bonhoeffer insisted, "The response of the disciples is an act of obedience, not a confession of faith in Jesus." They did not consider his claims, make up their minds, and then decide whether to follow—they simply heard and obeyed. Their response is "a testimony to the absolute, direct, and unaccountable authority of Jesus." The call is all. Jesus is the reason. The only way to follow is to leave everything and follow him. Here is a call that makes short work of all our questions, objections, and evasions. Disciples are not so much those who follow as those who *must* follow.

Later on this unsettling sternness mounts. Mark records that Jesus set his face toward Jerusalem, "while those who followed were afraid." Oswald Chambers called this "the discipline of dismay." In the beginning of our discipleship we think we know all about Jesus. Abandoning everything for him is a dawn-fresh delight, but now as the day wears on, we are not so sure. He is out front and the look on his face is strange. Chambers continued:

> There is an aspect of Jesus that chills the heart of a disciple to the core and makes the whole spiritual life gasp for breath. This strange Being with His face "set like a flint" and His striding determination, strikes terror into me. He is no longer Counsellor and Comrade, He is taken up with a point of view I know nothing about, and I am amazed at Him. At first I was confident that I understood Him, but now I am not so sure. I begin to realize there is a distance between Jesus Christ and me; I can no longer be familiar with Him. He is ahead of me and He never turns round; I have no idea where He is going, and the goal has become strangely far off.

Do you know only the soft-gospel invitation of our convenience-loving age, or have you been mastered by the no-concession summons of God's call? Have you experienced "the discipline of dismay"? Chambers is almost as stern as his master when he writes: "If we have never had the experience of taking our commonplace religious shoes off our commonplace religious feet, and getting rid of all the undue familiarity with which we approach God, it is questionable whether we have ever stood in His presence. The people who are flippant and familiar are those who have never yet been introduced to Jesus Christ."

Today we have deflated the phrase "let God be God." We laughingly apply it to presidents or children, usually as a form of indulgence—"let Reagan be Reagan" or "let Johnny be Johnny" we say condescendingly. But for Martin Luther who coined the phrase, the context was the unrelenting call of God before which he trembled.

But if the phrase needs recovery, how much more the reality of God's authority in our lives? At its heart, the modern world is a decisive challenge to the authority of God outside our private lives. This is true not because a few atheists trumpet that "God is dead" but because our entire culture, Christians included, so relies on the gifts of the modern world that we have "no need of God" in practice.

No more urgent task faces the church today than the recovery of the authority of faith over the modern world. Those who imagine this can be done solely through strong institutions, more authoritative leadership, sharper formulations of orthodoxy, and ever more aggressive political movements will be disappointed. In a world as dynamic, flexible, and individualistic as ours, there can be no return to the authority of faith without a return to the understanding of calling as every follower of Jesus Christ "lets God be God" in practice.

Luther again shows the way. Many people have commented on the fact that in Luther's first hearing before the Emperor Charles V at the Diet of Worms in April 1521, he was visibly overwhelmed. Uncharacteristically hesitant, he asked for time "to think it over." Surely, his enemies thought, the simple monk and miner's son was overawed in the presence of the brilliant young prince, heir of the long line of Catholic sovereigns, son of the house of Hapsburg, lord of Austria, Burgundy, the Low Countries, Spain, and Naples.

But that was not the reason. As his friends knew, and Roland Bainton later wrote in his biography *Here I Stand*, what overpowered Luther was "not so much that he stood in the presence of the emperor as this, that he and the emperor alike were called upon to answer before Almighty God." Called as he had been, Luther feared God more than he feared the emperor. That is why he could say the next day, "My conscience is captive to the Word of God. I cannot and I will not recant anything, for to go against conscience is neither right nor safe. God help me. Amen."

Faith in Christ will regain its decisive authority in the modern world only when we who follow Christ fear God more than we fear the powers and favors of modernity—when we hear God's call and are so captured by his summons that we say with Luther, as the earliest printed reports add, "Here I stand, I cannot do otherwise."

Do you want to "let God be God" and know a decisive
authority in your life that will brook no refusal? Listen to Jesus
of Nazareth; answer his call.

9

THE AUDIENCE OF ONE

July 27, 1881, was the happiest day in the life of Andrew Carnegie. A Scottish weaver's son, he had risen from a Pittsburgh "bobbin boy" at $1.20 a week to America's "King of Steel," "the Industrial Napoleon," "the *Homo Croesus Americanus*," "St. Andrew" (Mark Twain's nickname)—and one of the world's most fabled rich men. He was always proud to be called "the star-spangled Scotchman," and he had set his heart on a triumphal return to Dunfermline, the city of his birth in the east of Scotland. "What Benares is to the Hindu, Mecca to the Mohammedan, Jerusalem to the Christians, all that Dunfermline is to me," he purred as he saw the city from the Ferry Hills above it.

Carnegie's trip had been long planned. With his mother and a select group of friends, he crossed the Atlantic from New York, set out from Brighton on the south coast of England, and slowly traveled north to Scotland and Dunfermline in a carriage that was royally built and furnished. At four o'clock in the afternoon, the coach and four rolled up St. Leonard's Street, greeted by banners reading "Welcome Carnegie, generous son" and passing the flags of Scotland, England, and the United States.

Then the official parade began, led by the Lord Provost, the guilds, and town councilors in their carriages. The procession passed the little stone cottage where Carnegie had been born and a similar cottage nearby from which his poverty-stricken family had fled to Pittsburgh thirty-three years earlier.

The climax of the day was Carnegie's bestowal of a new, handsome public library on the city of his birth, the first such bequest outside the United States. But long before then, his mother Margaret, who throughout the entire trip had ridden on top of the coach, had asked to sit inside so that she could weep freely but unseen on her day of triumph.

Homecomings, alumni reunions, visits to ancestral countries . . . most people can identify with the feelings of a native son returning home. But Andrew Carnegie's pride that day had another source too. Years earlier, when he was a young boy and he and his family lived in penury in Pittsburgh, he found his mother weeping in a moment of despair. Cradling her hands in his, he urged her not to cry and tried to console her.

"Some day I'll be rich," he assured her, "and we'll ride in a fine coach driven by four horses."

"That will do no good over here," his mother snorted, "if no one in Dunfermline can see us."

That was the moment when young Andrew solemnly resolved that someday he and his mother would make a grand entry into Dunfermline in a coach and four, and the whole town would witness it. For his mother's sake, he would "show them." A Pittsburgh audience would not be enough for that. He had to prove the Carnegie family's success before his hometown audience.

Needless to say, Andrew Carnegie was no poll-taking, crowd-pleasing politician. Early on he spoke of business as a game of "solitaire"; his favorite line was Robert Burns's "Thine own reproach alone do fear"; and his personal creed—Social Darwinism—gave him a ruthless streak never wholly offset by the legendary generosity of his philanthropy. But Carnegie was not simply the "robber baron," the entrepreneurial capitalist egotist of his enemy's attacks.

Among the softening factors was his evident desire to please. A special drawer in his desk was labeled "gratitude and sweet words," and one of his secretary's daily tasks was to cut out favorable comments from the press and file them for Carnegie's enjoyment. Above all, he longed to win the approval of the few audiences he valued—especially the city of his birth. "It's God's mercy I was born a Scotchman,"

Carnegie the atheist avowed with no sense of contradiction when he crossed the Scottish border on July 16. And then more straightforwardly: "Ah, you suit me, Scotia, and proud I am that I am your son." Unquestionably, Andrew Carnegie and his mother Margaret had "shown them."

A GYROSCOPE OR A GALLUP POLL?

The preceding story, which is told so well in Joseph Frazier Wall's biography *Andrew Carnegie,* highlights a vital point for understanding calling. When we discuss our plans and endeavors, we automatically think of notions like "aims," "ambition," "achievements," "assessment," and so on. But we often overlook the vital part of "audience."

Only madmen, geniuses, and supreme egotists do things purely for themselves. It is easy to buck a crowd, not too hard to march to a different drummer. But it is truly difficult—perhaps impossible—to march only to your own drumbeat. Most of us, whether we are aware of it or not, do things with an eye to the approval of some audience or other. The question is not *whether* we have an audience but *which* audience we have.

This observation underscores another vital feature of the truth of calling: *A life lived listening to the decisive call of God is a life lived before one audience that trumps all others—the Audience of One.*

In Genesis Abraham's call is to live a life of trust in God as he journeys before God. Usually God calls Abraham, but at one point he appears and says, "I am God Almighty; walk before me and be blameless." Behind the voice of God is the eye of God and behind the eye the face and behind the face the heart. To follow the call of God is therefore to live before the heart of God. It is to live life *coram deo* (before the heart of God) and thus to shift our awareness of audiences to the point where only the last and highest—God—counts.

Jesus intensifies this same emphasis. He reminds those he calls that their Father "knows" and "sees." God notes the sparrow hopping on the ground, and he numbers the very hairs of his followers' heads. Contrary to the universal human desire to parade virtue and to give in order to be recognized and honored, Jesus required that our good deeds be secret. "Then your Father, who sees what is done in secret, will reward you."

This stress on living before the Audience of One was prominent among the Puritans. John Cotton expands on the theme of audience. Quoting St. Paul's letter to the Ephesians, he describes the calling of servants as "not with eye-service as man-pleasers." Rather, he says, "we live by faith in our vocations, in that faith, in serving God, serves men, and in serving men, serves God." But is this language simply Puritan word play? Far from it. Living before the Audience of One transforms all our endeavors—"he doth it all comfortably though he meet with little encouragement from man, whereas an unbelieving heart would be discontented that he can find no acceptance, but all he doth is taken in the worst part."

That is why Christ-centered heroism does not need to be noticed or publicized. The greatest deeds are done before the Audience of One, and that is enough. Those who are seen and sung by the Audience of One can afford to be careless about lesser audiences.

When asked why he was not stung by a vicious attack from a fellow Member of Parliament, Winston Churchill replied, "If I respected him, I would care about his opinion. But I don't, so I don't." Similarly we who live before the Audience of One can say to the world: "I have only one audience. Before you I have nothing to prove, nothing to gain, nothing to lose."

Needless to say, the modern world is light years from the Puritan world. We have moved from the "inner directed" world of the Puritans, in which calling acted as an inner compass, to the "other directed" world of modern society, in which our contemporaries are our real guides—and a roving radar ranges to pick up their cues. We see this in teenagers listening to their peers, women following the beguiling images of womanhood in magazines and designer fashions, politicians aping polls and slavishly following focus group findings, and pastors anxiously following the latest profiles of "seekers" and "generations." One large church pastor told me, "I'm haunted when I look into the eyes of my congregation and realize they are always only two weeks away from leaving for another church."

Curiously, the twentieth century, which began with some of the strongest leaders in all history—some good like Winston Churchill and Franklin Roosevelt, many bad like Lenin and Stalin—ended with a weak style of leadership codependent on followership: the leader as panderer.

"I hear it said," Churchill remarked in a speech in the House of Commons on September 30, 1941, that "leaders should keep their ears to the ground. All I can say is that the British nation will find it very hard to look up to the leaders who are detected in that somewhat ungainly posture." "Nothing is more dangerous . . . ," he said another time, "than to live in the temperamental atmosphere of a Gallup Poll—always feeling one's pulse and taking one's temperature."

Though almost always impressive before audiences and sometimes dazzling, Churchill himself was described by his friend Violet Bonham Carter as being "as impervious to atmosphere as a diver in his bell." Similarly Harry Truman, whose presidency included such momentous decisions as the Marshall Plan and the first use of the atomic bomb, once said: "I wonder how far Moses would have gone if he had taken a poll in Egypt."

By contrast, as great a genius as Wolfgang Amadeus Mozart could write (in a letter to his father in 1778), "I am never in a good humor when I am in a town where I am quite unknown." Extreme examples of "other-direction" or "outside-in" thinking are easy to find and poke fun at. For instance, an old French story tells of a revolutionary sitting in a Paris café who suddenly hears a disturbance outside. He jumps to his feet and cries, "There goes the mob. I am their leader. I must follow them." Churchill's friend and colleague (and later prime minister) David Lloyd George was famed for his acute sensitivity to public opinion. Lord Keynes was once asked what happened to Lloyd George when he was alone in the room. Keynes replied, "When Lloyd George is alone in the room there is nobody there."

Screen goddess Marlene Dietrich even issued recordings of her cabaret ovations—two sides of nothing but applause. Her biographer tells us that she frequently gathered friends to listen and insisted on playing both sides to Judy Garland and Noel Coward. "That was Rio," she told them solemnly, "That was Cologne. That was Chicago."

Such narcissism may be fatuous, but we are all affected by the overall shift. The Puritans lived as if they had swallowed gyroscopes; we modern Christians live as if we have swallowed Gallup polls. Or as Martin Luther King wrote in his *Letter from Birmingham Jail,* "in those days the church was not merely a thermometer that recorded the ideas and principles of popular opinion; it was a thermostat that transformed the mores of society." Leaders or panderers? Gyroscope or Gallup poll? Thermostat or thermometer? Only those who practice the presence of the Audience of One can hope to attain the former and escape the latter.

Growing awareness of the Audience of One has greatly helped me in the vicissitudes of my own calling. Part of my calling, as I have discovered it and tried to fulfill it, has been to make sense of the gospel to the world (as an apologist) and to make sense of the world to the church (as an analyst). I have sought to do both in a way that stands between high, specialized, academic knowledge and ordinary, popular thinking.

This attempt to bridge means that no single human audience is my sole, natural audience. In fact, each audience sometimes scorns the effort to reach the other. No sooner does one side dismiss the effort as hopelessly "intellectual" than the other disdains it as "mere popularizing." So I find it a tremendous comfort as well as a continual challenge to remember that above and beyond the impossible-to-satisfy constituencies is the one audience that matters—the Audience of One.

To live before the Audience of One truly makes a demonstrable difference. The character and life of the great nineteenth-century Christian soldier General Charles Gordon, sometimes known as "Chinese Gordon" or "Gordon of Khartoum," is a striking example. In his book on the recapture of Sudan, Winston Churchill described General Gordon as "a man careless alike of the frowns of men or the smiles of women, of life or comfort, wealth or fame." But these words came almost directly from Gordon himself. "The more one sees of life . . ." Gordon wrote, "the more one feels, in order to keep from shipwreck, the necessity of steering by the Polar Star, i.e. in a word leave to God alone, and never pay attention to the favors or smiles of man; if He smiles on you, neither the smile or frown of men can affect you."

General Gordon was eventually abandoned and left to die in the siege of Khartoum because of the moral cowardice of Prime Minister William Gladstone and his Cabinet in London. His end at the hand of the Mahdi and his fanatical followers is legendary. But his calling-inspired strength was equally legendary through-out his entire life.

"Do you know, Gordon Pasha," snarled the cruel King John of Abyssinia in an earlier incident, "that I could kill you on the spot if I liked?"

"I am perfectly well aware of it, Your Majesty," Gordon replied. "Do so at once if it is your royal pleasure. I am ready."

"What, ready to be killed?"

"Certainly. I am always ready to die. . . ."

"Then my power has no terrors for you?" the king gasped.

"None whatever!" Gordon answered, and the king left him, amazed.

After Gordon's death John Bonar, a Scottish friend, wrote to Gordon's brother. "What at once, and always struck me was the way in which his oneness with God ruled all his actions, and his mode of seeing things. I never knew one who seemed so much to 'endure as seeing Him who is invisible.'" Gordon, he concluded, seemed "to live with God, and for God."

General Charles Gordon, peerless military strategist, legendary commander, and mostly all-conquering victor, lived so closely before the Audience of One that when his time came, he had only a short step home. Like all for whom God's call is decisive, it could be said of him, "I live before the Audience of One. Before others I have noth-ing to prove, nothing to gain, nothing to lose."

*Do you wish to be inner-directed rather than other-directed
and truly make one audience decisive, the Audience of One?
Listen to Jesus of Nazareth; answer his call.*

10

OUR UTMOST FOR HIS
HIGHEST STILL

Once, when Winston Churchill was on holiday staying with friends in the south of France, he came into the house on a chilly evening, sat down by the fireplace, and stared silently into the flames. Resin-filled pine logs were crackling, hissing, and spitting as they burned. Suddenly his familiar voice growled, "I know why logs spit. I know what it is to be consumed."

Human beings consume and are consumed by many things—food, drink, possessions, ambition, love, to name a few. Many of these things only shrink and debase us. But in the great person and with the great cause, the consuming force may become a magnificent obsession and a heroic destiny.

Winston Churchill himself was consumed by an extraordinary sense of providence and personal destiny—leading a nation and championing the cause of freedom against a vile tyranny at overwhelming odds. On the night of May 10, 1940, Churchill was invited by King George VI to form a government and lead Britain against the forces of Nazism that menaced Europe and threatened the free democracies. Churchill later recounted, "I felt as if I were walking with destiny, and that all my past life had been but a preparation for this hour and for this trial."

For some people the grand passion is art, music, or literature; for others the dream of freedom and justice; for yet others the love of a man or a woman. But search as you will, there is no higher or more ultimate passion than a human being ablaze with a desire for God.

79

Moses was such a person. By nature he was a man of action and not, as he said to God, "a man of words." He was transformed as he learned the failure of his own self-styled actions and the power of his halting words when they come from God himself. Twice he reverted to character as a man of action, once striking an Egyptian dead and once striking the rock to produce water. The first action turned out to be a failure; the second an act of disobedience.

Slowly, incident by incident, test by test, Moses was shaped to be a man of God and a prophet, a hero of the moral word. Supremely, facing the rebellion of the Golden Calf in the deepest crisis of his life, with his own survival as well as his leadership on the line, he prayed audaciously to know all of God that God will allow and a fallen human being can stand to know. "Lord, show me your glory," he asked and his request was granted. From then on his eyes had quite literally seen the glory of the coming of the Lord and he lived to tell the story.

Little wonder Moses was later given the tribute, "Since then, no prophet has risen in Israel like Moses, whom the Lord knew face to face." But how was this great intimate of God called? He was arrested at the sight of a bush, burning yet not burned up—as if God were telling him from the very beginning that his call would set his life on fire, but the fire would not consume him.

Nearer our own time Blaise Pascal was another such person on fire with passion for God. Mathematical genius, inventor, grandfather of the computer and modern risk theory, renaissance thinker well versed in physics, philosophy, and theology as well as mathematics, among the most elegant prose stylists in the French language, Pascal is one of the supreme human thinkers of all time and author of a great masterpiece of Western literature—*Pensées*.

But almost no one in Pascal's day and still too few in ours know of the experience that kept these achievements in perspective and lay at the core of his brief, intense, pain-filled, flame burst of a life. On the evening of Monday, November 23, 1654, he was thirty-one years old and had just experienced a close brush with death in a carriage driving accident. That night he had a profound encounter with God that changed the course of his life. Pascal was a notoriously fast driver and skeptics were ready with their scorn. "My friend," Voltaire scoffed to Condorcet, "never weary saying that since the accident on the Neuilly Bridge, Pascal's brain was damaged!"

Pascal's experience lasted from 10:30 P.M. until 12:30 A.M. It is often called his "second conversion," to distinguish it from his first, more formal conversion at Rouen when he was twenty-four. What he went through strained and finally shattered the capacities of his language. He could only title it in one word: *fire*. But the experience was so precious and decisive to him that he sewed the parchment record of it into the lining of his doublet and wore it next to his heart. For the remaining eight years of his life he took the trouble to sew it into every new doublet he bought, and it was only found by his sister, who felt the odd bump it formed, after his death in 1662 at the age of thirty-nine. The opening half of his "Memorial" reads:

Fire

"God of Abraham, God of Isaac, God of Jacob,"
    not of philosophers and scholars.
Certainty, certainty, heartfelt, joy, peace.
God of Jesus Christ.
God of Jesus Christ.
My God and Your God.
"Your God shall be my God."
The world forgotten, and everything except God.
He can only be found by the ways taught in the Gospels.
Greatness of the human soul.
"O righteous father, the world had not known thee,
    but I have known thee."
Joy, Joy, Joy, tears of joy.

Most of us cannot begin to understand Pascal's mathematical accomplishments, and we would not wish to experience the pain and suffering of his short life. But what lit and fanned into a blaze the deep potential of his character and gifts is something open to us all—the call of God. The call came to Pascal so deeply that he became a man consumed by a divine fire that touched his life and work. As such Pascal illustrates a further aspect of the wonder of calling—*God's calling is the key to igniting a passion for the deepest growth and highest heroism in life.*

FOR CHRIST'S SAKE, EXCELLENCE!

Heroism, it is often said, has fallen on hard times in the modern world. Many reasons have been given, but two are especially prominent. One is the modern habit of debunking. Aleksandr Solzhenitsyn described Stalin as so suspicious that "mistrust was his worldview." But following the three grand masters of suspicion, Nietzsche, Marx, and Freud, we have all been schooled in the art of mistrust. Heroism is therefore automatically suspect today. As modern people, we look straightaway not for the golden aura but for the feet of clay, not for the stirring example but for the cynical motive, not for the ideal embodied but for the energetic press agent.

Only then, we say to ourselves, will we know we are not being duped. But the trouble is, only rarely do we suspend disbelief. So even if there are genuine heroes today, it is difficult for us to admire them long enough to emulate them.

The other reason commonly given for the crisis of heroism is that, in fact, there are fewer heroes—because of the role of the press and media in creating the modern celebrity and widening the gap between fame and greatness, heroism and accomplishment. Formerly, it is pointed out, heroism was linked to the honor of accomplishment. Honor was accorded to the person with some genuine achievement, whether in character, virtue, wisdom, the arts, sport, or warfare.

Today, however, the media offer a shortcut to fame—instantly fabricated famousness with no need for the sweat, cost, and dedication of true greatness. The result is not the hero but the celebrity, the person famously described as "well-known for being well-known."

A big name rather than a big person, the celebrity is someone for whom character is nothing, coverage is all.

Powerful and important though they are, these two factors pale beside a third reason for the crisis of heroism—the so-called death of God in Western society or what should be termed more accurately the drowning out of the call of God in modern life.

Psychologist Ernest Becker clearly recognized this problem. In his book *The Denial of Death* he acknowledged: "One can only talk about an ideal human character from a perspective of absolute transcendence." Becker therefore saw that Søren Kierkegaard's formula for what it means to be a man was apt and inspiring. To be a great human being was to be "a knight of faith," which Becker describes sympathetically:

> This figure is the man who lives in faith, who has given over the meaning of his life to his Creator, and who lives centered on the energies of his Creator. He accepts whatever happens in this visible dimension without complaint, lives his life as a duty, faces his death without a qualm. No pettiness is so petty that it threatens his meanings; no task is too frightening to be beyond his courage. He is fully in the world on its terms and wholly beyond the world in his trust in the invisible dimension.

Becker readily acknowledged the beauty of this calling. The knight of faith is "surely one of the most beautiful and challenging ideals ever put forth by man." But he concluded sadly, "One cannot give the gifts of the knight of faith without first being dubbed by some Higher Majesty." Just as there is no calling without a Caller and no age of faith unless the purpose of life is placed beyond life, so—for people without God—there are no knights of faith because there is no Higher Majesty to dub them.

But what of the person of faith whose life is an answer to the call of God, who has been dubbed by a Higher Majesty? Following the call becomes the secret of growth and a key to heroism in two ways. First, God's call always challenges us directly to rise to our full stature as human beings. As we saw earlier, human beings who come face to face with the presence and call of God typically react like many in the Old Testament—falling flat on their faces in awe and wonder. But when they do, God's response is to say, as to Ezekiel at his call, "Stand up on your feet and I will speak to you."

In other words, there is more to God's call than simply sending us out—the commissioning, as calling is usually thought to be. Certainly, it ends by "sending us out," but it begins by "singling us out"—we are called by name—and it continues by "standing us up." As we respond to the call of our Creator, we rise to our feet, not only physically but also in every sense of the word, to be the people he alone knows we are capable of being. Like a coach bringing out the full capacity of each member of the team, or a conductor bringing out the deepest potential of the orchestra, God's call resonates in us at depths no other call can reach and draws us on and out and up to heights no other call can scale or see.

C. S. Lewis well captures this thrilling theme. The higher and different sort of life of God's call is as far above normal life, as spiritual life is above biological life. Certainly there is a resemblance, as between a photo and a place, or a statue and a man. But someone rising to the call and passing from the biological life to the spiritual life "would have gone through as big a change as a statue which changed from being a carved stone to being a real man. And that is precisely what Christianity is about. This world is a great sculptor's shop. We are the statues and there is a rumor going round the shop that some of us are some day going to come to life."

Second, God's call to follow him is vital to growth and heroism because it includes the element of imitation that is at its heart. Even with human heroism, the hero is the person of worth on whom we model our lives and pour forth our surging aspirations, and thereby grow higher than we ever would on our own. But merely human heroes are always fallible, sometimes disappointing, and they often compete with our other heroes for our loyalty. Concerning them we can agree with Nietzsche: "One repays a teacher badly if one always remains a pupil only." Jesus Christ, fully God and fully man, is the one true hero. He alone will never be surpassed, but neither will we surpass what we grow to be if we model ourselves on him.

Following God's call therefore says that as we run the race of faith, "let us fix our eyes on Jesus, the author and perfecter of our faith"— the Greek word for pattern and role model. Similarly, the apostle Paul wrote to the disciples in Corinth, "Be imitators of me as I am of Christ." Or as Dostoevsky's Father Zossima said, "What is Christ's word without an example?"

Paul's use of the word *imitators* is important. Modeling—observing and copying—is vital to discipleship because of the biblical view of the way disciples must learn. There is always more to knowing than human knowing will ever know. So the deepest knowledge can never be put into words—or spelled out in sermons, books, lectures, and seminars. It must be learned from the Master, under his authority, in experience. When we read in the Gospels that Jesus chose twelve "to be with him," their being with him was not some extra privilege they enjoyed. It was the heart and soul of their discipleship and learning.

The theme of tutoring and imitation, which goes far deeper than current notions of "mentoring," is conspicuous in the teaching of the early church. We grow through copying deeds not just listening to words, through example as well as precept, through habit and not just insight and information. Calling therefore creates an ethic of aspiration, not just of obligation. Ignatius of Antioch urged the Philadelphians "to imitate Jesus Christ as he imitated the Father." Clement of Alexandria wrote, "Our tutor Jesus Christ exemplifies the true life and trains the one who is in Christ. . . . He gives commands and embodies the commands that we might be able to accomplish them."

Clement's last sentence is noteworthy. Some Christians are suspicious of imitation because it sounds like a form of self-help spirituality. Modeling seems to smack of a foolproof method of growth that is as mechanical as the instructions for assembling a model airplane. But they misunderstand imitation. For one thing, genuine "originality" is God's prerogative, not ours. At our most "creative," we are only imitative. For another, imitating a life is far from wooden. Real lives touch us profoundly—they stir, challenge, rebuke, shame, amuse, and inspire at levels of which we are hardly aware. That is why biographies are the literature of calling; few things are less mechanical.

No one apart from Jesus and Paul has been more influential on the church than Augustine. Not only do we have his many writings but we also have his unique *Confessions*. Yet when Augustine died, his contemporaries, who also knew his live sermons, appreciated most of all his life. His friend Possidius wrote: "Yet I think that those who gained most from him were those who had been able actually to see and hear him as he spoke in Church, and, most of all, those who had some contact with the quality of his life among men."

Importantly, imitating Christ is not a form of do-it-yourself change because it is part and parcel of responding to the call—a decisive divine word whose creative power is the deepest secret of the change. Think of Ezekiel's vision of the valley of the dry bones or the astounding miracle of Jesus calling the dead Lazarus out of the tomb. Can anyone listen to that voice, see what it effects, and still say the hearers responded by themselves? Do dry, brittle bones ever reassemble into a body on their own? Can a corpse shake off death by itself?

No more do we change by ourselves as we imitate Christ. The imitation of Christ that is integral to following him means that, when he calls us, he enables us to do what he calls us to do.

Has anyone said it better than Oswald Chambers in his matchless description of the disciple's master passion, "My utmost for his highest"? Often I hear it said that Christians have no equivalent of the Greek notion of excellence—the ideal that each person or thing is to achieve the highest standard of perfection of which it is capable. That is not true. However, the pursuit of excellence that for the Greeks could be achieved by human endeavor alone is only possible for the follower of Christ in response to the high call of God.

Do you long to rise to the full stature of whom you are created to be? To know the passion of the intensity of life at its fullest? To be your utmost for his highest? Listen to Jesus of Nazareth; answer his call.

11

WHERE THE BUCK
STOPS, THERE STAND I

Pablo Picasso's creative genius towers over twentieth century art. But in his relationships, especially with women, he could be a devouring monster. The "Minotaur" was his own name for himself, and "monster" was the word used by friends such as sculptor Alberto Giacometti. "When I die," Picasso said, "it will be a shipwreck, and as when a huge ship sinks, many people all around will be sucked down with it."

Sadly, Picasso was right. After he died in 1973, aged ninety-one, three of those closest to him committed suicide—his second wife Jacqueline, an early mistress Marie-Thérèse, and his grandson Pablito—and several others had psychiatric breakdowns, including his first wife Olga and his most famous mistress Dora Maar. This destructiveness showed itself from his early days. His own mother warned his first wife: "I don't believe any woman could be happy with my son. He's available for himself but for no one else."

In *Life with Picasso,* Francoise Gilot recounts the story of her ten years as his third mistress, forty years his junior. He was so compelling, she wrote, that there were "moments when it seemed almost a physical impossibility to go on breathing outside his presence." But as Picasso admitted, there were only two kinds of women in his world—"goddesses and doormats"—and sooner or later everyone went from the first category to the second. Dora Maar, who preceded Gilot as Picasso's mistress, eventually told him, "You've never loved anyone in your life. You don't know how to love." And Gilot once told him he was "the devil"—whereupon Picasso branded her with a cigarette held to her cheek, stopping only because "I may still want to look at you."

Picasso himself said to Francoise Gilot, "Every time I change wives I should bury the last one. That way I'd be rid of them. . . . You kill the woman and you wipe out the past she represents." Gilot called this Picasso's "Bluebeard complex," and there is no question it was linked to his atheism. An avowed follower of Nietzsche, Picasso held that God was dead and was heard muttering, "I am God, I am God." In the nihilistic vacuum that Picasso created, among the forces that remained were a demonic drive to keep producing art and exercising power over people.

But, needless to say, Pablo Picasso remained not only a great artist but also a human being made in the image of God. For all his destructiveness, he still showed yearnings that pointed in another direction. One of the most poignant examples startled Gilot with its contradiction. One day, three years into their relationship, they were at Antibes in the south of France when Picasso suddenly steered Gilot toward a little church and guided her into a dark corner near the front.

"You're going to swear here that you'll love me forever," Picasso said.

"I can swear that anywhere," Gilot replied, taken aback, "if I want to commit myself to that extent. But why here?"

"I think it's better done here than just anywhere," he said.

"Here or somewhere else, it's all the same," she replied.

"No, no," Picasso said, "well, yes, of course, it *is* all the same, but it's one of those things. You never know. There may be something to all that stuff about churches. It might make the whole thing a little surer. Who knows?"

So Gilot swore, she says, and Picasso swore, and he seemed satisfied.

Was Picasso's insistence superstition or intuition? Picasso was unquestionably superstitious and fatalistic. He had taught Gilot bleakly that "any love could last only for a predetermined period"—so much so that she wrote: "Every day I felt that ours had one less day to go." But he was also incurable in his longing. "I guess I'll die without ever being loved," he said another time. After all, as an old ballad puts it, "If love is not forever, what's forever for?" But such a yearning points beyond the frailties of human relationships. It cries out for an eternal reference point. Only an eternal standard can hold accountable a desire for enduring love. So Picasso, the atheist still made in the image of God whom he denied, intuitively headed to the church to hold himself responsible as he and his lover declared their love to each other.

RESPONSIBILITY TO OR FOR?

This incident from Picasso's life highlights a further aspect of the importance of calling: *The notion of calling is vital to the modern search for a basis for moral responsibility and to an understanding of ethics itself.*

The Western world is awash today with equal parts of hand wringing over the moral crisis and pious calls for greater responsibility to remedy it. For religious people and many conservatives the two are closely linked—moral responsibility is the answer to the moral crisis. For some secular people there is no real moral crisis, only new challenges in a secular society where religion is less relevant and responsibility is the respectable way to talk about morals without talking about religion. For other secular people the crisis of modern morals is very real—ethics has collapsed into a "morally ungrounded morality"—but what saves us, they say, is the bedrock of responsibility. To be "moral" does not mean to be "good" but to exercise one's freedom and responsibility as either an author or actor in choosing between good and evil.

Contemporary calls for responsibility are legion. They range from the 1948 World Council of Churches slogan about a "responsible society" to the 1994 Republican Party's "Personal Responsibility Act" in the *Contract with America*. No discussion of morals is complete without this all-purpose, high-status word. "Responsible" doubles for "good" in ethics, for "nice" among neighbors, for "professional" in the world of business, and for "reasonable" and "reliable" in a score of *New York Times* editorials. Apparently the common remedy for criminals, welfare junkies, unwed mothers, deadbeat dads, teenagers, and presidential candidates alike is greater "responsibility."

Curiously, few people stop to ask what it means to "take responsibility for our responsibility" or to ask whether "responsibility" can possibly be responsible for the weight of all these expectations. Signs are that it can't. First, the notion of responsibility has all the marks of a "sunset value"—like the sun, it is most colorful and appreciated just as it is setting. Second, the novelty of its current prominence should make us pause. Prior to the nineteenth century, responsibility was assumed as a foundation of virtue, but it was not considered a virtue in itself. Only as the classical virtues disappeared has it become one of the few virtues left—in a reduced pantheon of virtues, it lingers on with such modern virtues as tolerance. Third, and most important of all, the notion of responsibility has been severed from its roots, without which it is fated to wither and die. Modern responsibility, contradicting its origins, is all "responsibility *for*" and no "responsibility *to*."

Put differently, calls to modern responsibility lay heavy burdens on us. We are told we are responsible *for* ourselves, *for* our personalities, *for* our bodies, *for* our futures, *for* our families, *for* our communities, *for* our environment, *for* our societies, and *for* the planet Earth. But this seems ever more hopeless and unfair. On the one hand, many of those things appear bigger, more complicated, and less controllable every year. On the other hand, we are no longer told *to* whom we are responsible for those burdens. For modern, secular, freedom-loving people responsibility to God is out of the picture and responsibility to society is out of the question.

So when we feel overwhelmed, it's easier to throw off the responsibility altogether. It's true that the charge of "irresponsibility" assumes a standard of "responsibility." It's true too, paradoxically, that only "bad people" have "good consciences." But when we are called to be responsible *for* too much and responsible *to* no one, then responsibility itself collapses.

Thus we are living in a time when leaders "take full responsibility" for mistakes and solemnly intone that "the buck stops here"—but never resign or appear to acknowledge any guilt. In practice responsibility seems little different from irresponsibility. Those preaching about "taking responsibility" one moment can be heard claiming "victim status" the next. Rejecting an impossible responsibility and refusing all responsibility are closer than many realize.

In stark contrast to this sad situation, the truth of calling provides a profound basis for responsibility. "In the beginning was the Word"—and in each of our beginnings was a Word to us. Each of our lives is therefore relational and aural at core. All we are is a hearing and a response. We are responsible because we are response-able. Between the first word of God's creation and the last word of his judgment our ways of life are our response to God's Word to us. There is no God but God. There is no word but God's Word. There is no way of life but God's way of life. But for the time being our response is up to us; we are not forced to say yes. Indeed, as Kierkegaard insists, "All the shrewdness of 'man' seeks one thing: to be able to live without responsibility."

Jesus therefore adds after his teaching, "If you have ears to hear, then hear." Of course those who heard him all had ears; of course they didn't all hear. Being responsible, we will be held responsible one day if not today.

Hitler's propaganda minister Joseph Goebbels based all of his strategy on the maxim, "Whoever says the first word to the world is always right." But he was wrong: The last word is the word that counts. For while we may debate our freedom to choose, there is no doubt that we are not free *not* to choose. Those who reject God's first word never escape his last. The Day of Judgment is one day on which responsibility comes home to roost. For once in our lives the buck will stop where the buck belongs.

In the meantime we who are followers of Christ must pick up and shoulder this challenging view of responsibility. Answering the call by its very nature is a stepping forward to responsibility. Responsibility is obedience by another name. We do not have the excuse of the careless silence, the awkward silence, or the desperate silence of those without a Caller. We have heard the call, and we acknowledge and assume our responsibility. Thus, to adapt Shakespeare, where the buck stops, there stand I. Our calling is the sphere of our responsibility. But we are not responsible to our calling. We are responsible to God, and our calling is where we exercise that responsibility.

The responsibility of calling must not become cant or cliché. Faith's significance for society, Kierkegaard wrote, "ought to be to do everything to make every man eternally responsible for every hour he lives, even for the least thing he undertakes, for this is Christianity." Today we must make responsibility real in the teeth of empty modern bombast and at a time when accountability is down and alibis are up. For as the Picasso story suggests, responsibility is most difficult when we are anonymous or invisible to everyone but God.

The fact is that much traditional morality was accountability. Both those who did right and those who did not do wrong often acted as they did because they knew they were seen by others. Their morality was accountability through visibility. Situations of anonymity are not, of course, new. But for most people most of the time, their villages or towns were sufficiently cohesive and their relationships sufficiently close that behavior was held in check. In small towns neighborliness was often "nosiness" just as in cities anonymity was often "liberation." But the point still stands—traditional morality was closely tied to accountability.

In the modern world, however, anonymity has risen sharply. Admiral Lord Nelson remarked that "every sailor is a bachelor when beyond Gibraltar." But what sent shivers down the spines of naval wives and sweethearts in the eighteenth century now raises questions for all concerned with right and wrong. For much of modern life is lived "beyond Gibraltar." More of us today are more anonymous in more situations than any generation in human history. Humanly anonymous and invisible, we must consciously hold ourselves responsible to the one audience—the Audience of One—or succumb to irresponsibility.

In his *Letters to Olga* Václav Havel asked, "Why is it that when we are traveling alone (a single stop) in the second car of a conductorless streetcar, so that obviously no one could catch us not paying, we still usually—though perhaps after an inner tussle—drop our fare in the box? Why do we do good at all even when there is clearly no personal advantage in doing so (for instance when no one knows about it and never will)?"

The answer, Havel argues, is more than conscience and upbringing. We are responsible human beings and responsibility means "vouching for ourselves" and "standing behind everything we do" before whatever is behind life. But, again, Havel is unusual. For everyone who behaves like him there are scores who don't. Why are there more temptations in a hotel room in a distant city than at home? Why do more people "flame" on the Internet than would ever lose their cool in an office? Travel and technology are only two of the ways modern life thrusts us from the world of the face-to-face to the world of the impersonal and the invisible. What we do then, when no one sees but God, is the test of our true responsibility.

The Genesis story of Joseph and Potiphar's wife shows calling in action. Invited by his master's wife to sleep with her, Joseph is completely unseen by human eyes—at that moment he has no father, no brothers, no master, no colleagues to witness his response. But his reply is unequivocal: "How then could I do such a wicked thing and sin against God?" Joseph had no human audience. But one audience was enough, the Audience of One.

Dietrich Bonhoeffer stated the same point simply in his *Ethics*: "Who stands fast? Only the man whose final standard is not his reason, his principles, his conscience, his freedom, or his virtue, but who is ready to sacrifice all this when he is called to obedient and responsible action in faith and in exclusive allegiance to God—the responsible man, who tries to make his whole life an answer to the question and call of God. Where are these responsible people?"

Where are these responsible people? In *Genealogy of Morals* Friedrich

Nietzsche described the search for human responsibility as "the task of breeding an animal entitled to make promises." Picasso the lover, Havel the poet-philosopher, and countless other would-be promise keepers would agree. But those who have heard the call go further. What entitles us to make promises when on our own we frail humans would do better to pray than vow? Apart from the call there is no responding and no responsibility. Only with this responsibility are we enabled, not entitled, to make promises that echo even weakly the covenant behind the call.

Do you wish to stand fast and be a responsible person, one "who tries to make his or her whole life an answer to the question and call of God"? Listen to Jesus of Nazareth; answer his call.

12

PEOPLE OF THE CALL

There are two things, it has often been said, that human beings cannot gaze at directly without going mad—the glory of God and the darkness of human evil. After years of studying human cruelty, Philip Hallie, professor of philosophy at Wesleyan University and a veteran of World War II, must have felt close to madness. Working on a project on Nazi cruelty, he focused on the medical experiments Nazi doctors conducted on Jewish children in the death camps.

"Across all these studies," Hallie wrote later, "the pattern of the strong crushing the weak kept repeating itself and repeating itself, so that when I was not bitterly angry, I was bored at the repetitions of the patterns of persecution. . . . My study of evil incarnate had become a prison whose bars were my bitterness toward the violent, and whose walls were my horrified indifference to slow murder. Between the bars and the walls I revolved like a madman . . . over the years I had dug myself into Hell."

During this time Hallie came across a short article about a small town of three thousand in the mountains of southern France, which was the only safe haven for Jews in all of German-occupied Europe. Reading with academic objectivity in his effort to classify types of cruelty and forms of resistance to it, he was about halfway down the third page of the story when he became "annoyed by a strange sensation on my cheeks." Reaching up to wipe away a piece of dust, he felt tears—"Not one or two drops; my whole cheek was wet." Those tears, Hallie wrote, were an instinctive "expression of moral praise."

What Hallie was reading was his introduction to the citizens of Le Chambon and their heroic rescue of more than five thousand Jewish children in the Second World War. Later written up in his modern classic *Lest Innocent Blood Be Shed*, Hallie came to realize the rightness of a summary by one of his readers: "The Holocaust was storm, lightning, thunder, wind, rain, yes. And Le Chambon was the rainbow." Yes, he concluded, "I realized that for me too the little story of Le Chambon is grander and more beautiful than the bloody war that stopped Hitler."

What emerges in his story is the strands of the stubborn courage of the Chambonnais. They were Huguenots, French Protestants fired by their faith in Christ and the experience of three hundred years of persecution following the revocation of the Edict of Nantes. And they were led, taught, and encouraged by their indomitable pastor, André Trocmé, and his equally heroic wife, Magda. But what comes across repeatedly is their character and the down-to-earth, no-nonsense quality of their faith.

Many French let themselves be deceived by the infamous "night and fog" propaganda with which the Germans concealed the death camps. But the Chambonnais simply did what had to be done, what they'd been taught to do, what Christ would have expected them to do—they sheltered and saved their neighbors, the Jews, who were in danger.

The evening Pastor Trocmé himself was arrested illustrates the whole story. The pastor and his wife had been invited to dinner by church members who, knowing they often forgot such invitations, sent their daughter to remind them. But when she entered the dining room, she saw the police arresting her pastor. So the word flew around the village: André Trocmé had been arrested.

Typically, however, Magda Trocmé invited the two policemen to have dinner with them. Friends were later incredulous and upset with her. "How could you bring yourself to sit down to eat with these men who were there to take your husband away, perhaps to his death? How could you be so forgiving, so decent to them?"

Madame Trocmé always gave the same answer: "What are you

talking about? It was dinner-time; they were standing in my way; we were all hungry. The food was ready. What do you mean by such foolish words as 'forgiving' and 'decent'?"

Such a response was typical. The Chambonnais shrugged off praise again and again. They would look Hallie in the eye and say, "How can you call us 'good'? We were doing what had to be done. Things had to be done, that's all, and we happened to be there to do them. You must understand that it was the most natural thing in the world to help these people." An outsider's words of moral praise, Philip Hallie concluded, are "like a slightly uncomfortable wreath laid upon a head by a kind but alien hand."

The story of Le Chambon is a stirring but all too rare example of the church of Christ in action as a corporate body in the modern world. It is also a reminder of a dimension of calling that modern believers tend to forget—*the call of Jesus is personal but not purely individual; Jesus summons his followers not only to an individual calling but also to a corporate calling.*

THE COVENANT COMMUNITY

When Margaret Thatcher was prime minister of Great Britain, she systematically dismantled much of the country's social welfare system in her successful bid to unleash the dynamism of a free market economy. One of her most famous justifications for her policy was more controversial: "There is no society, only individuals and their families."

The prime minister's remark annoyed liberals because she was using liberal language to attack liberalism. But it also dismayed conservatives because it ignored the rich texture of groups and associations that make up the worlds in which we all live. "Society" may be too abstract to exist for most people, but to assume that individuals and families can make up the whole picture is little better.

Community, of course, has fallen on hard times in the modern world. First, all modern people live with a greatly weakened sense of community compared with traditional people—due to modern travel, modern mobility, modern media, modern work and lifestyles, and the saturation of modern relationships.

To be sure, our nostalgia—literally homesickness—for a lost world tempts us to romanticize community in the traditional world. Doubtless it was often rigid and claustrophobic rather than liberating. To be sure too the benefits of the modern world are staggering. But there is a huge cost in the shift from involuntary community to voluntary groupings. And no amount of talk of "virtual community" can overlook the fact that communication that is person-to-person but not face-to-face amounts to a severe loss. The plain fact is that for most modern people, community is either a rare experience or a distant, even mocking, ideal.

Second, modern people are prone to a recurring bias against all institutions, especially large institutions. They are, we are almost raised to believe, impersonal, alienating, and dehumanizing. Protesters in the 1960s became famous for such slogans as "do not fold, spindle, or mutilate"—human beings were being handled as impersonally as IBM cards. But the widespread concern that became the cry of that decade has far earlier roots in a host of critiques of the rise of the modern world.

The great German social scientist Max Weber, for example, was the first to provide a penetrating analysis of modern bureaucracy. But his vision is best captured in the novels of Franz Kafka, especially *The Castle* and *The Trial*. The world of *The Castle* is the domain of bureaucratic power and authority. Telephone exchanges produce more muddles than connections. Bureaucracy drowns human beings in a deluge of files and forms. A stifling hierarchy makes it impossible to get through to a person above anyone. Countless petty officials work endless overtime and get nowhere. Innumerable interviews take place, but none of them comes to any purpose. In *The Castle* human beings are reduced to files and in *The Trial* to cases. As Kafka once said of such a world, "The conveyor belt of life carries you on, no one knows where. One is more of an object, a thing, than a living creature."

Third, believers in the modern world have had their sense of the corporate nature of the church weakened further by the rise of the voluntary associations. In a much-quoted passage in *Democracy in America,* Alexis de Tocqueville wrote, "Americans of all ages, all conditions, and all dispositions constantly form associations. . . . Whenever at the lead of a great undertaking you see the government in France, or a man of rank in England, in the United States you will be sure to find an association."

These words usually conjure up pictures of an earlier golden age of voluntarism, but in fact you cannot trace back American voluntarism to colonial beginnings. The seeds of the idea were there—the voluntary church, with its voluntary membership and voluntary contributions, is the historical prototype of the voluntary association. But from Thomas Hobbes's *Leviathan* to George Washington's Farewell Address, a powerful current of suspicion runs against voluntary association, because of the fear of "faction." (Since nothing should exist apart from state control, Hobbes wrote, voluntary associations were "worms in the entrails of Leviathan.")

Voluntary associations actually flowered only slightly before the arrival of Tocqueville, urged on by such evangelical leaders as Lyman Beecher of Connecticut. They were the products partly of the Second Awakening, partly of the second wave of disestablishment in the early nineteenth century, and partly of the precedent of successful evangelical associations in Britain in the era of William Wilberforce. But what matters is the effect: The rise of voluntary associations shifted the emphasis of moral agency in public life from local churches as institutions to individual Christians acting as individuals in public life—in association.

The outcome was overwhelmingly beneficial. Voluntary associations led to an outburst of diverse, creative enterprises that no local church could have matched. And Christian individuals in association could enter spheres and engage issues that no local church could risk. But they also came with a cost. Voluntary associations (and later "parachurch" organizations) reinforced the trend toward individualism and further eclipsed the corporate nature of the church in most Christians' minds.

These three major factors have been reinforced by a number of lesser factors—not least the fact that the business corporation has virtually taken over all language of corporate institutions. When we say "corporation" today, we almost always mean business corporation. This is both a far cry from the humble beginnings in the incorporation of the East India Company and a drastic shrinking of the idea that bodies (corporations) of more than one human being can have personal characteristics.

In short, experiencing the corporateness of the church of Christ, let alone the decisive influence of a local church like that of Le Chambon, is rare for many of us as modern believers. However strong our individual callings are, our sense of corporate calling is often very faint.

The call of Jesus runs counter to all these modern trends because it is inescapably a corporate calling. Our word *church* translates the common, secular Greek word for a popular "assembly." But with its root meaning in the word for "called out" and its Old Testament meaning in the idea of a "called out people," the church is the assembly of God's people, called out by him and belonging to him. Each of us is summoned individually and therefore uniquely and personally. But we are not summoned to be a bunch of individual believers, rather to be a community of faith.

In the New Testament, it is not so much that there are different churches in different places as that there is one church in many places. Each local church embodies and represents the whole church, so the church is both local and universal, visible and invisible, militant and triumphant. Yet the idea does not evaporate into vague mysticism—because of calling: The called-out assembly of God's people, which is subordinated to Christ as its head and coordinated with its fellow members of the body, lives its life by its practical obedience to God's call in Christ.

The story of the church, like the story of Israel, is the story of a people, not just of individuals. Prior to the exodus from Egypt, the Bible tells us of God's call to individuals and to families. But the phrase "the people of Israel" is first used in Exodus. The descendants of these same individuals and families are now fused into a people and a community by the founding acts of liberation and covenant.

Thus over against history's involuntary groupings, such as the tribe, the city-state, and the nation, there now stands a new community composed of willing members—the assembly of God's called-out ones. These are bound together by a covenant and living out a corporate calling that both complements and transcends their callings as individuals.

Is any part of our calling harder than this one? For many of us a living sense of corporate calling has to be rebuilt slowly and painfully like someone learning to walk again after a stroke. But some of the main challenges are plain.

First, commitment to our corporate calling means we must resolutely guard against modern proneness to casual individualism. Exploding denominationalism is one example. According to the *World Christian Encyclopedia* (1982) there were an estimated 1,900 Christian denominations at the beginning of the twentieth century and an estimated 22,000 at the end. Under the influence of the modern world, the historical "accident" of denominations has become a theological disaster for anyone believing in one church.

How much better the generosity of spirit of John Bunyan: "I would be, as I hope I am, a Christian. But for those factious titles of Anabaptist, Independent, Presbyterian, and the like, I conclude that they come neither from Jerusalem nor from Antioch, but from Hell or Babylon." Or of George Whitefield: "Father Abraham, whom have you in heaven? Any Episcopalians? No! Any Presbyterians? No! Any Independents or Methodists? No, no, no! Whom have you there? We don't know those names here. All who are here are Christians. . . . Oh, is this the case? Then God help us to forget party names and to become Christians in deed and truth." Or of William Wilberforce: "Though I am an Episcopalian by birth, I yet feel such a oneness and sympathy with the cause of God at large, that nothing would be more delightful than communing once a year with every church that holds the Head, even Christ."

For many people another challenge of individualism is closer and easier to change: commitment to faithful, regular worship. One of the most bizarre features of the Western church is the incidence of

Christian leaders who are undisciplined about regular worship in the assembly of God's people. Excuses are legion—the busyness of schedules, the richness of alternative fellowship, a proper disdain of legalism, and the supposed distraction of a well-known Christian attending a service. But the outcome is a casualness about worship that is a sorry contradiction of their leadership.

Second, commitment to our corporate calling means that we must honor the purpose and interests of the church of Christ in all our individual callings. One way in which we fail to do this is through the error of "particularism"—the idea that there is only one particular Christian way to do a thing and, of course, that our way is "the Christian way."

The fallacy of particularism stems from the fact that God has not spoken definitively to us about everything. Obviously he did not intend to. It is an error for Christians to make relative what God has made absolute. But it is equally an error for Christians to make absolute what God has left relative. As G. K. Chesterton wrote, "If there is one thing worse than the modern weakening of major morals it is the modern strengthening of minor morals."

Put differently, where God has not spoken definitively, we can legitimately say, "This practice (political decision, lifestyle, or whatever) is *not* Christian"—if it contradicts the teaching of the Bible. But we cannot legitimately go on to say, "This practice *alone* is Christian."

This point means that there is no one Christian form of politics any more than there is one Christian form of poetry, raising a family, running an economy, or planning a retirement. Many ways are definitely *not* Christian, but no *one* way alone is. We should especially beware of Christian voluntary associations using the title "The Christian X, Y, or Z." All too often, and especially with Christian political organizations, such names are not only improper in principle but also confusing in practice because they mislead the watching world into identifying the group with the church as a whole. Christian political organizations that also disregard the maxim, "Do God's work in God's way," make the situation even worse. Christian means that do not serve Christ's end will subvert Christ's end and tar the whole church with the brush of their lack of wisdom.

Third, commitment to our corporate calling means remembering the need for ongoing reformation and even for the reformation of reformation. As we saw earlier, the Carthusian monastic movement was proud of its motto, "Never reformed because never deformed." But in a fallen world the Reformation maxim *Semper Reformanda* ("always reforming") is nearer the mark. We are all always in need of reformation.

Today our deepest need is not just for reformation but for the "reformation of reformation" as well. Throughout much of Christian history, the impulse toward reformation has been carried by the voluntary principle and the voluntary movement—whether earlier Catholic movements such as the Benedictine and Franciscan orders or more recent Protestant movements such as missionary societies and some parachurch organizations. These special kinds of reforming voluntary associations were the *ecclesiola in ecclesia* ("the little church in the large church").

Now, due to the modern eclipse of the corporate church by exploding individualism, the reforming principle has run amok. Many of the "little churches" of the voluntary associations have become an end in themselves. They deform rather than reform the church—and need reforming themselves. The business of "the little church" is to put itself out of business by feeding its wisdom and concern back into "the large church" and so contribute to the reformation of the one body that is central to God's purpose for all time. Yet many Protestant organizations are as much in need of dissolution as the monasteries in Henry VIII's England.

Needless to say, such implications of our corporate calling as members of the church of Christ raise difficult questions and challenges. But if calling is to be honest and practical, and not just a pious figure of speech, we must not duck the issue.

The eminent French statesman and priest Talleyrand said well, "Without individuals, nothing happens; without institutions, nothing survives." But the corporateness of the church goes far beyond institutional realism and survival. It is a matter of the mystical unity of the followers of Christ comprising "the body of Christ."

Psychologist Jean Piaget attacked the Christian faith for this mystical sense of corporateness. He wrote in his *Moral Judgment of the Child*, "Only in theology, that is to say, in the most conservative of the institutions, does the idea of Original Sin keep alive the idea of collective responsibility." But we may wear his criticism as a compliment. Not only "Original Sin" but more positive notions of corporateness, too, such as the church as "the body of Christ" and "the communion of saints," are part of the glory of the gospel. Keep alive an appreciation of the corporateness of the life of faith and we remain true not only to our calling but also to the full reality of humanness.

Are you frustrated with "the institutional church," as if there is such a thing as a noninstitutional church? Is your communal expression of faith only a spiritual equivalent of a "lifestyle preference" and a "lifestyle enclave"? Or are you committed to the holy, catholic, and apostolic church? Is your allegiance truly to a nonpolitical and nonethnic assembly of people designed to gather all nations to itself, on the basis not of tribe or nation but the call of God in Christ? Listen to Jesus of Nazareth; answer his call.

13

FOLLOWERS OF THE WAY

Arthur F. Burns, the chairman of the United States Federal Reserve System and ambassador to West Germany, was a man of considerable gravity. Medium in height, distinguished, with wavy silver hair and his signature pipe, he was economic counselor to numerous presidents from Dwight D. Eisenhower to Ronald Reagan. When he spoke, his opinion carried weight and Washington listened.

Arthur Burns was also Jewish, so when he began attending an informal White House group for prayer and fellowship in the 1970s, he was accorded special respect. No one in fact knew quite how to involve him in the group and, week after week when different people took turns to end the meeting in prayer, Burns was passed by—out of a mixture of respect and reticence.

One week, however, the group was led by a newcomer who did not know the unusual status Burns occupied. As the meeting ended, the newcomer turned to Arthur Burns and asked him to close the time with a prayer. Some of the old-timers glanced at each other in surprise and wondered what would happen. But without missing a beat, Burns reached out, held hands with the others in the circle, and prayed this prayer: "Lord, I pray that you would bring Jews to know Jesus Christ. I pray that you would bring Muslims to know Jesus Christ. Finally, Lord, I pray that you would bring Christians to know Jesus Christ. Amen."

Arthur Burns's prayer has become legendary in Washington. Not only did he startle those present with his refreshing directness, but he also underscored a point about "Christians" and "Christianity" that needs repeating regularly. It highlights another important aspect of the truth of calling: *Calling reminds Christians ceaselessly that, far from having arrived, a Christian is someone who in this life is always on the road as "a follower of Christ" and a follower of "the Way."*

THE ONE UNANSWERABLE OBJECTION

Think of the three terms *Christ, Christian,* and *Christianity.* How would you describe the progression from the first to the second to the third? Conjure up all the associations each word has and you find yourself moving in one of two directions: either from the personal to the impersonal or from the fresh and direct to the institutional, ideological—and, too often, corrupt. For everyone attracted by Christ, there are scores bored or repelled by "Christianity."

The reason, of course, lies in the nature of the fallen world. Due to the twin factors of the presence of sin and the passing of time, no personal relationship or spiritual experience is self-perpetuating. Each must be nourished, sustained, and fanned into flame again and again or it will die. Not even spiritual revivals last. The natural course of entropy in things personal and spiritual is toward decline and death, or toward the atrophying ugliness that such words as *formalizing* and *routinizing* aim to convey. With repetition the extraordinary becomes ordinary and the revolutionary routine. Whereas "Christ" is free and fresh, "Christianity" is often formal and dead—or worse.

The trouble is not just that "this too shall pass away." Unlike old soldiers, old expressions of faith and old religious institutions do not simply fade away—they lumber the ground with outgrowths that stultify, distort, and even contradict their original purpose. That is the reason for a sad fact: Over the course of two thousand years, there is one unanswerable objection to the Christian faith—Christians. An American T-shirt simply states, "Jesus, save me from your followers."

Happily, most people know at least some followers of Christ whose lives express the spirit of Christ and attract people to Christ. But sadly, the story of the church as a whole is the story of frequent lapses from the pattern of Christ and periods when "Christianity" was an open advertisement for the Christian view of evil rather than for Christ.

The critics and enemies of the church are no more objective and fair than any other critics and enemies. But what is troubling is a recurring motif in their accusations: Only rarely and with a special spite is "Christianity" indicted for being too Christlike; far more commonly it is convicted of being not Christ-ian enough.

Clearly there is a direct link between the profession of faith, the practice of faith, and the plausibility of faith. Practice what you preach and you commend your faith; don't and you contradict it. "By this all men will know you are my disciples," Jesus said, "if you love one another." Or as Erasmus reminded his contemporaries a millennium and a half later in a more corrupt generation, "If we would bring the Turks to Christianity, we must first be Christians."

History shows that the very shift in focus from "Christ" to "Christianity" is itself a mark of corruption. The direct relationship and the dynamic way of life become a religious ideology and institution (which is why you won't find any use of the term *Christianity* here, apart from its use in quotation marks or in the quotations of others). "Every Stoic was a Stoic," Ralph Waldo Emerson wrote, "but in Christendom, where is the Christian?" "In truth there was only *one* Christian, and he died on the cross," wrote Friedrich Nietzsche. Or as George Bernard Shaw quipped, "Christianity might be a good thing if anyone ever tried it."

There is certainly a silver lining to this cloud. Comedian Lenny Bruce remarked that "every day people are straying away from the church and going back to God." But nevertheless there is a cloud over the church, and the best spokespeople for the faith have lamented it. G. K. Chesterton expressed one side of the matter: "The Christian ideal has not been tried and found wanting. It has been found difficult; and left untried." But Archbishop William Temple expressed the other: "'I believe in the Holy Catholic Church,' and I only regret it does not exist." Or as Søren Kierkegaard wrote from Denmark in his Christian *Attack upon Christendom*, "The most dreadful sort of blasphemy is that of which 'Christendom' is guilty: transforming the God of Spirit into . . . ludicrous twaddle."

Kierkegaard, a Lutheran writing four centuries after Luther, reduced his protest to "a thesis—only a single one":

> O Luther, thou hadst 95 theses—terrible! And yet, in a deeper sense, the more theses, the less terrible. This case is far more terrible: there is only one thesis. The Christianity of the New Testament simply does not exist. Here there is nothing to reform; what has to be done is to throw light upon a criminal offense against Christianity, prolonged through centuries, perpetrated by millions (more or less guiltily), whereby they have cunningly, under the guise of perfecting Christianity, sought little by little to cheat God out of Christianity, and have succeeded in making Christianity exactly the opposite of what it is in the New Testament.

As he so often did, C. S. Lewis hit the nail squarely on the head. "If ever the book which I am not going to write is written, it must be the full confession by Christendom to Christendom's specific contribution to the sum of human cruelty. Large areas of the world will not hear us until we have publicly disowned much of our past. Why should they? We have shouted the name of Christ and enacted the service of Molech."

Thomas Linacre, after whom Linacre College, Oxford, is named, was king's physician to Henry VII and Henry VIII of England, founder of the Royal College of Physicians, and friend of the great Renaissance thinkers Erasmus and Sir Thomas More. Late in his life he took Catholic orders and was given a copy of the Gospels to read for the first time. The Bible, of course, was still the preserve of the clergy and not in the hands of ordinary people. And Linacre lived through the darkest of the church's dark hours—the papacy of Alexander VI, the Borgia pope whose bribery, corruption, incest, and murder plumbed new depths in the annals of Christian shame.

Reading the four Gospels for himself, Linacre was amazed and troubled. "Either these are not the Gospels," he said, "or we are not Christians."

LIFE AS JOURNEY

How does the truth of calling help safeguard us against this slippage from *Christ* to *Christian* to *Christianity*? First, calling by its very nature reminds us that we are only followers of Christ when in fact we follow Christ—in other words, when we leave all other allegiances and walk after him, doing what he says and living as he requires. Jesus himself put the point bluntly to those whose deeds did not match their words: "Why do you call me, 'Lord, Lord,' and do not do what I say?" Christians who contradict Christ are Christians who are not following his call.

The point is easily overlooked: "The Way" is for traveling. Either we progress, however slowly and unsurely, or we are not on the Way. Anything purely theoretical, anything that is only good intentions, anything merely static and settled, let alone exclusive, hidebound, and hypocritical, is out of the question for those for whom one person, Jesus, is everything and all that matters is progress—pilgrim's progress—toward him and in his steps.

Christian is certainly a term used in the New Testament, but by outsiders and with the suggestion of an insult. To others, Christians were *Christianoi*—"Messiah's men." But among themselves, the preferred term for disciples was *followers of Jesus* or *followers of the Way*. John the Baptist had prepared "the way for the Lord." Jesus had constituted his disciples with two decisive words: "Follow me." So there was no "Christianity" abroad on the earth, only a radical, new "Way" and a motley band of "brothers" and "sisters" who were "followers of the Way."

Second, calling reminds us that to be "a follower of the Way" is to see life as a journey, which, while we are still alive on the earth, is an incomplete journey that cannot be finally assessed. The idea of life-as-journey should not be esoteric today. Journey and movement are major themes in the twentieth century. Less obvious perhaps than such grand triumphs as the moon landing or such dark tragedies as Auschwitz, travel is so typical of our times that ours is literally a world on the move.

From Mexicans crawling through Southern Californian ravines to Vietnamese boat people bobbing on the South China Sea to terrified Tutsis fleeing the murderous wrath of the Hutus in Rwanda, millions of our fellow human beings experience the twentieth century as life on the move in an age of displacement and migration. Because of war, disease, hunger, persecution, and genocide, the number of people driven out of countries rivals the number of those shut up inside.

More and more people have been uprooted and made to feel at home nowhere. Thus ours is a day of exiles, émigrés, expatriates, immigrants, refugees, deportees, illegal aliens, undesirable aliens, resident aliens, migrant workers, drifters, vagabonds, and bums. The journeying of the pilgrims, explorers, conquerors, and colonizers of the past have been overshadowed by the restlessness of the modern nomads and the wandering of today's stateless.

There is of course a very positive side of modern migration, as represented by the history of the United States as a "nation of immigrants" and epitomized by Ellis Island and Emma Lazarus's poem on the Statue of Liberty. It is true too that much of our awareness of journeying has been heightened by the creative insights of exiles and expatriates themselves. Dante and Petrarch wrote as exiles from Florence, John Calvin as an expatriate from France, Jean-Jacques Rousseau from Switzerland, and John Keats from England. But the volume of exiles and expatriates in the twentieth century has risen to a flood, led by American writers and artists in Paris, Henry James and T. S. Eliot in England, Albert Einstein in Princeton, W. H. Auden in New York, Aleksandr Solzhenitsyn in Vermont, and countless refugees from Nazism and communism in the United States at large.

Enormous differences divide these twentieth century travelers—differences of geography, culture, and psychology. But all experience some sense of a loss of home, of history, and of a sense of "the fatherland," the "mother tongue," the "language of childhood," and therefore the "homesickness" of nostalgia that is the experience of our time. Too many of us, in W. H. Auden's words, feel that we are "altogether elsewhere."

But the greatest dimension of our sense of journey is deeper still. It is created by the nearly universal intuition that journeying is the most apt metaphor for human life itself—or at least that the human odyssey at its highest is life with a quest for purpose, meaning, destination, and home. Human life is not only life on the road but also life in search of home.

"Midway on our life's journey I found myself in a dark wood." So begins Dante's metaphysical adventure story *The Divine Comedy*, his three-part pilgrimage to discover the fate of souls after death. From the Hebrew Exodus to Homer's *Odyssey* to Virgil's *Aeneid* to John Bunyan's *Pilgrim's Progress* to Mark Twain's *Huckleberry Finn* to Herman Hesse's *Siddhartha*, no picture of human life is more universal than to see it as a journey, a voyage, a quest, a pilgrimage, a personal odyssey. We are all somewhere on life's journey—at some point unknown to us between the beginning and the end of this odyssey of our human existence.

For those who live life as a journey and see faith as a journey, calling has an obvious implication. It reminds us that we are all at different stages on the way and none of us alive has yet arrived. Trouble comes when we forget this fact and pretend that life is static and settled, as if everything were a matter of sharp lines, clear boundaries, precise labels, and final assessments. So that some are in, some out; some have arrived, others not.

When mighty Rome was sacked in A.D. 410 by Alaric's barbarians, Augustine jotted down the observation that the seeming permanence of a city was sought by unfaithful Cain, not faithful Abel. "The true city of the saints is in heaven," he wrote in *The City of God*. Here on earth Christians travel "as on a pilgrimage through time looking for the Kingdom of Eternity."

Certainly we who follow Christ know why we have lost our original home. We know the home to which we are going. And we know not only the One who awaits us there, who makes it home, but also the

One who goes with us on the journey. But we are still on a journey, and we are truly travelers. We are not wanderers, but we are wayfarers. We have discovered that he is the way, but we are still on the road. Our faith is a pilgrim faith essentially at odds with place and settlement.

In all our testimony this sense of "progress report" or "work in progress" changes everything. Just imagine what we might have been without Christ. Novelist Evelyn Waugh, for example, was notoriously contentious and at times nearly paranoid. Yet he admitted to a friend, "I know I am awful. But how much more awful I should be without the Faith." C. S. Lewis expanded on this point in *God in the Dock:*

> Take the case of a sour old maid, who is a Christian, but cantankerous. On the other hand, take some pleasant and popular fellow, but who has never been to Church. Who knows how much more cantankerous the old maid might be if she were *not* a Christian, and how much more likeable the nice fellow might be if he *were* a Christian? You can't judge Christianity simply by comparing the *product* in these two people; you would need to know what kind of raw material Christ was working on in both cases.

Third, calling reminds us that, recognizing all the different stages people are at, there are many more who are followers of Jesus and on the Way than we realize. To forget this and insist that everyone be as we are, at the same stage and with the same stories as ours, is to be a Christian Pharisee. For the Gospels tell us it was the Pharisees who were shocked at those following Jesus. "While Jesus was having dinner at Levi's house, many tax collectors and 'sinners' were eating with him and his disciples, for there were many who followed him." Exclusiveness and exclusion always result from making a false idol of purity. Pharisaism, in fact, is the result of a perverted passion for theological purity just as ethnic cleansing is for racial purity.

Is this situation any different today? Are we saved by believing in Jesus or by trusting theologically correct formulations of believing in Jesus? Are only creed-carrying pillars of orthodoxy to be counted as true Christians? Or should we expect to find that some of the followers that Christ loves most are as unlikely as the wise men from the East, the loose-living foreign woman at the well, or the centurion from the army of the hated occupying power? Even the best and quickest of the disciples took three years of following Jesus to come close to seeing who he was. And no sooner had they seen it than they misunderstood it and betrayed him. Are we going to make the process simpler, surer, more routine?

Are we to say, like Oswald Chambers, "I am so amazed that God has altered me that I can never despair of anybody"? Or are we, like Dostoevsky's Grand Inquisitor, to say to Christ with all the superiority of "Christianity," with its cleaned-up theological creeds and moral codes, "We have corrected Your work"?

God forbid! Until Christ identifies and welcomes home the disciples he has called, we his followers can expect to be as unfinished and unvarnished as we are unlikely—but we are on the road, and we are followers of the Way.

Do you wish to live life as a journey? Are you eager to know the Way? Deeply desiring to reach the goal of your quest? Willing to lead an examined life, travel with those who use the same signposts, and associate with all who long for the same home? Listen to Jesus of Nazareth; answer his call.

14

THERE BUT FOR THE
GRACE OF GOD GOES GOD

I would give the greatest sunset in the world for one sight of New York's skyline. . . ," Ayn Rand wrote in her novel *The Fountainhead*. "The sky over New York and the will of man made visible. What other religion do we need?"

At first sight nothing seems farther from the aggressive humanism of modern skyscrapers than the soaring majesty of medieval cathedrals. Built patiently over many generations rather than by a short, sharp bench-press of modern engineering, designed and adorned by countless anonymous craftsmen rather than raised by a firm of internationally renowned architects, the cathedrals are surely a symphony in stone to the glory of God rather than a humanist tract on "the will of man made visible."

But in some cases the difference is not that clear. Bernard Mandeville wrote in *The Fable of the Bees* (1714) that "pride and vanity have built more hospitals than all the virtues together." It doesn't take a cynic to believe that pride and vanity have also painted paintings, composed music, written novels, dispensed fortunes, given extravagant gifts—and built cathedrals.

Such is the theme of William Golding's novel *The Spire*. When the foundation stone for Salisbury Cathedral was laid on April 28, 1220, there was neither a spire in the plans nor the foundation on which to build one. Completed in 1266, the cathedral is a perfect example of early English style, with a rare architectural unity as well as grace. Yet today Salisbury Cathedral is known for its elegant spire, the highest in England.

The spire was added in the fourteenth century, supposedly as a monument to the monomaniacal egotism of a dean who built it against all the architectural wisdom of the time. Present-day visitors to the cathedral can judge the result with the naked eye—severe buckling in the pillars.

The protagonists in Golding's moral fable are Dean Jocelin, the proud, powerful, and relentlessly driven priest who champions the spire, and Roger, the veteran Masterbuilder who counsels caution and warns of the heavy architectural and human costs. At one point, alone together as they survey the scene like hawks from hundreds of feet up, Roger passionately expounds on "the sheer impossibility of the spire!" He climaxes his argument dramatically by saying, "I've seen a building fall."

The Dean had listened with his eyes shut and his teeth gritted. Inside his head he had felt the spire shudder and begin to collapse, like a "dunce's cap a hundred and fifty feet tall." But when the Masterbuilder counseled, "Stop building," he barked back from the very core of his being, "No, no, no, no."

Then, digging deep into his own will, Dean Jocelin opened his heart.

"Now I'll tell you what no one else knows. They think I'm mad perhaps; but what does that matter? They'll know about it one day when I—but you shall hear it now, as man to man, on this very stump of a tower, up here with no one else to listen. My son. The building is a diagram of prayer; and our spire will be a diagram of the highest prayer of all. God revealed it to me in a vision, his unprofitable servant. He chose me. He chooses you, to fill the diagram with glass and iron and stone, since the children of men require a thing to look at. D'you think you can escape? You're not in my net—oh yes, Roger, I understand a number of things, how you are drawn, and twisted, and tormented—but it isn't my net. It's His. We can neither of us avoid this work. And there's another

116

thing. I've begun to see how we can't understand it either, since each new foot reveals a new effect, a new purpose. It's senseless, you think. It frightens us, and it's unreasonable. But then—since when did God ask the chosen ones to be reasonable? They call this Jocelin's Folly, don't they?"

"I've heard it called so."

"The net isn't mine, Roger, and the folly isn't mine. It's God's Folly. Even in the old days He never asked men to do what was reasonable. Men can do that for themselves. They can buy and sell, heal and govern. But then out of some deep place comes the command to do what makes no sense at all—to build a ship on dry land; to sit among the dunghills; to marry a whore; to set their son on the altar of sacrifice. Then, if men have faith, a new thing comes."

Noah, Job, Hosea, Abraham. . . . Dean Jocelin summons to his argument these biblical heroes of audacious faith. They saw the impossible, they attempted the impossible, they achieved the impossible. And why not? Like the Dean, they were called by God.

But was Dean Jocelin truly called? Or was he using God to countersign his own vision and energy raised to the level of hubris? God only knows. The line is impossible for us to draw. But in fact the odds were defied and the spire was built. More than six hundred years later the spire still stands. The "devouring Will" of the Dean overpowered the reluctance of the Masterbuilder and forced the project upward to its logic-defying success.

One man alone. Entrepreneurial vision and drive at their best, his admirers say. Roger's conclusion, before the two men descended the scaffolding, was different: "I believe you're the devil. The devil himself."

THE SIN OF THE NOBLE MIND

Golding's tale is well told and his characters vividly drawn. They highlight a darker side of calling we must face: *The reverse side of calling is the temptation of conceit.* It's an illusion to think that recovering doctrines is simple and straightforward, that they need only to be reaffirmed to be rediscovered. Far from it. All truth in a fallen world is vulnerable to distortion. In fact, each truth has its own foreseeable distortions that are its shadow side. Each also has a sort of magnetic attraction to distortions prevalent in the people who believe the truth and the times in which they live. To help keep our feet on the ground, this chapter and the next three examine some of the major temptations surrounding calling.

The closeness between calling and conceit is easy to see. After all, to be called is to hear God whisper three things to you in a hundred intimate ways—"You are chosen; you are gifted; you are special." Let those three things sink in for longer than the first precious moments and you will inevitably hear another voice, honeyed and smooth: "Yes, you really are chosen . . . gifted . . . special."

All too soon, if you are anything like most of us, you will find yourself saying in response to the devil's echo of God—to yourself, of course, never out loud: *I'm chosen. I'm gifted. I really must be special.* And before you know it, the wonder of calling has grown into the horror of conceit.

Chosenness and conceit have grown so close that many people confuse the two. Chosenness *is* egocentrism, they say, an elegant theological fig leaf to cover self-flattery. But the original difference is plain. As the Old Testament insists, Jewish "chosenness" did not mean the Jews were better, wiser, or more deserving than others. It was a miracle of God's love. Nor did chosenness bring or imply any special privileges and benefits for the Jews alone. It was a summons that brought a higher task, a heavier burden, and a sterner judgment. The purpose of Israel's choosing is universal. Israel's significance is for all humankind.

The temptation, however, is inescapable—for us as much as the Jews. During World War II, Winston Churchill's governing coalition included, as president of the Board of Trade, Sir Stafford Cripps, later the Socialist Chancellor of the Exchequer. Cripps was a teetotaler and a vegetarian and, in Churchill's eyes, somewhat crabbed in personality. His only concession to pleasure was smoking cigars. But Cripps renounced that habit too, declaring to a wartime rally that he was giving up cigars as an example of sacrifice for the cause.

"Too bad," Churchill whispered to a colleague on the same platform, "it was his last contact with humanity."

Cripps was also a strong Calvinist and, in Churchill's eyes, Cripps's sense of the providence of God had seeped across into his own sense of self-importance. His self-regard, we might say, was a trifle high. One day, Cripps left the cabinet room and Churchill turned to the others and said: "There but for the grace of God goes God."

Such expressions of pride and vanity are not uncommon among people with a profound sense of calling. Henry Luce, the founder of *Time* and a Presbyterian, was described by his Yale contemporaries as speaking as if he were "God's classmate." The great seventeenth-century poet John Milton was a Puritan with a highly developed conviction of calling. In *Defense of Himself* he wrote, "Singular indeed is the favor of God toward me, that he has called me above all others to the defense of liberty." One later critic wrote, not altogether unfairly, "One may still wonder which came first: Was it that Milton believed in God or that Milton believed in Milton (and believed that God did too)?"

The greatest artistic creators may be especially prone to this conceit. Creators, like God, they come to see themselves as challengers to God. D. H. Lawrence felt it in himself: "I always feel as if I stood naked for the fire of Almighty God to go through me—and it's rather an awful feeling. One has to be terribly religious, to be an artist." Critic George Steiner glimpses it in the "awesome encounters between God and the more god-like of his creatures. To have carved the figures in the Medici Chapel, to have imagined Hamlet and Falstaff, to have heard the *Missa Solemnis* out of deafness is to have said, in some mortal but irreducible manner: 'Let there be light.' It is to have wrestled with the angel."

But, Steiner asks, "How much mastery over creation can a man achieve and yet remain unscathed?" Jacob limped away from wrestling at the Jabbok. Steiner suggests there was some similar appropriate justice in Milton's blindness, in Beethoven's deafness, and in Tolstoy's haunted flight toward death. Maxim Gorky, after all, described Tolstoy's attitude to God as the relationship of "two bears in one den."

What happens to individuals can also happen to groups and even nations. For example, America's "Manifest Destiny," or more broadly America's sense of exceptionalism, can be traced to various roots, geographical and economic, but the deepest root is theological. The English Puritans saw their revolution as "God's own Cause" and their Commonwealth (in poet Andrew Marvell's words) as "the darling of heaven." So when their revolution failed and they migrated from the Egypt of England to the Canaan of New England, they transferred the sense of destiny. They were "the Lord's first born," entrusted with a "pious errand into the wilderness." In short, with America destiny preceded discovery.

To be fair to the Puritans, they neither coined the term *manifest destiny* nor believed in the idea. They believed that God had a providential purpose for *all* nations, including the United States. It was not for the United States alone. The term *manifest destiny* was first used in 1845 by John L. Sullivan, the editor of *Democratic Review*. It was a secular, nationalistic distortion of calling that needs to be challenged in a nation as much as in an individual. The old saying, "God takes care of babies, drunks, and the United States," is pure conceit.

When individuals debase calling, the consequences are mostly limited because individuals are. When nations do, it is more dangerous but also more rare. But as *The Spire* illustrates, one of the most common, subtle, and manipulative distortions of all is in religious empire building. God only knows how many churches, missionary societies, charities, colleges, crusades, reforms, and acts of philanthropic generosity have trumpeted the call of God and advanced their leaders' egos. In a generation's time this flaw will probably be seen as the single greatest problem of the megachurch movement. More than any part of the church of Christ should, today's big churches and parachurch organizations rise and fall by the strength of a single person.

"My cause (whatever it is) is God's gift to the world," the heroic founder says in effect. "His (or her) calling (whatever it is) is God's gift to our cause," loyal followers repeat in a hundred reverent ways. So the call of God is enlisted to camouflage ego, stifle disagreement, excuse failure, decry opposition, and gild the commemorative plaques of success. There but for the grace of God. . . .

Needless to say, the Jewish people have had a terrible safeguard against this conceit—suffering. "You have chosen us from among the nations" is a recurring phrase in their daily prayers; "Why did you have to pick on the Jews?" is the characteristic Yiddish counterpoint.

Pride has traditionally been viewed as the first, worst, and deadliest of the seven deadly sins. But the contemporary world has tried to transform this vice into a virtue—through changing the definition of pride to self-respect. So pride no longer "goeth before a fall," it cometh before a promotion, provided you have sufficient self-confidence and self-esteem. "Pride has always been one of my favorite virtues," actress Dame Edith Sitwell wrote. "I have never regarded it, except in certain cases, as a major sin. . . . I despise anything which reduces the pride of Man."

But the deadly sin is not pride in the sense of self-respect, a justifiable sense of one's own worth. The sin of pride is wrong because it is inordinate and overweening. Consider its synonyms: egotism, arrogance, hubris, selfishness, vanity, haughtiness, presumption, boastfulness, big-headedness, self-satisfaction, self-centeredness, and the like. None of them is admirable and neither is the conceit that is the rotten fruit of calling. "The greatest curse in spiritual life," Oswald Chambers wrote, "is conceit."

Notice how conceit twists calling in two characteristic ways. First, people who are called are especially vulnerable to pride because of the very nobility of calling. Temptation is always the tempter's compliment to the tempted, so the strongest temptations are the subtlest. Put differently, temptation tempts most temptingly when it is a shortcut to realizing the very highest at which we aim. So the twisting of our highest aspirations will be twice as evil as the twisting of our lowest. Dorothy Sayers's warning applies to calling: "The devilish strategy of Pride is that it attacks us, not in our weakest points, but in our strongest. It is preeminently the sin of the noble mind."

Second, we who are called are vulnerable to a special form of pride because of our desire to wean ourselves from human audiences and live before the Audience of One. The trouble comes, of course, when we truly live before an Audience of One, but the audience is not God but us. As C. S. Lewis observed in *Mere Christianity*, that is why vanity is the least bad and most pardonable form of pride—the vain person is always angling for praise and admiration, living before the Audience of Thousands. In contrast, "The real black, diabolical Pride comes when you look down on others so much that you do not care what they think of you." The outcome, as the prophet Ezekiel wrote of the proud city of Tyre, is the point when we say, "I and who but I?" Or, as it was said of Charlie Chaplin's tyrannical and conceited meanness as a film director, it was all "me, me alone, and that's enough."

The practical outcome of such conceit in Christian organizations today is lack of genuine accountability for leaders. All too often such leaders have no tough-minded peers to hold them to account. Generally, those who work for them are younger. Inevitably they take on something of the attitude of groupies.

At times the church of Christ has created institutional ways of challenging pride. Few are more moving than the burial ceremony of the Habsburg emperors, who were laid to rest in the vaults of the Capuchin monastery in Vienna. When Emperor Franz Josef died, the grand cortège arrived at the closed doors of the monastery and a herald knocked at the gate. From within the voice of the Abbott could be heard asking:

"Who are you, who knocks?"

"I am Franz Josef, Emperor of Austria, King of Hungary," the herald replied.

"I don't know you. Tell me again who you are."

"I am Franz Josef, Emperor of Austria, King of Hungary, Bohemia, Galicia, Lodomeria, and Dalmatia, Grand Duke of Transylvania, Margrave of Moravia, Duke of Styria and Corinthia . . ."

"We still don't know you. Who are you?" the sepulchral voice reiterated. Whereupon the herald knelt down and said:

"I am Franz Josef, a poor sinner humbly begging for God's mercy."

"Thou mayest enter then," the Abbott said and the gates were flung open.

We might wish for a similar challenge to our presidents, prime ministers, and all the elected officials who strut the various stages to which we have elevated them. Or a similar challenge to our religious leaders. But what we really need is a daily challenge to ourselves, a reminder as regular as looking in the mirror. G. K. Chesterton warned: "For if a man can say, 'I like to find something greater than myself,' he may be a fool or a madman, but he has the essential. But if a man says, 'I like to find something smaller than myself,' there is only one adequate answer—'You couldn't.'"

Do we feel the wonder of being called? It is all a gift and all of grace. And contrary to expectations, grace is not a matter of God's welcoming the lawbreaker as well as the law-abiding, the disreputable along with the respectable, the prodigal son as well as the stay-at-home.

Quite the reverse. Pride is the first and worst sin, so grace is most amazing when it embraces the fruits of pride rather than the fruits of gluttony or lust, when it reaches the Pharisee soul rather than the profligate Mary Magdalene, when it wins the proud person made prouder still by calling rather than the sinner feeling unworthy to be addressed.

Only grace can dissolve the hard, solitary, vaunting "I" of the sin of pride in each of us. But the good news is that it does.

⚜

Do you think you are worthy of God's call? Do you act as if calling was for you alone, designed exclusively for your wishes,

dreams, plans, titles, and achievements? Or do you know
yourself so well that you know beyond a shadow of a doubt
calling is all a gift and all of grace? What will you say at the
gates of heaven when you are asked, "Who are you?" Listen to
Jesus of Nazareth; answer his call.

15

WHAT IS THAT TO YOU?

People often ask me what it was like to grow up in a family with a name like ours and wealth like ours. Sometimes I tell them honestly: 'Can you imagine living your life at the bottom of a deep well with a millstone around your neck? That is what it was like to grow up as I did.'"

I will never forget the pathos with which this was said to me by the heir of one of the world's wealthiest families. Most people find it hard to take seriously the sorrows of a "poor little rich kid." They would be only too glad to be tempted just once with such wealth. But not only people rich in money feel the burden; people rich in talents feel it too. Up to a certain point, it seems, we can wrap ourselves flatteringly in our giftedness, but a point comes when the talent is so utterly extraordinary that we cannot deny it is a gift. It is so obviously beyond us.

Then the sense of burden may enter. If the gift is that extraordinary, how can the gifted person discharge the responsibility for it? And to whom? And there is often the special insecurity of the hugely talented: Do people appreciate them for themselves or only for their gifts?

Wolfgang Amadeus Mozart would unquestionably be among a tiny handful of people elected without contest to the highest circle of human genius. "A wonder child," "a prodigy of nature," "a veritable miracle," "sublime," "celestial," "precocious beyond belief," "surpassing all imagination"—awed tributes have poured forth in response to his gifts as a composer and musician ever since he burst onto the world's musical stage in 1763, at the age of seven, under the tutelage of his father Leopold.

Not surprisingly, such utterly extraordinary, seemingly transcendent giftedness has been seen as the focus of a matching envy—most famously in connection with his contemporary Antonio Salieri. Five years older than Mozart, Salieri had been established seven years as Court Composer and Conductor of the Italian Opera in Vienna before Mozart moved there. For thirty-six years—that is, for thirty-three years after Mozart died—he occupied the even loftier position of the Emperor's Court Kapellmeister in Vienna. So from the perspective of the court and the public, Salieri had every reason to pity Mozart, not to envy him, and there is no evidence for the rumor that Salieri confessed the year before he died in 1825 that he had poisoned his younger rival.

Yet the dramatic potential of this rumored rivalry has attracted playwrights such as Alexander Pushkin, whose *Mozart and Salieri* was set to music by Rimsky-Korsakov, and Peter Shaffer, whose award-winning *Amadeus* was made into an award-winning film by Milos Forman.

At one point in Shaffer's play, Salieri finds himself alone in the room with a portfolio of Mozart's compositions on the desk in front of him. He reaches out to take it, but as if fearful of what he might find, he pauses—then he snatches it, tears off the ribbon, and opens the case. His eye falls on the opening bars of Mozart's Twenty-Ninth Symphony, in A major.

> She had said that these were his original scores. First and only drafts of the music. Yet they looked like fair copies. They showed no corrections of any kind. It was puzzling—then suddenly alarming. What was evident was that Mozart was simply transcribing music completely finished in his head. And finished as most music is never finished. . . . Displace one note and there would be diminishment. Displace one phrase and the structure would fall. . . . I was staring through the cage of those meticulous ink strokes at—an Absolute Beauty.

Stunned, Salieri collapses senseless to the floor, where he lies quite still, his head next to the score of the heavenly music. As the clock strikes nine he raises his head and addresses God.

Capisco! I know my fate. Now for the first time I feel my emptiness as Adam felt his nakedness. . . . Tonight at an inn somewhere in this city stands a giggling child who can put on paper, without actually setting down his billiard cue, casual notes which turn my most considered ones into lifeless scratches. *Grazie, Signore!* You gave me the desire to serve You—which most men do not have—then saw to it the service was shameful to the ears of the server. *Grazie!* You gave me the desire to praise You—which most men do not feel— then made me mute. *Grazie tanti!* You put into me perception of the Incomparable—which most men never know!—then ensured that I would know myself forever mediocre. *Why?* . . . *What is my fault?* . . . Until this day I have pursued virtue with rigor. I have labored long hours to relieve my fellow men. I have worked and worked the talent You allowed me. You know how hard I've worked! Solely that in the end, in the practice of the art which alone makes the world comprehensible to me, I might hear Your Voice! And now I do hear it—and it says only one name: MOZART! . . . And *my* only reward—my sublime privilege—is to be the sole man alive in this time who shall clearly recognize Your Incarnation! *Grazie e grazie ancora!* So be it! From this time we are enemies, You and I! I'll not accept it from You—*do you hear?* . . . They say God is not mocked. I tell You, *Man* is not mocked! . . . *I* am not mocked! . . . They say the spirit bloweth where it listeth: I tell you NO! It must list to virtue or not blow at all!

Shaffer's play, in both its stage and film versions, has moved audiences profoundly around the world. But the evidence of Mozart's actual life also challenges us to feel the burden of the gift from his point of view.

Dying in 1791 at the age of thirty-five and buried in a pauper's grave, Mozart lived a short life that was a tragedy comprised of certain obvious components. He was controlled by a domineering father, betrayed by a faithless wife, hounded by financial worries, condemned to spend a third of his life in travel, and above all he was caught in the shift from the world of "court music" in which the musician was little higher than a flunky to the world of "artist's music" in which the musician was potentially an independent genius and a free agent of his own works.

But what gives excruciating poignancy to Mozart's tragedy was the interplay between his gifts, his desires, and his sense of obligation. The citizens of his native Salzburg were unappreciative—"When I play or when any of my compositions are performed, it is just as if the audience were all tables and chairs." He was quite literally booted out of the employment of Count Colloredo, the archbishop of Salzburg. But what gave meaning to his life was his extraordinary gift and his sense of duty to God because of it. "I am a composer and was born to be a Kapellmeister. I neither can nor ought to bury the talent for composition with which God in his goodness has so richly endowed me."

Closely tied to Mozart's giftedness was his deep desire for the love of a woman he could trust and a Viennese public that would appreciate the music he created. Both things he tasted briefly and both things he came to feel he lost. And with the loss came an inconsolable sense of failure and loneliness. It has been suggested that Mozart died from more than medical reasons but not from poison. One scholar wrote, "Perhaps in the end he simply gave up and let go." Sadly, many have said, in large measure he wrote his final *Requiem* for himself.

Two hundred years later, when the name Mozart is synonymous with genius and sublime musical delight, the thought is agonizing: How could such a gifted creator possibly have been so unappreciated? Could the withholding of love and favor actually have hastened him prematurely to the grave with who-knows-how-many unborn creations dying with him? Mozart's life in both its real and fictional forms has poignant and tragic dimensions that stir us to the depths— and uncovers perspectives on another facet of calling: *The truth of calling touches closely on the link between giftedness and desire and the almost inescapable temptation of envy.*

THE REVENGE OF FAILURE

In his excellent book *The Seven Deadly Sins Today*, journalist Henry Fairlie suggests that the motto for our times might be "The Revenge of Failure." If we cannot paint well, we destroy the canons of painting and pass ourselves as painters. If we cannot or will not read, we dismiss linear thinking as irrelevant and dispense with reading. In area after area, if we are not inclined to submit to the rigors of the discipline, we destroy the standards and pass ourselves off as acceptable.

And the reason? Fairlie finds it in the corrupt egalitarianism of a soft-minded democracy. "To pit unequals against unequals as if they were equals is to make a breeding ground for Envy. . . . What we are unable to achieve, we will bring low. What requires talent and training and hard work, we will show can be accomplished without them."

Fairlie's analysis is a merciless uncovering of the cancer of envy in modern society—as seen in our debunking biographies, leveling interviews, gossip columns, attack-ad electioneering, and the "boom to bust" cycle of our expectations of our leaders. Deeper still it is a reminder of the historical role of envy in corrupting democracy. And deepest of all it is an incisive modern commentary on the biblical and classical view of the vice of envy in the human heart.

Traditionally envy was regarded as the second worst and second most prevalent of the seven deadly sins. Like pride, it is a sin of the spirit, not the flesh, and thus a "cold" and highly "respectable" sin, in contrast to the "warm" and openly "disreputable" sins of the flesh, such as gluttony. Its uniqueness lies in the fact that it is the one vice that its perpetrators never enjoy and rarely confess.

As with pride, modern people tend to duck the sting of the classical view by changing the definition of envy. Is it wrong, they say, to see someone succeed (in business or sports, say) and aspire to succeed too? Aspiration, emulation, competition—aren't they what drives an open society and a free market?

But envy is not simply aspiration or ambition. Those themes, after all, are constructive and central to calling. Rather, envy—in Thomas Aquinas's famous definition—is "sorrow at another's good." Envy enters when, seeing someone else's happiness or success, we feel ourselves called into question. Then, out of the hurt of our wounded self-esteem, we seek to bring the other person down to our level by word or deed. They belittle us by their success, we feel; we should bring them down to their deserved level, envy helps us feel. Full-blown envy, in short, is dejection plus disparagement plus destruction.

Dorothy Sayers summed up envy succinctly. "Envy begins by asking plausibly: 'Why should I not enjoy what others enjoy?' and it ends by demanding: 'Why should others enjoy what I may not?'" When he was asked to give an example of envy, Sir John Gielgud replied with both candor and typical self-deprecation, "When Sir Laurence Olivier played Hamlet in 1948, and the critics raved, I wept."

There are important reasons why calling is vulnerable to envy, as the rivalry of Mozart and Salieri illustrates. First, envy strikes at the place where our giftedness and our deepest desires are intertwined with our sense of calling. To understand ourselves, we need to know not only our gifts but also the deepest desires we long to fulfill. Our desires, needless to say, are not simply to fulfill God's call because for every similar good and conscious desire we have other desires less conscious and often much less worthy.

Over the years these deep, primordial desires grow fixed in a form that helps drive us in adult life, though many of them are rooted and reinforced through the entire trajectory of our past. Fulfill them and life feels full of meaning and satisfaction. Deny them and the most sophisticated and tenacious of beliefs can seem meaningless. Confuse them with calling and the unfulfilled, perhaps unfulfillable, elements of desire become a breeding ground for envy.

Second, envy corrupts calling by introducing the element of

competition. Like pride, envy by its very nature is comparative and competitive. Or more precisely, pride is competitive and envy is the result of pride wounded in competition. As C. S. Lewis wrote in *Mere Christianity*, "Pride is *essentially* competitive. . . . Pride gets no pleasure out of having something, only out of having more of it than the next man. We say people are proud of being rich, or clever, or good-looking, but they are not. They are proud of being richer, or cleverer, or better-looking than others."

Lewis's point about pride also applies to calling. Once the element of competition comes in, envy will not be far behind. For what happens if you pause for a moment in the path of your calling and look across at other people in theirs? You can always find someone who has a happier marriage, more delightful children, a higher income, greater public recognition, or whatever surface successes touch on the subterranean depths of your desires.

Just let such comparisons mix with your less worthy desires and envy will rear its head again—an envy that increases, not lessens, with age; an envy that may be petty but will be all-consuming; an envy that focuses on those most competitive, and therefore closest, to your own gifts and calling; an envy that is finally self-destructive because what the envier cannot enjoy, no one is allowed to.

Third, envy attacks calling especially because calling goes back directly to God and envy is essentially profane. Fairlie explained, "Envy cannot bear to think that mere accident or fortune—or some other unknowable power, fate, or destiny, or perhaps even God—has conferred a good on someone else. . . . This is what is profane in Envy. It will not embrace what is fate-given, chance-given, or God-given."

If someone else's success that belittles me is due to that person's calling, then finally my grudge is not simply against the other person but against God. So the fictional Salieri turns on God, just as Cain did out of jealousy of Abel and Saul out of jealousy of David. Some people respond in anger, some in complaint, and some by piously expressing disappointment in God. But as Fairlie concluded, in each case the envy is "all the more tormenting because it springs from an inordinate self-love."

In his novel *Doctor Faustus,* Thomas Mann described the subtle dance of envy of a later generation of Viennese musicians, reminding us once more that we are always most vulnerable to envying those closest to our own gifts and callings. Musicians generally envy musicians, not politicians; politicians other politicians; sportspeople other sportspeople; professors other professors; ministers other ministers; and so on.

> Wolf, Brahms and Bruckner lived for years in the same town—Vienna, that is—but avoided each other the whole time and none of them, so far as I know, ever met the others. It would have been penible, too, considering their opinions of each other. They did not judge or criticize like colleagues; their comments were meant to annihilate, to leave their author alone in the field. Brahms thought as little as possible of Bruckner's symphonies; he called them huge, shapeless serpents. And Bruckner's opinion of Brahms was very low. He found the first theme of the D-minor Concerto very good, but asserted that Brahms never came near inventing anything so good a second time.

There are many counterpoints to envy in the Scriptures, but there is no skirting the uncomfortable fact that Jesus deals with the roots of calling-envy severely and summarily. At the close of John's Gospel, Jesus spells out a sobering description of Peter's future: "I tell you the truth, when you were younger you dressed yourself and went where you wanted; but when you are old you will stretch out your hands, and someone else will dress you and lead you where you do not want to go." Jesus then concluded to Peter, "Follow me!"

For whatever reason, Peter, turning and seeing John, asked Jesus, "Lord, what about him?"

To which Jesus answered, "If I want him to remain alive until I returned, what is that to you? You must follow me."

When Jesus calls, he calls us one by one. Comparisons are idle, speculations about others a waste of time, and envy as silly as it is evil. We are each called individually, accountable to God alone, to please him alone, and eventually to be approved by him alone. If ever we are tempted to look around, compare notes, and use the progress of others to judge the success of our own calling, we will hear what Peter heard: "What is that to you? Follow me!"

Do you have the habit of looking around at others with callings close to yours? Do you feel called into question by their achievements? Do you feel that their success is more than they deserve and yours somehow less? Are you disappointed, even angry, at the gap between your desires and your accomplishments? Listen to Jesus of Nazareth; answer his call.

16

More, More, Faster, Faster

The decisive question for the West is its capacity to direct and discipline capitalism with an ethic strong enough to do so. I myself don't believe the West can do it." When the Singapore economist I mentioned in chapter 7 delivered that blunt assessment a few years ago, a shiver of excitement ran through the room. There were no academic ifs, ands, or buts. Here was a plain-speaking, "one-handed" economist who would have delighted Harry Truman.

Such a challenge makes many Westerners uncomfortable. Yet another tiresome assault on our materialism? But the unease is odd because the criticism is not new, and it is Christian in origin. It forms the so-called gravedigger thesis, the notion that capitalism may undermine itself by its very success. This idea got a bad name because of its association with Karl Marx—"What the bourgeoisie produces above all is its own gravediggers." But in Christian history it was a key part of Puritan analysis before Marx picked it up. In eighteenth-century America, for example, Cotton Mather warned that unless there was vigilance, a sense of calling would bring forth prosperity, only to result in prosperity's destroying the sense of calling.

In our own generation a distinguished professor from Harvard University has called attention to the "cultural contradictions" of capitalism. Originally, he argued, the menace of unrestrained economic impulse was held in check by the Protestant ethic—people worked in response to their calling. But now, with this ethic dissolved, including its moral attitudes toward hard work and saving, only hedonism remains. "The greatest single engine in the destruction of the Protestant ethic," he wrote, "was the invention of the installment plan, or instant credit. Previously one had to save in order to buy. But with credit cards one could indulge in instant gratification." Or as another scholar put it simply: Capitalism, having defeated all challenges, such as socialism, now faces its greatest challenge—itself, because it devours the very virtues it needs to thrive.

In short, the Singapore salvo is to the point. Following the collapse of communism from its own inner contradictions, the triumph of capitalism is unarguable on market grounds but far less assured on spiritual, moral, and social grounds. Is any belief or ethic strong enough to corral capitalism?

MONEY IS A SPIRITUAL ISSUE

What does this challenge have to do with calling? The answer is, everything. The issues of the global economy reveal the issues of our human hearts, projected onto a world screen. We therefore face another side of the truth of calling—*calling, which played a key role in the rise of modern capitalism, is one of the few truths capable of guiding and restraining it now.*

The task of guiding and restraining the explosive power of capitalism is daunting. At its core is an unavoidable issue: No one can master money without mastering the *meaning* of money. This in turn requires us to remove two modern myths that form roadblocks to understanding money. One is the myth that the making of money matters more than the meaning of money, as thousands of salespeople, schemes, and seminars trumpet daily. The other is the myth that money is simply neutral, merely a medium of exchange. As a Texas oil billionaire claimed, "Money is nothing. It's just something to make bookkeeping convenient."

The truth is that money is much more than a monetary issue. It

135

was, and is, a spiritual issue. Trying to solve the problem of money through tinkering with economics or by switching systems altogether will always fail. Money is money regardless of whether it exists in a free market or a centralized market, and it must be understood as such. In an obvious sense we take money too seriously today. But less obviously, we do so only because we don't take money seriously enough—seriously enough to understand it.

At the heart of the meaning of money lie a number of questions, such as, "Why is there a problem?" Significantly, the dominance of money in modern society coincides with the disappearance from modern thinking of the notion of avarice—the most radical view of why money is a problem. Throughout history the most universally acknowledged problem with money is that its pursuit is insatiable.

As we seek money and possessions, observers note, the pursuit grows into a never-satisfied desire that fuels avarice—described by the Bible as a vain "chasing after wind" and by moderns as an "addiction." The very Hebrew word for money (*kesef*) comes from a verb meaning "to desire" or "languish after something." This emphasis is important because avarice is often confused with an Ebenezer Scrooge-like hoarding. Traditionally, however, it has been better described as a form of spiritual dropsy or a thirst that can never be slaked. The insatiability touches two areas—getting what we do not have and clutching on to what we do.

Second, the insatiable pursuit of money is commonly tied to a dangerous narrowness—the narrowness of a single-minded devotion to the goal of making money. Most people dream of being rich because they think of all they could do with the money—and therefore divert themselves and thwart the fulfillment of their dreams. But people in high pursuit of money think only of *making* money. One of Henry Ford's biographers, for example, described him as "a sort of human dynamo, made to run purposefully along a single track."

Third, the insatiability has always been seen as a sign of other needs—for power, protection, approval, and so on. Howard Hughes, for example, had an extraordinary need to possess people and places. He hired a man to spend months in a hotel room waiting for a call that never came. And he kept at least five young starlets in mansions, with cars, chauffeurs, guards, and restaurant charge accounts—and although he never visited them, he hired private detectives to make sure no one else did.

Fourth, insatiability is commonly linked to being consumed. Individuals and societies who devote themselves to money soon become devoured by it. Or as the Bible reiterates, we become what we worship. Money almost literally seems to eat people away, drying up the sap of their vitality and withering their spontaneity, generosity, and joy. Descriptions vary: Andrew Mellon was called "a wisp" and "shadow of a man" and Howard Hughes was described as looking like "a witch's brother." A recurring theme is the evaporation of life juices in the very rich and an inability to take pleasure in the fruits of their wealth.

Fifth, and most important, the problem of insatiability provides a boost for the other great problem accompanying money—"commodification." This rather forbidding word describes the process whereby money assumes such a dominant place in a society that everything (and everyone) is seen and treated as a commodity to be bought and sold. The term may be new, but the problem, as the Greek legend of Midas shows, is old. Among notorious early examples of commodification are the moneychangers in the Jewish temple and the papal selling of indulgences by Johann Tetzel in the medieval era.

The charge of commodification is not a criticism of the marketplace itself—buying, selling, merchandising, and marketing are all legitimate in their place. But not everything can or should be given a market price. The line drawn between "For Sale" and "Not for Sale" is a prime indication of a nation's or group's values. The sign of a good society is the level and number of things acknowledged to be beyond market values—and thus appreciated for their own sake and not for extrinsic, especially financial, rewards. As the early church father Tertullian stated, "There is no buying and selling of any sort in the things of God. Though we have our treasure chest, it is not made up of purchase-money, as of a religion that has its price."

G. K. Chesterton wrote that the "chief heresy" of vulgar capitalists is "the fundamental falsehood that things are not made to be used but made to be sold." In our own day it is said that following the collapse of Soviet totalitarianism, our chief Western danger is "market totalitarianism," or "economic imperialism." "What does an economist economize on?" the question has been asked. The answer is "love." Under a market system operating strictly on profit and loss, a society can get by with less love than under any other system. The "commodifying" society economizes on love.

The overall lesson of insatiability is that money alone cannot buy the deepest things we desire. Money never purchases love, or eternity, or God. It is the wrong means, the wrong road, the wrong search. That is why the pursuit is vanity. "Nothing gained" is the final lesson of insatiability.

Yet the pursuit continues. We keep upping the ante. The horizon recedes as we approach. We still don't stop. As Sam Walton's wife Helen admitted, "I kept saying, Sam, we're making a good living. Why go out, why expand so much more? The stores are getting farther and farther away. After the seventeenth store, though, I realized there wasn't going to be any stopping it."

When John D. Rockefeller, Sr., was asked how much money it takes to make a man happy, he gave the immortal reply, "Just a little bit more." It is always over the next horizon, after we've conquered the next summit. It's always tomorrow.

ALL IN OUR MINDS

The insatiable desire, of course, is in our *minds*. It acts, as Plutarch put it, "like a tapeworm." The artist Delacroix once asked James Rothschild, of the great banking family, to pose for a painting of a beggar, since he had "exactly the right hungry expression." Rothschild, who was a friend of the artist, agreed, and appeared the next day, suitably garbed in a disreputable costume. The masquerade was so convincing that a passerby gave him money. Similarly, a Texas oil billionaire's colleague commented of him, "No matter how much money he had, he was *always poor in his own mind.*"

Many people acknowledge the problem in theory. Andrew Carnegie wrote this famous memorandum in 1868 when he was thirty-three and stuffed it away in a drawer: "Man must have an idol—the amassing of wealth is one of the worst species of idolatry—no idol more debasing than the idol of money." But in 1905 President Theodore Roosevelt wrote reluctantly of Carnegie himself, "I have tried hard to like Carnegie, but it is pretty difficult. There is no type of man for whom I feel a more contemptuous abhorrence than for one who makes a God of mere money-making."

Carnegie's biographer observed that just as Napoleon drove his soldiers with the slogan that every footsoldier carried a marshal's baton in his knapsack, so Carnegie taught his employees to believe that every worker carried a partnership in his lunch pail. But then the insatiability and restlessness kicked in. Carnegie offered them rewards and the promise of a glittering prize at the end but in words that are an eerie real-life parallel to Tolstoy's story, "How Much Land Does a Man Need?": "It was always 'more, more, faster, faster.' The race went on and on and the casualties were heavy. But still they ran, with Carnegie alternately cheering and cursing them on."

Such observations of insatiability should make us pause. From the Greeks and Romans down to many modern people, a simple piety has reigned: the notion that we can solve the problem of money by distinguishing between "needs" and "surplus," between "necessities" and "luxuries." Carnegie, for example, held that philanthropy was the business of "administering *surplus* wealth." But what if we can never settle on the balance? What if one person's luxuries are another's necessities? Can't we always rationalize how much is enough?

Jesus gave a very different answer that was far more realistic. The problem is that money can assume an inordinate place in our lives until it becomes a personal, spiritual, god-like force that rules us—Mammon.

Jesus' use of *Mammon* (Aramaic for *wealth*) is unique—he gave it a strength and precision that the word never had before. He did not usually personify things, let alone deify them. And neither the Jews nor the nearby pagans knew a god by this name. But what Jesus says in speaking of Mammon is that money is a power—and not in a vague sense, as in the "force" of words. Rather, money is a power in the sense that it is an active agent with decisive spiritual power and is never neutral. It is a power *before* we use it, not simply as we use it or whether we use it well or badly.

As such, Mammon is a genuine rival to God. The recurring biblical demand confronts us: "You shall not worship the work of your hands." Jesus challenged his hearers to choose one master or another—God or Mammon. Either we serve God and use money or we serve money and use God. Ultimately we follow what we have loved most intensely to its natural destination—eternity or death—"for where your treasure is, there will your heart be too."

Before we blithely invoke calling to resist Mammon, we must face up to a stark truth. As the earlier mention of Cotton Mather underscores, calling has been undermined by prosperity once before. So the task will not be easy, and the more successful calling is, the more vulnerable it will be again to its tendency to undermine itself.

Mather wrote in *Magnalia Christi Americana,* "Religion brought forth prosperity and the daughter destroyed the mother." In other words, there was a disastrous shift between the early Puritans, whose calling gave them an edge in success because it made them "diligent in the world but dead to it," and the later Puritans, of whom it was said that "they came to do good and did well."

The crass heresy of the prosperity doctrines and the "health and wealth gospel" is the bastard child of corrupted calling. A century after Cotton Mather, and two centuries after his grandfather John Cotton, Alexis de Tocqueville wrote of preachers he heard on his travels in America, "It is often difficult to ascertain from their discourses whether the principal object of religion is to procure eternal felicity in the other world or prosperity in this."

Certainly, no truth is more manipulable than calling when it is corrupted. But certainly too, no truth is more potent than calling when it is reformed. And the truth of calling speaks to a money-saturated, market-dominated culture at two vital points.

First, calling means that, for the follower of Christ, there is a decisive, immediate, and moment-by-moment authority above money and the market. The choice between Masters has been made. There is one God, there is no God but God, and there is no rest for anyone whose god is anyone but God. So the answer to Mammon once and for all, and without reservations, is no.

Second, and more practically, calling introduces into society a different style of operating that directly counters the market mentality. We do what we do in life because we are called to it rather than because we get paid for it. Under Mammon and its "market totalitarianism," the principles, habits, and outlooks of the commercial economy reign supreme and cover the whole of life like an Arctic freeze. Not only products but also ideas and people are bought and sold. Everything is. Work, politics, sports, leisure, art, education, relationships, religion—nothing and no one has a sanctity that is immune. The core motivation of humanness, it is claimed, is rational calculation of how to maximize our best interests.

Ironically, a "free market" does not create a society as free as many think, for the constant pricing and charging of everything acts like a series of customs tolls blocking the free flow of ideas and relationships. Equally ironically, we eventually cannot afford what we most desire—deep relationships. For if "time is money" and people take time, then the "opportunity costs" of relationships (the gain that we would earn by doing something else) will be prohibitive and intimate friendships will be few. "Spending" time with friends is costly; we could "invest" it better elsewhere.

The spirit of calling counters this spirit of commerce by knocking holes in the ice. Thus there are, if you like, two economies—a "calling economy" as well as a "commercial economy"—and for followers of Christ the former, not the latter, is supreme. Contrary to the ways of commerce, calling means that life is lived for God's sake or for its own sake under God. Intrinsic satisfaction outweighs external rewards, such as pay, advancement, and recognition.

Calling, in this sense, helps foster the old amateur ideal. There are many things we do, not for profit, but for the sheer love of doing them. Whether we are doing it for our own sake or the sake of others, we are happy to be doing it, even if nobody is watching us and nobody pays us. We do it *gratis pro deo* ("free and for God"), as earlier generations put it. David Lean, the film director and maker of such epics as *Bridge on the River Kwai* and *Lawrence of Arabia,* used to say that this was the difference between directors and producers. As a director rather than a producer, he said, "I have to do it. It's in my blood." The producers he knew were simply after money. "Practically every day I thank God I'm doing what I'm doing, and I bet you that none of those people thank God that they're doing what they're doing."

The novelist Joseph Conrad wrote, "The artist appeals to that part of our being . . . which is a gift and not an acquisition—and therefore permanently enduring." Works of art, like many of the best things in life, can be products of both calling and commerce, but only the former is essential. A work of art can be sold on the market or it can survive without the market. But it must not be reduced solely to a commodity. Without the giftedness and inspiration that come from calling, it is not true art.

Such implications of calling must be worked back into our lives and into our society. That way "everyone, everywhere, and in everything" will live life unto God and profane Mammon decisively by stripping money down to its size—as a medium of exchange rather than an idol.

Do you allow money to dominate your priorities, assessments, relationships, and time? Do you allow consumer society to

contrive your wants? Or do you do what you do, above all, for God's sake and the sheer love of it? Are you so free from anxiety about money that you can be carefree in giving to those in need? Listen to Jesus of Nazareth; answer his call.

17

COMBATING THE
NOONDAY DEMON

I would prefer not to." More than twenty-five times in little over as many pages Herman Melville's character repeats these five words, delivered politely but firmly, to bring America's most ambitious and energetic street to a standstill. "Bartleby the Scrivener: A Story of Wall Street," a short story published in 1853, no longer startles as it must have done its first readers in the nineteenth century. But its haunting central figure remains as unsettling as a modern homeless vagrant, and it brilliantly evokes the world of resigned forlornness and absurdity that such writers as Franz Kafka and Samuel Beckett have portrayed in our own century.

Melville's narrator is "a rather elderly man," an unambitious lawyer with chambers in Wall Street. He had done work, we are told, for robber-baron John Jacob Astor. From his youth upward he had been "filled with a profound conviction that the easiest way of life is the best." He was soon to meet his match. He already employed three people, two scriveners (or copyists of legal papers) and an errand boy—known in the office by their nicknames, Turkey, Nippers, and Ginger Nut. Gratified by his growing business, he advertised for a new scrivener and finds on his office threshold a figure "pallidly neat, pitiably respectable, incurably forlorn!"— Bartleby.

At first, Bartleby distinguishes himself by his industry. He did an extraordinary quantity of writing both by sunlight and by candle light—"As if long famishing for something to copy, he seemed to gorge himself on my documents."

But then, on only his third day of work, when asked to help with some document checking, Bartleby confounds both his boss and his fellow-workers when "in a singularly mild, firm voice, [he] replied, 'I would prefer not to.'"

These words become Bartleby's five-word creed. Is the request politely repeated? "I would prefer not to," he replies. Does his boss insist? Is work put in front of his nose? Do the other workers ask him to assist them? "I would prefer not to," he intones. Is Bartleby asked to explain himself? Is he offered other jobs? Is he fired and told to find other work? Is he ordered to quit the premises once and for all? Sometimes Bartleby doesn't answer at all; he stands in one of his profound "dead-wall reveries." More often he simply says, "I would prefer not to."

Naturally, Bartleby's noncompliance initially baffles and in the end infuriates his boss. In between, the narrator feels every emotion known to a caring employer and a decent human being. But nothing succeeds. Nothing gets through. The story rolls relentlessly toward its climax in "the Tombs," Manhattan's infamous nineteenth-century House of Detention. Bartleby, finally refusing even food, wastes away and dies, "his face towards a high wall."

What explains Bartleby's strange behavior? Is he "a little luny," as twelve-year-old Ginger Nut believes? Or fully deranged as the bystanders think? Is his noncompliance an intuitive political protest, a nineteenth-century precursor to Gandhian nonviolent resistance? Or is Bartleby, as modern critics have written, a case of "terminal *acedia*" (or sloth) at the heart of modern capitalism?

Melville leaves such questions like hooks buried in our minds and consciences. All he adds is "one little item of rumour" that the narrator heard a few months after the scrivener's death. Bartleby had come from Washington, D.C., where he had lost his job because of a change in administrations. He had been "a subordinate clerk in the Dead Letter Office" (for the storage and disposal of undeliverable mail).

"Dead letters!" Melville writes at the story's conclusion. "Does it not sound like dead men? Conceive a man by nature and misfortune prone to pallid hopelessness: can any business seem more fitted than that of continually handling those dead letters, and assorting them for the flames? . . . On errands of life, these letters speed to death. Ah Bartleby! Ah humanity!"

It is hard not to read something of Melville's own life into this story. When he was thirty-three he felt a failure. His great masterwork *Moby Dick*, published two years earlier in 1851, had sold only 2,300 copies and had been savaged by reviewers on both sides of the Atlantic. *Pierre*, published in 1832, sold only 2,030 copies over thirty-five years (earning over his lifetime the princely sum of $157). So as Melville complained in a letter in 1851 to his Massachusetts neighbor Nathaniel Hawthorne, "Dollars damn me." If sales are the public's letter to an author, Melville was not encouraged by his mail. He had tried to express in *Moby Dick*, he wrote, "the sane madness of vital truth," but the world was not interested.

Like Bartleby, Herman Melville felt his life had taken him down a blind alley and all he seemed to see was dead, blank walls. Or, as he wrote to Hawthorne, using the picture of a stagecoach changing horses while carrying mail (the theme of messages again): "Lord, when shall we be done changing? Ah, it's a long stage, and no inn in sight, and night coming, and the body cold."

BETTER BARBARISM THAN BOREDOM?

Whether "Bartleby the Scrivener" is read on its own or read against the backdrop of its author's life, it sharpens our appreciation of yet another aspect of the truth of calling—*calling is the best antidote to the deadly sin of sloth.*

Sloth, the fourth of the seven deadly sins, is today the most misunderstood of all—which is ironic because, properly understood, it is the characteristically modern sin. For a start, sloth must be distinguished from idling, a state of carefree lingering that can be admirable, as in friends lingering over a meal or lovers whiling away hours in delighted enjoyment. In W. H. Davies's famous lines, "What is this life, if full of care, / We have no time to stand and stare?" Or, as George Macdonald argued, "Work is not always required of a man. There is such a thing as sacred idleness, the cultivation of which is now fearfully neglected."

But sloth must also be distinguished from the modern notion of couch-potato lethargy ("Nearer my couch to thee," as *The New York Times* headlined it). Sloth is more than indolence and physical laziness. In fact, it can reveal itself in frenetic activism as easily as in lethargy because its roots are spiritual rather than physical. It is a condition of explicitly spiritual dejection that has given up on the pursuit of God, the true, the good, and the beautiful. Sloth is inner despair at the worthwhileness of the worthwhile that finally slumps into an attitude of "Who cares?"

Defined in this way, it is plain, as Evelyn Waugh observed, that "sloth is not primarily the temptation of the young." It is what the medievals spoke of as "the noonday demon." It is a sluggishness of spirit, feeling, and mind that eventually overcomes the body like an after-lunch languor. A far cry from the early morning idealism and enthusiasms of youth, it is captured in such phrases as the listlessness of life, despondency over meaning, career doldrums, moral burnout, paralysis of will, and the expressive French words *ennui* and *anomie.*

There are three principal points of entry for modern sloth, overlapping at times but quite distinct, and calling runs counter to them all. The first is philosophical. Loss of faith in God, and therefore in eternity and immortality, leads inexorably to an erosion of vitality in life itself. Max Weber wrote of the secularizing of the modern world as "disenchantment." The magic and mystery of life viewed under the aspect of eternity is systematically reduced and destroyed. But C. S. Lewis wrote more aptly of our modern "enchantment," and Blaise Pascal wrote earlier still of the "incomprehensible spell" and "supernatural torpor" of the sloth that comes from loss of faith.

"One needs no great sublimity of soul," Pascal wrote in *Pensées,* "to realize that in this life there is no true and solid satisfaction, that all our pleasures are mere vanity, that our afflictions are infinite, and finally that death which threatens us at every moment must in a few years infallibly face us with the inescapable and appalling alternative of being annihilated or wretched throughout eternity." Therefore, Pascal writes, "I make an absolute distinction between those who strive with all their might to learn and those who live without troubling themselves or thinking about it."

Pascal's warnings about the danger of indifference have been amply proved true in our century. Friedrich Nietszche may have written of the "death of God" with excitement ("We philosophers and 'free spirits' feel ourselves irradiated as by a new dawn by the report that the 'old God is dead'"). Bertrand Russell may have felt inspired by his atheistic vision of a "Free Man's Worship" ("Only on the firm foundation of unyielding despair can the soul's habitation henceforth be safely built"). But for countless modern people, the world without God and without faith is closer to Bartleby's dead-end passivity or to the murky alienation of Joseph K in Kafka's *Trial* and the forlorn pointlessness of Samuel Beckett's two tramps in *Waiting for Godot*.

The year after Beckett arrived in Paris, literary circles were rocked by the suicide of the writer Jacques Rigaut because it was such a contradiction of his earlier weariness: "There are no reasons for going on living, but no more are there any reasons for dying. . . . The only manner left us in which we can evidence our disdain for life is by accepting it. . . . Life is not worth the trouble of leaving it."

In his *Letters to Olga*, Václav Havel commented on the incidence of intelligent modern people who are cynical and have "lost faith in everything." Such "giving up on life," he said, is "one of the saddest forms of human downfall." But the important thing to note is that "it was not the evil of the world that ultimately led the person to give up, but rather his own resignation that led him to the theory about the evil of the world."

"The temptation of Nothingness," Havel mused, "is enormous and omnipresent, and it has more and more to rest its case on, more to appeal to. Against it, man stands alone, weak and poorly armed, his position worse than ever before in history." And then, in words reminiscent of Pascal, he concludes, "The tragedy of modern man is not that he knows less and less about the meaning of his own life, but that it bothers him less and less. . . ."

The second point of entry for sloth is cultural. We think of the rise of the modern world as the story of dynamism, energy, progress, and achievement—which it is. But we often overlook its other side. The world produced by such dynamism is a world of convenience, comfort, and consumerism. And when life is safe, easy, sanitized, climate-controlled, and plush, sloth is close.

The flipside of dynamic optimism is corrosive boredom. The couch potato is the half-brother of the astronaut. Equally the flipside of consumerism is complacency. The most compulsive of shoppers and channel-surfers move from feeling good to feeling nothing.

Søren Kierkegaard was a passionate earlier rebel against this modern sloth. "Let others complain that the age is wicked," he wrote of the mid-nineteenth century, "my complaint is that it is wretched, for it lacks passion. . . . Their lusts are dull and sluggish, their passions sleepy. They do their duty, these shopkeeping souls, but they clip the coin a trifle." Also in the nineteenth century, Charles Baudelaire wrote that "ennui, fruit of dreary apathy, takes on dimensions of everlastingness." And in a dark prophecy of modern boredom-bred violence and vandalism, Théophile Gautier wrote: "Better barbarism than boredom!"

The thought is arresting. Does the lethargy of sloth breed an itch for action, violence, and chaos? What is undeniable is that when comforts and convenience sap our energies and idealism, inactivity secretes sloth into our minds like a poison in the blood. Then, as lethargy, tedium, and futility overtake us, we progressively lower our ideals and succumb. The result, as Dorothy Sayers wrote devastatingly, is a slump into the sin of sloth—"the sin which believes in nothing, cares for nothing, seeks to know nothing, interferes with nothing, enjoys nothing, loves nothing, hates nothing, finds purpose in nothing, lives for nothing, and only remains alive because there is nothing it would die for." We have known it far too well in the twentieth century, Sayers concluded. "The only thing perhaps that we have not known about it is that it is mortal sin."

When the Bible describes the occasion of King David's sin of adultery and then murder, it says revealingly, "In the spring, at the time when kings go off to war, David sent Joab out . . ." Relaxed when he should have been on the job, inactive when he would normally be under arms, David was more than halfway open to temptation.

The third main entry point for sloth is biographical. There are natural points in our lives when each of us is especially prone to losing a sense of the worthwhileness of the worthwhile. Throughout history the most common moment is the experience of discouragement through failure. Today the most talked about is the pent-up frustrations of a "midlife crisis." Probably the worst of all is the combination of a midlife crisis that pivots on failure. For few things are more ignominious than failing at something that was not worth doing in the first place.

Midlife crises that are genuine and not simply fashionable are generally due to the tensions between three very different desires: for successful careers, for satisfying work, and for rich personal lives. Early in life the differences between our personal lives and our work may not be marked or obvious. But as life goes on, and especially if success in one sphere is not complemented by success in the other, a yawning chasm will open that leads to deep frustration. Sadly, studies show, a few people enjoy neither their work nor their personal lives; more enjoy their work but not their personal lives; only a few say they enjoy both.

Crises created by a contradiction between successful careers and satisfying work are even more fateful. For when we set out in youth and choose careers for external reasons—such as the lure of the salary, the prestige of the position, or pressure from parents and peers—we are setting ourselves up for frustration later in life if the work does not equally suit us for internal reasons, namely our giftedness and calling. "Success" may then flatter us on the outside as "significance" eludes us from the inside.

At that point many people jump to the opposite extreme where another frustration looms. They go wrong in thinking that "success" failed to satisfy because it was secular whereas "significance" will be fulfilling because it is religious. That is actually the "Catholic distortion" again. The troublesome contradiction is not between secular and religious work but between work that is inspired by gifts and calling (whether secular or religious) and work that is directed solely by career.

Any contradiction between our callings and our careers condemns us to be square pegs in round holes. But while the resulting midlife crisis may be severe, it may also serve as a wake-up call that turns out to be an opportunity as much as a crisis. Careers that express calling are as fulfilling as careers that contradict calling are frustrating.

The truth of calling addresses all these entry points of sloth. Personally summoned by the Creator of the universe, we are given a meaning in what we do that flames over every second and inch of our lives. Challenged, inspired, rebuked, and encouraged by God's call, we cannot for a moment settle down to the comfortable, the mediocre, the banal, and the boring. The call is always to the higher, the deeper, and the farther.

Awakened to our deepest gifts and aspirations, we know that consideration of calling always has to precede considerations of career and that we can seek the deepest satisfaction in work only within the perspectives of calling.

In short, every time the marsh gas of sloth rises from the swamps of modern life and threatens to overcome us, the call of God jerks us wide awake. Against the most sluggish temptation to feel "Who cares?" calling is the supreme motivation, the ultimate "why." God has called us, and we are never more ourselves than when we are fully stretched in answering. There is no yawning in response to this call.

Do you long to escape the smallness of a life with no purpose higher than your own? To rise above the mediocrity, tedium, and quiet desperation of so many around you? To know a purpose no odds can daunt and no failure can dismay? Listen to Jesus of Nazareth; answer his call.

_18_

A WORLD WITH
WINDOWS

To come of age and come to faith in a tumultuous decade like the 1960s was a bracing privilege. No one could take anything for granted. Nothing could remain secondhand. For those who thought and those who cared, everything had to be challenged, taken back to square one, thought through, and engaged with one's whole being and not just the mind. To adapt Nietzsche, "all truths were bloody truths for the children of the sixties."

Nowhere was this challenge more plain than in knowing what we believed and why. When I was studying philosophy as an undergraduate, for example, an aggressive humanism was the dominant faith on many campuses and the reigning philosophy was militantly atheistic. It actually trumpeted the maxim that "G-o-d was less meaningful than d-o-g." Later certain Protestant theologians became notorious through *Time*'s coverage of their suicidal affirmation of "God is dead" theology. And the ABC (or "anything but Christianity") mood of the decade often meant that any religion was fresh, relevant, and exciting so long as it was not Christian, orthodox, or traditional.

In particular, hundreds of thousands of young people in the 1960s followed the Beatles, in mind if not body, when they flirted with Eastern religions. First introduced to the Beat movement by poet Gary Snyder and popularized in the newly emerging "counterculture" by one-time Anglican counselor Alan Watts,

Eastern religions suddenly became the rage after the visits to the West of the Maharishi Mahesh Yogi and a bevy of Indian gurus and Zen masters. Meditation centers, vegetarianism, communes, reincarnation, sitar music all became as familiar as blue jeans and rock music. The *Bhagavad Gita, The Tibetan Book of the Dead,* and Herman Hesse's *Siddartha* seemed as widely read as the Bible.

As a new follower of Christ, my desire to understand those on the physical or spiritual road to the East was so strong that I took to the road myself—physically, not spiritually. For more than six months I ranged "the hippie trail," exploring such crowded meccas as Kabul, Goa, Benares, Rishikesh, Katmandu, and Thailand.

Among a host of memories, two stand out because they were linked by the same phrase—"the sleep of death." The first time I heard it used was in Rishikesh, the famous center of the gurus in the foothills of the Himalayas. I was there studying in an ashram not far from the Maharishi's, where the Beatles had gone. Most of those there were Indians, but my roommate was an Italian, a friend of film director Frederico Fellini, and there were at least twenty-five Europeans and Americans in various stages of initiation into Hinduism.

Repeatedly the guru, who spoke fluent English and was well versed in Western philosophy, would speak of the Westerners as "my refugees." When new people arrived, he would explain that they were refugees not just from the West but also from Western consciousness. They were "refugees from the sleep of death."

Sometimes the guru would expand on this phrase by referring to Plato's parable of the cave—like captive cave-dwellers, he said, Westerners had no idea of the world of awareness outside their reason-and-science-bound cave. Often he would just quote William Blake, the eighteenth-century English poet and artist: "May God us keep / From single vision & Newton's sleep!"

Not long after leaving the ashram, I went to Katmandu. Never will I forget the second time I heard the phrase—the first time I entered one of the cafés frequented by Westerners, accompanied by an English doctor who cared for those in the terminal stages of drug addiction. At least forty young Westerners were slumped with their heads down on the tables. As we entered, a shaft of sunlight broke into the smoky room, and half a dozen or so lifted their heads slowly and stared at us with glazed, unseeing eyes. They then settled down again to the zombielike stupor in which they spent their days.

Watching to see my reaction to this sight he knew so well, the doctor said simply: "Poor things. They started out to escape a metaphorical sleep of death, and they've ended by succumbing to a real one."

"The sleep of death," "single vision," "Newton's sleep"—what were the doctor, the guru, and the poet referring to? Clearly William Blake was speaking of the mechanistic view of life spread by the scientific discoveries of Isaac Newton in the seventeenth century. In his famous print "Newton," Blake painted a naked man sitting on a rock with his hand stretched out, measuring the arc and triangle of a mathematical diagram outline on a scroll. Head bowed in meditation, the man is entirely wrapped up in himself and his thoughts. He has almost become part of the rock, which itself appears to be in a cave—the scientific version of Plato's celebrated cave.

Mechanistic science, Blake believed, had petrified human life into a machinelike existence that was a form of captivity. Awareness of higher or different levels of reality, whether understood from a Christian, Hindu, or any supernatural viewpoint, was frozen out.

Elsewhere, in his even more famous poem "Jerusalem," William Blake wrote of the "dark Satanic mills" that were disfiguring the traditional landscape in the early industrial revolution. Today these modernizing forces, such as capitalism and industrialized technology, rather than Newton's ideas, would be held responsible for the "sleep of death." The technical name given to the process is "secularization."

Whatever the precise origin of the problem, secularization is a major challenge to the integrity and effectiveness of faith in the modern world because it affects the way we view reality. As stressed earlier, the modern world is not only the most nearly universal culture in history but also the most powerful culture so far. For all its truly wonderful advantages, its most obvious disadvantage is the damage it has done to traditional religion. And the first and greatest of its three adverse pressures on religion is secularization.

Yet here we see another dimension of the truth of calling—*calling directly counters the great modern pressure toward secularization because the call of Jesus includes a summons to the exercise of the spiritual disciplines and the experience of supernatural realities.*

A WORLD WITHOUT WINDOWS

The term *secularization* can be very confusing because so many people use it in so many different ways. Some people, for instance, wrongly use the term to refer to the disappearance of religion. And since many of them would like religion to disappear, they misuse the scientific term to provide a cloak of respectability for their hopes. But to their disappointment, religion has plainly not disappeared in the modern world and shows no sign of doing so. It has changed, certainly, and in some ways decidedly for the worse. But it has not disappeared.

Properly defined, secularization is *the process through which the decisive influence of religious ideas and institutions has been neutralized in successive sectors of society and culture, making religious ideas less meaningful and religious institutions more marginal. In particular, it refers to how our modern consciousness and ways of thinking are restricted to the world of the five senses.*

In traditional societies most human beings were open to a world beyond the natural, visible, and tangible. Certainly they spent most of their lives in the paramount reality of the "seven-to-eleven waking world" of mundane, everyday concerns and interests. Certainly most were somewhere between the extremes of the mystic and the skeptic in their attitudes to higher realities. And certainly many of the experiences that went beyond ordinary reality—for example, dreams—were not considered necessarily religious.

Nevertheless, the deepest experiences of all were held to be "religious," "sacred," "other," or "transcendent," however these terms were defined. Not only that, pursuits as down-to-earth as farming, business, sex, and politics were seen in the light of the world beyond.

Secularization has changed all that. Today, for some people all of the time and for most people some of the time, secularization ensures that *ordinary* reality is not just the *official* reality of the modern world but the *only* reality. Traditionally human life was lived in a house with windows to other worlds, however dirty, broken, or boarded up. Modern life, however, is lived in what Peter Berger aptly calls "a world without windows."

We need not stop to explain exactly why this has happened. In brief, less and less of life has been left to God, chance, or human spontaneity, as more and more of life has been classified, calculated, and controlled by the use of reason—in science and technology. What matters more is to recognize that secularization affects religious believers just as much as it does atheists and agnostics. The same vast assembly of plans and procedures that we use to put an astronaut on the moon or market a new computer chip can also be mustered to "grow a church" or "evangelize an unreached people."

In short, the modern world quite literally "manages" without God. We can do so much so well by ourselves that there is no need for God, even in his church. Thus we modern people can be profoundly secular in the midst of explicitly religious activities. Which explains why so many modern Christian believers are atheists unawares. Professing to be believers in supernatural realities, they are virtual atheists; whatever they say they believe, they show in practice that they function without practical recourse to the supernatural. An Australian business leader once told me when he shared his faith with a Japanese CEO, the response was dismissive: "Whenever I meet a Buddhist leader, I meet a holy man in touch with another world. Whenever I meet a Christian leader, I meet a manager at home only in this world like I am."

The call to follow Jesus Christ runs directly counter to this deadly modern pressure toward secularization. First, Jesus summons us explicitly to a kingdom and a life made qualitatively different by their supernatural dimensions. Dallas Willard, author of *The Spirit of the Disciplines* and a sure guide to this momentous aspect of faith, emphatically underscores that "spirituality is a matter of *another reality*." It is not merely a religious sentiment, a commitment, a lifestyle, let alone a political stance or a mystical-sounding buzzword. Spirituality for the follower of Christ is a matter of a different world with a different reality, different energies, different possibilities, and different prospects.

Unseen, spiritual reality is not unreal. In fact it is more real—decisive over the shadow reality of the seen world. A spiritual reality all around, above, and inside the secular reality of the world of our five senses, spirituality is a dimension we enter only when we are supernaturally born into it and learn, though the disciplines, to make it our regular habitat.

Do we take the supernatural, the world of the unseen real, seriously? Like Hamlet's friend, many of us need Shakespeare's reminder, "There are more things in heaven and earth, Horatio, than are dreamt of in your philosophy." Like Nicodemus, many of us need to be startled again by what Jesus said, "I tell you the truth, no one can see the kingdom of God unless he is born again." It is quite common for people to trumpet that they have been "born again" yet exhibit no signs of living in the supernatural dimensions of the reality they have been born into.

Second, Jesus not only calls us to follow him but shows us the essential place of spiritual discipline in his own life. Called by God at his baptism, he is driven into the wilderness to confront Satan's temptations, which he overcomes through spiritual warfare. Facing the crucial choice of twelve disciples to be the apostles on whom his worldwide movement will depend, he goes out to a mountainside to spend the night alone in prayer to God.

Pressured by crowds allowing him no space to move and no time to eat, he gets up early in the morning and goes off while it is still dark to a solitary place to pray.

For Jesus, spirituality is plainly not a life of contemplation divorced from a life of action. There is nothing in Jesus' life of either the super-spiritual "Catholic distortion" or the all-too-secular "Protestant distortion" we saw earlier. There is only a rhythm of engagement and withdrawal, work and rest, dispensing and recharging, crowds and solitude, in the midst of one of the shortest, busiest public lives ever lived.

If we are not to be dried up, our secular lives require supernatural refreshment too. But equally, if our supernatural experience is not to become an end in itself and a source of indulgence and pride, we must resolutely descend from the mountain peaks of vision to the valley of ordinary life where our callings take us. The New Testament knows no monasteries or monks, only spiritually disciplined disciples in a demanding, everyday world.

Third, Jesus calls us to specific spiritual disciplines that are vital to sustaining calling itself. Neither of the two terms in "spiritual discipline" comes easily to us as modern people—we are by nature neither spiritual or disciplined. But if we see discipline as the necessary training we undertake to help us do what we cannot do by direct ordinary effort, spiritual discipline operates on essentially the same principle as training for athletics or learning to play a musical instrument. In Dallas Willard's words, it is "nothing but an activity undertaken to bring us into more effective cooperation with Christ and his kingdom."

Take, for instance, the importance of solitude to the practice of living before the Audience of One. When Jesus and his disciples were so pressured that they couldn't even eat, he said: "Come with me by yourselves to a quiet place and get some rest." He then took them to "a solitary place." Like the other disciplines of abstinence (as opposed to the disciplines of engagement), solitude is vital for training us to stand against the excesses of our culture. Whereas normal life puffs up our sense of self-importance and

159

locks us into patterns of thought and behavior dependent on others, solitude liberates us from these entanglements by carving out a space from which we can see ourselves and our situation before the Audience of One.

Whether viewed as "the desert" or the "closet," solitude provides the private place where we can take our bearings and so make the Lord our North Star that we remain fixed on as we return to society. Thus solitude becomes not so much a place as a state of heart. It is a matter of aloneness, not loneliness. Wherever we go, whatever we face, solitude is the mobile altar in our lives that allows us to live as we worship—before the Audience of One.

Today we tend to talk of "work" and "leisure" as opposites. Work is serious, leisure is play, it is said. Work is drudgery, leisure is fun. Work is for pay, leisure is free. Work is what we do for someone else, leisure is for ourselves—and so on. But a moment's thought shows this is not so. Far closer to the mark is the observation that the modern world has scrambled things so badly that today we worship our work, we work at our play, and we play at our worship.

That confusion is worth pondering. But the more important point is that the relationship between work and leisure changes from society to society and from generation to generation in the same society. A holiday as "vacation," for example, is a recent invention that is quite different from the holiday as "holy day." So while it is fruitful to reflect on a Christian critique of society's view of leisure at any particular time, it is absolutely essential to think through Christ's view of rest and spiritual discipline for his disciples for all time. Only then can we answer the call and resist the sleep of death.

Do you live in a world without windows? Do you feel the time squeeze of those for whom managing time is a bigger problem than making money? Have you developed your gifts of reason

and practicality to the point where your eyes of faith are blind
and your weapons of spiritual warfare purely metaphorical?
Or do you see "the horses and chariots of fire all around"?
Listen to Jesus of Nazareth; answer his call.

19

LOCKED OUT AND
STAYING THERE

Karl Barth's famous description of himself is equally apt as a picture of Martin Luther. Painfully climbing up the steps of a medieval cathedral tower in the dark, he reached for the stair rope to steady himself and was amazed to hear a bell ring out above him—he had inadvertently pulled on the bell rope and woken up the whole countryside.

Far from a man with a comprehensive vision of reform and a well-calculated plan for carrying it out, Luther struggled painfully for salvation before God and was surprised to set off the cataclysmic sixteenth-century movement that we now call simply the Reformation.

Luther's wrestlings were cataclysmic, and in ways we find difficult to believe in a day when theology is marginal to society. The story is told, for example, of two young Dutch priests who eagerly followed news of Martin Luther's early reforms—brought to them by Guttenberg's new printing presses. In 1520, they read the revolutionary paragraphs in *The Babylonian Captivity* (mentioned in chapter 4). They were stunned. Their whole view of following Christ, and in particular their whole way of leading the church, was wrong. Their response was swift and decisive—the very next Sunday evening they locked the doors of their church.

Locked their church doors? What on earth for? For security reasons? Or were they hijacking their premises and transferring them forcibly to another denomination? There were in fact no "Protestant" churches at this stage, let alone "denominations." The priests' point was theological. At a time when "church" was typically equated with "clerical" and associated with buildings, institutions, and ecclesiastical hierarchies, Luther's rediscovery of calling blew apart the distortions of the medieval world.

Followers of Christ live by faith alone to the glory of God alone. As we saw earlier, there is no sacred vs. secular, higher vs. lower, perfect vs. permitted, contemplation vs. action where calling is concerned. Calling equalizes even the distinctions between clergy and laypeople. It is a matter of "everyone, everywhere, and in everything" living life in response to God's summons.

Yes, the church as a building is essential to worship and certain other aspects of the church's corporate life. But to make it more is to fall for the perennial "edifice complex." So the two priests locked the church doors on Sunday night as a statement that followers of Christ were to live their whole lives to God. The bricklayer with the trowel, the farmer behind the plow, the artist before the easel, the cook beside the oven, the magistrate presiding at the bench, the parent at the crib—each one was to live out his or her calling without regard to titles, hierarchies, and distinctions. Locked out of church, they were to stay out as a demonstration of the lordship of Christ over every inch and second of life.

This simple act by two Dutch priests grew into a robust tradition that has characterized the Dutch church at its best. The seventeenth-century painter Rembrandt van Rijn is its best-known exponent, but one of the most interesting stories of the influence of holistic faith on Dutch life is that of Abraham Kuyper, the remarkable nineteenth-century Christian leader destined to be the Netherlands' first twentieth-century prime minister. Born in Massluis in the south of Holland in 1837, Kuyper graduated from the University of Leiden and started his career at a time when faith in Christ was being squeezed between the rock of an unyielding secular liberalism and the hard place of a shrunken evangelical pietism—similar to one part of our problem today. In response Kuyper carved out a vision of faith and public life that was comprehensive, compelling, and enduring. He has been described as the Martin Luther King of his people.

A visionary thinker, though never a man of ideas only, Kuyper was a dedicated reformer whose energies propelled him higher and higher onto the national stage of the Netherlands. Trained for the ministry, he went from job to job, or rather added job to job, as his influence broadened. His résumé during the fifty-seven years of his public career was phenomenal. He was four years prime minister, ten years a pastor, ten years a member of parliament, seven years in the Upper House, twenty years a professor at the Free University of Amsterdam, forty-two years chairman of his political party, and forty-seven years an editor of a daily and weekly newspaper. At one time he actually held the roles of editor, party chairman, professor, and prime minister simultaneously. The bibliography of his writings lists 232 titles. He gave his followers not only powerful leadership and a practical example but the theoretical tools to carry their vision forward in later generations.

Critics of Kuyper point to three nervous breakdowns in his life. This renaissance thinker simply attempted to do too much, they say. But there were other factors in the crises. Neurasthenia, or "nervous prostration," was fashionable in the late nineteenth century and observers have traced the depressions to his relationship to his father. More important, Kuyper's Herculean portfolio of jobs was due not just to overwork and what his daughter called his "iron regimen" but to his inspiring vision of the lordship of Christ over the whole of life.

In 1903, when Abraham Kuyper as prime minister faced the railroad strike that was to ring down the curtain on his political career, he wrote to his daughter in the Dutch East Indies, "My calling is high, my task is glorious. Above my bed hangs a crucifix, and when I look up there it is as if the Lord is asking me each night: 'What is your struggle next to my bitter cup?' His service is so exalting and glorious."

It was this vision of his high calling, not drivenness, that lay behind Kuyper's famous banner statement mentioned earlier: "There is not one square inch of the entire creation about which Jesus Christ does not cry out, 'This is mine! This belongs to me!'"

This vibrant Dutch tradition has its flaws, but it often stands in marked contrast to the recurring feebleness of recent Anglo-Saxon pietism. And it points to yet another dimension of the truth of calling—*calling directly counters the great modern pressure toward privatization because of its insistence that Jesus Christ is Lord of every sphere of life.* To be more specific, calling keeps us from the deadly triangle of pitfalls currently bedeviling faith in public life.

LAUNCH OUT INTO THE DEEP

The first pitfall for faith in public life is "privatization," an ugly word, but the technical term for something of immense importance to religious believers in the modern world. Privatization is sometimes used to describe the dismantling of socialism and in particular the return of state-run companies to private control. That meaning is not our interest here. As used here, *privatization is the process by which modernization produces a cleavage between the public and private spheres of life and reinforces the private sphere as the special arena for individual freedom, fulfillment—and faith.*

Beyond question, the private sphere in modern life represents incredible freedom. More people can choose more, do more, buy more, see more, and travel more than ever before. The results may be chaotic or regrettable, but in opening up for us "a world of our own," the private sphere provides an unprecedented chance to think and act independently.

But at the end of the day we must not be beguiled: The results of privatized freedom are limited and limiting. There is unprecedented freedom, but only within the limits of the private sphere. What do we wish to pursue? Yoga? Satan worship? Spouse swapping?

Bridge playing? Speaking in tongues? A Bible study group? The choice is ours and the range of possibilities is truly fabulous. Money, time, and, to some extent, our neighbors' sensitivities are the only limits.

But woe betide the person who expects similar freedom in the public world of work—the world of Wall Street, Capitol Hill, IBM, and NASA. That is a different world with different ways. We may have prayer breakfasts *before* work maybe. Or a Bible study group in the lunch hour perhaps. But in much of the normal working world, personal convictions, along with hats and coats, are to be left at the door.

Lord Melbourne, British prime minister in the 1830s, once listened to a pointed sermon and made the indignant remark: "Things have come to a pretty pass when religion is allowed to invade the private life!" He was perceptive. In a day of formal public faith, personal faith was radical. In touching the personal life, it threatened to become a force that reached out into all of life and left nothing untouched. That, for a prime minister in the days of the British Empire, was a bit much.

But think where we are today. A historian in the 1970s commented on what he had observed of the Christian faith in the United States: "Socially irrelevant, even if privately engaging." In today's world things have come to a pretty pass in the lives of many believers if religion is allowed to invade the *public* life.

Many people fail to see that private life in the modern world is a harmless play area for believers. It serves as a sort of spiritual Indian reservation or Bantustan, a homeland for separate spiritual development set up by the architects of secular society's apartheid. And the trouble is, most Christians are unaware of the problem and simply love to have it so.

Why is this a problem? What privatized faith lacks, in one word, is *totality*. People may say and sing that "Jesus is Lord," but what they demonstrate is something else. Lordship is reduced to pocket size. Total life norms have become part-time values. Thus again and again and at point after point it has to be said: *The problem with Western*

Christians is not that they aren't where they should be but that they aren't what they should be where they are.

Luke in his Gospel describes how Peter was brought to his knees over this point. Jesus borrowed Peter's boat from which to teach a crowd and then told Peter to "put out into deep water, and let down your nets for a catch." Peter objects to the absurdity. He'd already fished out there all night. "Look here," his answer implies, "you're the rabbi. I'm the fisherman. I'll listen all day to you, but you leave the fishing to me."

Reluctantly Peter obeys, only to find his nets breaking and the two boats sinking because the catch is so large. Shown up, he hurries back to land and falls at Jesus' feet, "Go away from me, Lord; I am a sinful man."

Jesus is not a "religious leader" but Lord of all of life. Responding to his call touches the world of fishing as well as preaching, the depths of the lake, not just the shore. All that we are, all that we do, all that we have, and even all that we think and dream is called into question by this demand. Once again, it is a matter of everyone, everywhere, and everything.

But surely, it might be objected, privatization is hardly the word to describe faith at the turn of the millennium. Christians are far too active in public, critics say. Would that the church *were* that confined and innocuous, they suggest. Aren't Christians more often accused of extremism and stridency in public life? Of acting to "impose" their views on everyone else?

A careful look would show a more complicated picture. For all the recent high-profile public activism of some Christians, most Christians are probably still subject to the confines of privatization and its damage to the practice of faith in every part of life. But mention of politics is a reminder that privatization is not the whole story. Two other pitfalls have opened up, partly in reaction, to form the triangle of dangers menacing those who have responded to privatization with too little thought.

The second pitfall for faith in public life is "politicization," virtually a direct reaction to privatization. If it is wrong to make faith privately engaging but socially irrelevant, then surely politics is the lever to bring faith back into all of life. Or so many Christians have thought in recent decades. But if privatization lacks the "totality" of faith, the problem of politicization is the lack of "tension." Called to be "in" the world but "not of it," Christian engagement in politics should always be marked by tension between allegiance to Christ and identification with any party, movement, platform, or agenda. If that tension is ever lacking, if Christian identification with a political movement is so close that there is not any clear remainder, then the church has fallen for a particularly deadly captivity.

Political forms of this "Babylonian captivity" are a problem already writ large over European history and a central reason for modern Europe's rejection of the Christian church. Indeed, there is a direct and unarguable relationship between the degree of the church's politicization in a culture and the degree of the church's rejection by that culture—the French and Russian revolutions being the extreme examples of a volcanic reaction to corrupt state churches that were monopolistic and allowed no dissent. The revolutionary slogan of 1789 was typical of this backlash: "Strangle the last king with the guts of the last priest!"

For two hundred years the churches in the United States have avoided this pitfall—thanks largely to the genius of the First Amendment, the constructive separation of church and state, and the creation of the voluntary associations that shifted the moral agency from the local church as a corporate body to individual Christians acting in concert with others. But the last quarter of a century indicates a different story. Christians have every right to be in the public square and every right to take the positions they have. That is not the problem. But to the degree that Christian activism in public life becomes a politicization of the church—an identification with political movements on either right or left *without critical tension*—to that degree Christian activism will betray Christ and stoke the fires of its own and the church's rejection.

There are signs that an American equivalent of Europe's antipathy to politicized faith is already beginning to build. Few things are more fateful for the future of faith in the modern world than to see that this development stops.

The third pitfall for faith in public life is "pillarization," an odd-sounding word that goes back to the Netherlands of Abraham Kuyper. In the face of the problem of expanding pluralism, the Dutch response was to encourage each faith community to build its own network of institutions and organizations in its own sphere. Thus Protestants built not only churches but also Protestant schools, Protestant universities, Protestant newspapers, Protestant labor unions, and so forth. And of course the Roman Catholics and Humanists did the same, the latter without the churches.

The effect was to "pillarize" Dutch society. Like a classical Greek or Roman building resting on many pillars, Dutch society maintained its overall national unity while encouraging diversity within it.

A moment's thought shows that aspects of this solution are highly promising. Many believe it provides a way forward for all our societies today. It allows each faith to apply itself to its own spheres of life in ways that are coherent, comprehensive, and concrete. What more, one might wonder, would Christians want than to be given the freedom to be consistently Christian in their own spheres of life? Here, surely, is the solution to privatization and politicization.

But not so fast. For history gives us reason to pause. If privatization is a denial of the *totality* of faith and politicization is a denial of the *tension* of faith, pillarization has proved deficient too. In practice it undermines the *transformation* of faith. When Christians concentrate their time and energy on their own separate spheres and their own institutions—whether all-absorbing megachurches, Christian yellow-page businesses, or womb-to-tomb Christian cultural ghettoes—they lose the outward thrusting, transforming power that is at the heart of the gospel. Instead of being "salt" and "light"—images of a permeating and penetrating action—Christians and Christian institutions become soft and vulnerable to corruption from within.

Kuyper may have stayed immune to this problem by resolutely remaining engaged in public life, but many of his institutions were steadily secularized after his death. Many of his fellow-heirs of the Reformation today even trumpet the ideals of "transformation"— and then scurry back from the daunting challenges of public life to the safety of their Christian enclaves.

For well over a generation now the air in Christian circles has been thick with calls for a new empowerment of laypeople. "The hour has struck," we have been told repeatedly, "for unfreezing God's frozen people/putting the spiritually unemployed back to work/exploiting strategic careers/liberating the laity" and so on and so on. But the overall change has been small and the recurring calls have been hollowed out into clichés. Rhetoric alone is no match for the deadly triangle.

Many other things are required too—a rediscovery of the genius of voluntary associations and a clear articulation of a public philosophy, for a start. But nothing is more essential for the penetration of modern society with integrity and effectiveness than the recovery of calling. Calling resists privatization by insisting on the totality of faith. Calling resists politicization by demanding a tension with every human allegiance and association. Calling resists pillarization by requiring an attitude toward, and action in, society that is inevitably transforming because it is constantly engaged.

Grand Christian movements will rise and fall. Grand campaigns will be mounted and grand coalitions assembled. But all together such coordinated efforts will never match the influence of untold numbers of followers of Christ living out their callings faithfully across the vastness and complexity of modern society.

⚘

Is your faith privately engaging but socially irrelevant? Is it as consistent in your place of work as in your home? Are all your memberships and your allegiances relativized by your commitment to Christ? Are you acting as "salt" and "light," or do you need to be locked out of a Christian ghetto? Listen to Jesus of Nazareth; answer his call.

20

A FOCUSED LIFE

H is end was so ignominious that it overshadowed the glory of his triumph. In his own day, he simply did not survive to tell the tale and claim the kudos. In ours, his last stand is viewed as crossing the line from courage to recklessness, which lays him open to the charge of megalomania.

But the man known to his fellow-Portuguese as Fernão de Magelhães, to the Spanish as Hernando de Magellanes, and to the English-speaking world as Capitán-General Ferdinand Magellan would have been indifferent to criticism. The discoverer of the way around South America and the strait named for him, who was the first to encircle the globe (almost), and who became the greatest explorer in the greatest age of exploration was one of the strongest-willed and most single-minded humans that has ever lived.

Magellan was not tall, handsome, nor physically impressive in any way. Nor was he a favorite of the court, a member of the highest aristocratic class, or versed in courtly ways. But whatever advantage he might have lacked in one area or another, he made up for with one thing: He was a dreamer fired by an inner vision and fortified by devout faith, which made him, in the words of a fellow captain, "tough, tough, tough." Of few other human beings could it be said more accurately that he marched to a different drummer.

When Magellan weighed anchor and set sail from Spain in September, 1519, with his five ships and 265 member crew—the "Armada de Molucca"—he could have no idea his trip would take three long years, not the two he had planned, or that only one of his ships would return and that he would perish. Nor is it likely that he had much under-standing of the revolutionary character of his times or of the signifi-cance of his own discoveries. He was an explorer; his business was to discover the new. But as his biographers have pointed out, he couldn't even be certain what he was looking for until he found it.

Remarkably, Magellan does not seem to have mentioned his real motives even to his royal Spanish sponsors. In his audience with Carlos I, soon to be elected Holy Roman Emperor as Charles V, he does not speak of sailing around the world. His sponsors' bottom line was profit, his was discovery. They desired spices from the Moluccas to make them rich. He sought a passage around the Americas to allow him to circumnavigate the globe in order to show that the world was round.

The world of the Reformation and the Renaissance was revolu-tionary in many spheres, especially religion, art, science, and com-merce. But no revolution was more significant than the age of discovery. Within thirty short years, a few hundred small ships, setting out from a tiny part of Europe's southwestern coastline, discovered more of the world than all the world's discoverers had found until then. The modern world was born through them as much as through the pens of Luther, Erasmus, and Machiavelli, the paintbrushes of da Vinci and Michelangelo, and the telescope of Copernicus.

Magellan was as well informed as anyone could be about the largely unknown. Having pestered returning seamen and ransacked available reports, his mastery of winds and tides in areas he had never sailed was extraordinary. But what he wanted, nobody knew: the whereabouts of a break in the landmass, believed to be in the south, through which sailors could pass from the known Atlantic to the then unknown and unnamed Pacific.

The highlights of Magellan's epic voyage are well known to gen-erations of school children—his crushing disappointment on dis-covering that the Rio del Plato, off Uruguay, was an estuary and not the passage he was looking for. His ruthless quelling of the mutiny of three Spanish noblemen. His pressing farther south toward the Antarctic than any European had sailed before. His discovery of the Strait of Magellan in October 1520 when all his men were in despair.

His rare tears at the first sight of the Pacific. And his incredible 12,600-mile crossing of the vast and chartless waters of the earth's greatest ocean.

Whatever happened, Magellan's response was always, "Sail on, sail on!" Whatever the setback or the response of his crew, he would keep his promise to King Carlos and "sail on, sail on." His sailors may have been emaciated, the stores exhausted, the sails rotting, the rigging tattered, and the sun merciless. But he never flinched. It was always, "Sail on, sail on." At last, on March 6, 1521, Magellan's armada sighted land—first Guam and then the Philippines.

Sadly but understandably, Magellan was filled with an intense religious exaltation at his accomplishment. It led not only to his forced conversion of the hapless natives but also to a reckless, foolish assault on another island, against overwhelming odds, in which he lost his life.

Magellan's ships eventually reached home, but without him. His flagship *Trinidad* broke up in a storm, and the last of his five ships, the *Victoria*, carrying twenty-six tons of spices, limped home alone to Seville. Out of the original Armada crew of 265, only 18 spectral survivors completed the 39,300-mile round-the-world voyage. What they had achieved, their countrymen said, was a miracle—"the most wonderful and greatest thing that has ever happened in the world since God created it."

Magellan's character was far from perfect, and his world was very different from ours. But in his heroic single-mindedness, his unflinching conviction, his resolute indifference either to approval or rejection, and his stubborn defiance of discouragement, defeat, and death, Magellan demonstrated the fortitude of a life in focus. As such, his story opens a window on another side of calling—*calling directly counters the great modern pressure toward pluralization because the call of Jesus provides the priorities and perspectives that are essential for a focused life in an overloaded age.*

LIFE IS TOO SHORT TO . . .

Yet another ugly word, *pluralization* is the technical term for the third great pressure the modern world exerts on faith. *Pluralization is the process by which the proliferation of choice and change rapidly multiplies the number of options. This affects the private sphere of modern society at all levels, from consumer goods to relationships to worldviews and faiths.*

Unlike secularization, pluralization is neither radically new nor difficult to understand. (The church was born and flourished in the highly pluralistic conditions of the first century.) But it does run counter to the more normal human experience in which the range of things available was limited and the differences of work and rank were unified by the cohesive force of religion.

The modern world offers an endless range of choice and change, overwhelming traditional simplicities and cohesion. Crowded modern cities mean that we are all much closer, yet stranger, to each other. The modern explosion of knowledge means that other people, places, periods, and psyches are accessible as never before. Yet coherent wisdom to interpret it all eludes us. Modern travel whistles us to any part of the world. Modern media bring us the world and its dazzling array of options at the push of a button. Modern business makes the products of the whole world available in our neighborhood.

This intensification of choice and change has effects on many levels. The heightened awareness of the presence of others increases our awareness of possibilities for ourselves. *Their* cuisines, *their* customs, *their* convictions can become *our* choices, *our* options, *our* possibilities. Life has become a smorgasbord with an endless array of dishes. And more important still, choice is no longer just a state of mind. Choice has become a value, a priority, a right. To be modern is to be addicted to choice and change. These are the unquestioned essence of modern life.

Some of the effects of pluralization are devastating but subtle. For example, the increase in choice and change leads to a decrease in commitment and continuity—to everyone and everything. Thus obligation melts into option and givenness into choice. But other effects are terribly obvious—above all the way in which choice and change lead quickly to a sense of fragmentation, saturation, and overload. In the modern world there are simply too many choices, too many people to relate to, too much to do, too much to see, too much to read, too much to catch up with and follow, too much to buy.

Each choice sprouts with its own questions. Might we? Could we? Should we? Will we? Won't we? What if we had? What if we hadn't? The forest of questions leads deeper and deeper into the dark freedom, then to the ever darker anxiety of seemingly infinite possibility.

At some point different to us all a cut-off switch kicks in. We are overloaded, saturated. There is too much to do and too little time to do it. But life goes on. Neither planning nor juggling can span the gap. But life goes on. At the level of our relationships alone, their sheer number, variety, and intensity become impossible. But life goes on. One minute we feel the vertigo of unlimited possibility and the next the frustration of superficiality. But life goes on.

The result is not only overload but also a profound loss of unity, solidity, and coherence in life. Experience comes to us shredded into fragments and episodes. Each moment stands on its own, with neither roots in any yesterday nor consequences for any tomorrow. Like a sound-bite or a headline, each experience bursts into our attention and quickly fades from our memory. So today's rage is ridiculous tomorrow; today's celebrity is tomorrow's bore. Not surprisingly, attention-deficit is a contemporary disorder and genuine tradition is a scarce commodity.

Stone, it is said, was the medium for the ancients and steel for the early moderns; ours is plastic and the name of the game is recycling. "One-and-only" and "forever" are obsolete, and "needing more space" is our most readily given excuse. In our fragmented lives the one thing necessary is to "keep our options open." The art of "identity building" is more a matter of fluidity than fixture. And since the rules of the game change as fast as the games themselves, we are taught to avoid above all being "stuck" with commitments that might "mortgage" the freedom of tomorrow.

How does calling speak to this everyday modern predicament? Obviously it is not a magic wand that makes the array of choice and change disappear and pieces together our shredded lives. But the very character of calling counters the fragmentation and overload at key points and opens up the secret of a focused life in a saturated world.

First, calling subverts the deadly modern idolatry of choice. Choice in modern life is central, powerful, unquestioned, and enshrined in how we think and all we do—so much so that it cannot be undermined merely by an appeal to another choice. Choice for modern people is a right that overwhelms both responsibility and rationality. Witness how arguments against abortion on demand are shipwrecked on the rocks of choice. The label "pro-choice" attempts to settle the argument by seizing the unchallengeable term.

Arguments against choice need to recognize the special, godlike power of choice. But ultimately only one thing can conquer choice— being chosen. Thus, for followers of Christ, calling neutralizes the fundamental poison of choice in modern life. "I have chosen you," Jesus said, "you have not chosen me." We are not our own; we have been bought with a price. We have no rights, only responsibilities. Following Christ is not our initiative, merely our response, in obedience. Nothing works better to debunk the pretensions of choice than a conviction of calling. Once we have been called, we literally "have no choice."

Second, calling provides the story line for our lives and thus a sense of continuity and coherence in the midst of a fragmented and confusing modern world. The saturation and overload produced by pluralization, and reinforced by mobility, are a leading cause of modern alienation. If we have lived in too many places, had too many jobs, known too many people, and watched too much TV, how do we make sense of it all? Is there a story line to our lives or are they just a jumble of experiences that are "sound and fury, signifying nothing"? Are we condemned to what historian Arnold Toynbee called "telling one damn thing after another"? Or is there a meaning to our life-stories despite the dislocations?

Whenever we feel this dilemma, calling reminds us that there were nomads before modern mobility—and calling gave them meaning. Thus Abraham left Ur of the Chaldees and followed the call of God without knowing where he was going. The people of Israel

177

crossed a trackless desert following a pillar of cloud by day and a pillar of fire by night. In both cases their sense of direction and meaning came solely from God's call, not from their foresight, their wisdom, or their ability to read their circumstances. They were on their way to a land of promise. They did not always know the way God was leading them, but they always knew why they trusted God: His word was the promise and his call was the way.

Is it any different today? We are all nomads again. We may live in one town a long time or a short time. We may have a job that is poorly paid or well rewarded. We may have friendships that are rich and fulfilling or thin and disappointing. We may have a résumé that is checkered or impressive. But for the follower of Christ, none of these things finally determine the meaning of our lives. What matters is that we follow the call.

Life may still bear the marks of desert trials, but the pillars of cloud and fire are there to guide and protect. Follow the call of Christ despite the uncertainty and chaos of modern circumstances, and you have the story line of your life.

Third, calling helps us to be single-minded without being fanatics. Modern choice and change, reinforced by the pace and pressure of modern life, constantly threaten to diffuse our concentration and dissipate our energy. There is good reason for the prevalence of such phrases as "burnout," the "tyranny of the urgent," and the "dictatorship of the diary." And many strategies of response are as bad as the problems. The dangerous notion that "the need is the call" is a sure recipe for overload and confusion; the beguiling notion that "you deserve a break today" is a sure recipe for lassitude and drift.

The remedy, needless to say, lies in setting wise goals and setting aside everything else. But how? Long ago the writer of the Proverbs observed, "Folly may amuse the empty-headed; a man of understanding makes straight for his goal." More recently, Harvard philosopher George Santayana wrote, "In accomplishing anything definite a man renounces everything else."

The modern world makes the focused life harder and makes it virtually impossible simply to muddle through. W. H. Auden, poet and follower of Christ, stated his lesson: "To achieve anything today, an artist has to develop a conscious strictness in respect of time which in former ages might have seemed neurotic and selfish, for he must never forget that he is living in a state of siege." Otherwise, Solzhenitsyn agreed, an artist "has no other recourse if he does not want to overheat himself with ephemeral concerns and boil dry."

What is true for the artist is true for us all. Life itself is a state of siege. But a sense of calling helps because it provides the bull's-eye at the center of the widening concentric circles that are life's possibilities. Modern life assaults us with an infinite range of things we could do, we would love to do, or some people tell us we should do. But we are not God and we are neither infinite nor eternal. We are quite simply finite. We have only so many years, so much energy, so many gray cells, and so many bank notes in our wallets. "Life is too short to . . ." eventually shortens to "life is too short."

Yet, as we make our contribution along the line of our gifts and callings, and others do the same, there is both a fruitfulness and a rest in the outcome. Our gifts are used for the purpose for which they were given us. And we can rest in doing what we can without ever pretending we are more than the little people we plainly are. René Dubos's famous maxim, "Think globally, act locally," comes into its own in the context of calling.

In his great prayer before the crucifixion, Jesus prayed to his Father, "I have glorified thee on earth by completing the work thou hast given me to do." Some people interpret this by focusing on what Jesus did. Others equally correctly focus on what Jesus didn't do, such as write a book, found a college, or start a revolution—or heal everyone, teach everyone, and care for everyone. But both points are different sides of his one calling, to be God's Messiah.

The ideal of a life focused by gifts and calling meant a great deal to writer Dorothy L. Sayers. Referring to her writing and to her work on Dante, she said, "I feel it is, as Tennyson observed, 'one clear call for me.'" But Sayers didn't start out that clearly or find it easy to finish that clearly. When she worked for Basil Blackwell, the Oxford publisher and bookseller, he described her as mismatched in the business—"Like a racehorse harnessed to a cart."

Nor did Sayers find it easy to stick to her calling once she had found it. Frequently she grew angry with clergy who asked her to open garden fêtes, taking her away from her writing. "How dare they talk about Christian vocation, when at the same time they try to take me away from my vocation, which is to be a craftsman with words, to waste my time doing something for which I have no vocation and no talent, merely because I have a name."

Sayers was even uncomfortable when fame thrust her into the role of Christian apologist and church leaders urged her on. ("We must make you a prophet to this generation and hand you the microphone to use as often as you feel able.") "When I am doing this kind of thing," she wrote to a friend, "I am visited by a powerful sensation that it is not my proper job, and that I am doing something perilously like violating my own integrity."

Honors may be as distracting as fame and worthy projects. In 1951 when Winston Churchill returned to power as prime minister, his office wrote to C. S. Lewis inviting him to become a Commander of the British Empire. Lewis was an admirer of Churchill, but still he declined. His calling could be compromised by the honor. "There are always . . . knaves who say, and fools who believe, that my religious writings are all covert anti-Leftist propaganda, and my appearance in the Honours List wd. of course strengthen their hands. It is therefore better that I shd. not appear there."

Is a sense of calling your ultimate compass in life? In 1941 T. S. Eliot wrote: "Can a lifetime represent a single motive?" If the single motive is our own, the answer to Eliot must be no. We are not wise enough, pure enough, or strong enough to aim and sustain such a single motive over a lifetime. That way lies fanaticism or failure.

But if the single motive is the master motivation of God's calling, the answer is yes. In any and all situations, both today and tomorrow's tomorrow, God's call to us is the unchanging and ultimate whence, what, why, and whither of our lives. Calling is a "yes" to God that carries a "no" to the chaos of modern demands. Calling is the key to tracing the story line of our lives and unriddling the meaning of our existence in a chaotic world.

Do you lead a saturated, overloaded, and fragmented life? Are you pulled around by the nose through appeals to need? Are you frustrated at yourself over the times the best in your life is diverted by the good? Do you long to know the overriding passion and purity of heart of willing one thing? Listen to Jesus of Nazareth; answer his call.

21

DREAMERS OF THE DAY

So long as the exploits of his life are still told and retold, people will always be torn in response to the enigma of T. E. Lawrence, or "Lawrence of Arabia." For some, no amount of Lawrence's brilliance and bravery will ever divert their eyes from his darker side. Novelist Lawrence Durrell called him "a disgusting little thing." For others, all the innuendo in the world will never dim the qualities that made Lawrence such a hero. Winston Churchill described Lawrence as "one of the greatest beings alive in our time." John Buchan, author, statesman, and governor general of Canada, was no fool as a judge of men and women. His estimate was typical: "I would have followed Lawrence to the end of the world."

Even the spin-offs from T. E. Lawrence have been inspiring. Arguably, the Oscar-winning epic, *Lawrence of Arabia* is one of the two greatest films of all time—along with Orson Welles's *Citizen Kane.* Certainly, it is the best film of director David Lean, who himself has been described as "the poet of the far horizon." Steven Spielberg is only the best known of those who credit their entry into filmmaking to this film. "I was inspired the first time I saw *Lawrence*. It made me feel puny. It still makes me feel puny. And that's one measure of its greatness."

All the ingredients of ambivalence toward Lawrence can be traced to his youth. Anticipating Freud, Alexis de Tocqueville wrote, "The entire man is, so to speak, to be seen in the cradle of the child." Or as the Irish poet George Russell, wrote hauntingly:

In ancient shadows and twilights
Where childhood has strayed
The world's great sorrows were born
And its heroes were made
In the lost boyhood of Judas
Christ was betrayed.

T. E. Lawrence was born in Wales in August 1888, but moved to north Oxford with his parents and three brothers when he was eight. His parents, Thomas and Sarah Lawrence, were very different in age, temperament, and social standing. His father was an Irish baronet, his mother a Scottish nursemaid, and their personalities were discordant. More significantly, Lawrence was the name of neither of them and they were not married, so all the boys were illegitimate. But this dark secret was not only covered, it was compensated for by a deep but stern Christian faith that inspired both parents and animated the life of the family.

The Lawrence family had come to Oxford, in fact, because of the influence of a powerful but kind Anglican rector, Canon Christopher. His long ministry at St. Aldate's had touched the lives of thousands of Oxford students and reached out to the Lawrence family in their need. Canon Christopher remained the dominant spiritual and intellectual influence on the family until his death, aged ninety-three, just before World War I.

All three of T. E.'s brothers were deeply influenced by Christopher. The first became a medical missionary in China, the second a Christian teacher in India, and the third an eloquent speaker at Christian camps. Lawrence, too, was touched indelibly. Though he was to travel far from his evangelical roots and break explosively from his mother's puritanical control, he was active in his faith until his early twenties, and the imprint of his family's faith marked him always.

Educated at Oxford High School and Jesus College, Oxford, Lawrence was known for his flaxen hair, his brilliant blue eyes, his dreamer's vision—and his fascination with the East. Oxford, "the city of the dreaming spires," had bred a dreaming son.

Drawn by the lure of the Arab world and tutored by David Hogarth, an Oxford archeologist and Naval Intelligence officer, Lawrence might well have become a world traveler or gypsy scholar if World War I had not fired the furnace that cast his character and reputation forever. Caught up in helping the Arab Revolt that helped in the liberation of Jerusalem that helped in the downfall of the Ottoman Empire that helped in the creation of the modern Middle East, Lawrence—extravagantly promoted by American reporter Lowell Thomas—returned to England a mythic hero, a Prince of Mecca, and "Lawrence of Arabia."

Lawrence was partly fascinated by Thomas's show about his life, "The Last Crusade," which was viewed by more than a million people in London alone. He returned to the theater night after night to witness what he had become. Partly, though, he was horrified by the myth and its demands. He therefore changed his name by deed poll and disappeared into anonymity in the Royal Air Force as Aircraftman Ross, a deliberate act of self-degradation that he called "brain-sleep" and "mind-suicide." And before the many contradictions could be unraveled, he was killed in a motorcycle crash in 1935 that left him forever an enigma unsolved.

Did T. E. Lawrence have his own dark secret—the result of his childhood struggles with the shame of illegitimacy, his mother's fierce possessiveness, and the "rape at Deraa" when he was captured by the Turks? Arguments will continue, inconclusively. Was Lawrence a fabulist himself as well as the product of the fantasies of others? To some extent, certainly. But when all the dust has settled and the smoke cleared, one thing is beyond question. T. E. Lawrence made an original and significant contribution to the rise of the modern Middle East, including the state of Israel and the Arab world—and he did so as a dreamer and a visionary whose imagination was the main spring of his action.

Dreaming sets the stage for Lawrence's *Seven Pillars of Wisdom*. He told a friend he had "collected a shelf of titanic works, those distinguished by greatness of spirit, *Karamazov, Zarathustra,* and *Moby Dick*. Well, my ambition was to make a fourth." First written in Paris during the Peace Conference, from notes written daily on the march, the book is his heroic account of his part in "an Arab war waged and led by Arabs for an Arab aim in Arabia." Almost at once he speaks lyrically of "the sweep of the open places, the taste of the wide winds, the sunlight, and the hopes in which we worked. The morning freshness of the world-to-be intoxicated us. We were wrought up with ideas inexpressible and vaporous, but to be fought for."

These dreams, Lawrence admits, were betrayed. "Youth could win, but had not learned to keep and was pitiably weak against age." He had worked for a new heaven and a new earth; the old men's solution was "a peace to end all peace." But one thing always drove him, he says hundreds of pages later in the closing words of the book, "I had dreamed, at the City School in Oxford, of hustling into form, while I lived, the new Asia which time was inexorably bringing up on us. . . . Fantasies, these will seem, to such as are able to call my beginning an ordinary effort."

Lawrence's most stirring statement on vision is in his introduction to *Seven Pillars of Wisdom*. "All men dream: but not equally. Those who dream by night in the dusty recesses of their minds wake in the day to find it was vanity: but the dreamers of the day are dangerous men, for they may act their dreams with open eyes, to make it possible. This I did."

It is a long way from the Oxford City High School to Aquaba and Wadi Rumm. But is the distance farther or it is in fact closer from a dreaming teenage schoolboy to a thirty-year-old colonel acting his dreams for the Arabs of "an inspired dream-palace of their national thoughts"? Dreamers of the day respond to the gap between vision and reality by closing it.

It would be fanciful to link Lawrence's vision too closely to a Christian understanding of vision—though the schoolboy dreaming he cites exactly coincides with the period of his most ardent faith. But Lawrence's term, "dreamers of the day," is an apt description of answering the call, and it illustrates another highly distinctive feature of calling: *Calling, by breaking through with an outside perspective on the present, is a prime source of Christian vision and Christian visionaries.*

WITH FIRE IN THEIR HEARTS AND WINGS ON THEIR FEET

In practical-minded circles today, it is fashionable to disdain "the vision thing." It is dismissed as idle, dangerous, or a passing phase of life. Certainly vision is a springtime feature of youth, a natural product of energy, idealism, and frustration with the ways things are. The journalist Malcolm Muggeridge, for example, was a convert to faith late in life and celebrated for his irreverent, if not cynical, debunking of pretension and pomposity. But as a young man he was different.

Just after his college days at Cambridge, Muggeridge wrote his own epitaph to a friend: "Here lieth one whose soul sometimes burned with great longings. To whom sometimes the curtain of the Infinite was opened just a little, but who lacked the guts to make any use of it."

Others, however, have made lasting use of vision and imagination—not only in youth but also as a wellspring of life itself. Benjamin Disraeli's climb to eminence as a nineteenth-century statesman was both swift and unlikely. But a clue to the secret of his success can be traced to an early diary entry: "The utilitarians in Politics are like the utilitarians in Religion. Both omit imagination in the systems, and Imagination governs Mankind."

What was true of Disraeli is true too of his whole people. H. L. Mencken wrote in an essay, "Jews, from time immemorial, have been the chief dreamers of the human race, and beyond all comparison its greatest poets." So as with calling itself, the visionary faith that calling inspires in followers of Christ goes back to the experience of the people of Abraham, Isaac, Jacob, and Moses. There is no god but God and no rest for anyone who has any god but God. God is on the move. Faith therefore means restlessness. The Caller may be unseen and the destination unknown, but those who follow his call have a voice above and vision ahead that subverts every status quo and unsettles every resting place.

Indeed, vision is so central to calling and so explosive in its consequences that it is wise to set it out in direct contrast to the counterfeits that give it a bad name. More particularly, calling's vision must be guarded at three main points. First, we must beware of spurious visions. God's calling inspires and guarantees only those visions that are truly the result of calling. For on the one hand, as the Bible warns, the momentous faculty of imagination has fallen and become the chief human means to aspire to godhead. In the words of the King James translation of the story of the tower of Babel, "And now nothing will be restrained from them which they have imagined to do." But power was not the builders' problem. Their fallen imagination—aided by technology and a universal language—enticed them to reach beyond the limits of the human condition and seek to rival God. After all, Marx, Hitler, and Mao Tse Tung were dreamers too.

On the other hand, vision and imagination, cut loose from the anchor of God's calling, are vulnerable to debunking. Freud distinguished fantasy and daydreaming from artistic creativity and dismissed the former as the product of unsatisfied wishes: "Every single phantasy is the fulfillment of a wish, a correction of an unsatisfying reality." Daydreaming, he says, "hovers, as it were, between three times." Examine it closely and you see that unfulfilled hopes string together past, present, and future "on the thread of the wish that runs through them." Look into a person's fantasies of winning the lottery or lazing on a Tahitian beach and you see what that person thinks of his or her present life.

In short, it is easy to abuse vision and make it serve as chaplain to our conceits or bellhop to our desires. Christian vision, by contrast, must be held accountable because it is inspired directly or indirectly by the call of God. It is an act of imaginative seeing that combines the insight of faith, which goes to the heart of things below the surface, and the foresight of faith, which soars beyond the present with the power of a possible future. This combining of the not-yet-combined is the secret of visionary faith. Vision and reality, word and fulfillment, present and future, situation and possibility, restlessness and reaching out, anger at what is wrong and an aim for what is better—whatever the contrast between the pairs, visionary faith is out to close the gap. This is what makes Lawrence's "dreamers of the day" different from daydreamers—and it is also why they are dangerous: "They act their dreams with open eyes."

Hebrews 11 is the great honors list of visionary faith, a stirring catalogue of men and women whose vision of God called them to live and work against the customs, values, and priorities of their generation. They marched to a different drummer. Their sights were on a different goal. Their home was in a different country. They looked forward to a different city. By their faith they called the entire world into question, and the author of Hebrews says of them, "Those who use such language show plainly that they are looking for a country of their own."

The secret of visionary faith lies in that sentence. How did they manage to transcend their times, surmounting the immediate, living against the generally accepted, looking for the possible beyond the impossible? Called by God, their whole lives were speaking and acting with the language and logic of the alternative vision that is proper to faith. These are the sort of people of whom the newly elected Pope says in Morris West's *The Shoes of the Fisherman*, "Find me men with fire in their hearts and wings on their feet."

Second, we must guard visionary faith by watching out for the pitfalls toward which genuine vision pulls us. Calling-born vision means that followers of Christ do not easily fit into the camps most people join—for example, conservatives and progressives or radicals—yet the fact that we are children of our age means that powerful currents pull us toward one shoal or another.

An obvious example is the difference between the traditional and modern worlds and their tendency to exploit calling in opposite directions. The traditional world had a natural bias toward conservatism and, both then and later, calling was often mistakenly used to justify the status quo. In his *Treatise of the Callings* William Perkins lays down the rule: "For ever as the soldier in the field must not change his place wherein he is placed by the general, but must abide by it to the venturing of his life, so must the Christian continue and abide in his calling without change or alteration." Like many at the time, Perkins based this advice on Paul's instructions in 1 Corinthians 7, "Abide in your callings"—not realizing that calling is not the word in the original; it had been mistranslated by Luther.

John Calvin had guarded against such a static understanding. "It might seem," he wrote commenting on the same passage, "as though the words conveyed this idea, that everyone is bound to his calling, so that he must not abandon it. Now it were a very hard thing if a tailor were not at liberty to leave another trade, or if a merchant were not at liberty to betake himself to farming. I answer, that this is not what the Apostle intends." What Paul is condemning is "that restlessness, which prevents an individual remaining in his condition with a peaceable mind."

Yet in spite of Calvin, calling was misused to justify the status quo in both the English and the American Civil Wars. In the seventeenth century John Cheke of Cambridge used it to attack the Parliamentary side. Search the Scriptures, he wrote to Oliver Cromwell's supporters, and "we learn not only to fear [God] truthfully, but also to obey our King faithfully and to serve in our own vocation." Worse still, in the United States in 1863 a Southerner attributed the loyalty of four hundred slaves on a North Carolina plantation to regular biblical instruction, including the teaching of 1 Corinthians 7. A Richmond paper of the same period declared, "May we not hope and pray that large numbers [of slaves] will be savingly converted to Christ, thus becoming better earthly servants while they wear with meekness the yoke of their master in heaven?"

In the modern world, by contrast, we have such a bias toward change and progress that this heavy-handed abuse of calling on behalf of conservatism appears ludicrous. But that is because our temptation is the progressive bias, not the static. We insist on choice, we expect change, we prize relevance, we are unthinking believers in the-newer-the-truer, the-latest-is-greatest, and what's in and what's out. We instinctively admire sentiments like George Bernard Shaw's, quoted by Robert F. Kennedy: "You see things as they are and ask 'Why?' But I dream things that never were and ask 'Why not?'"

But we are then led by such biases to our own extremes. Since the cultural revolution of the 1960s, "Why not?" has served far more than dreams of justice; it has become the magic word with which to challenge restraint and defy prohibitions. "Why not?" and "So what?" we ask. "It is forbidden to forbid"—"Everything is permitted" in our Lotus-land of freedom. The result of our casual nihilism is a careless demolition of tradition and the creation of a spiritual, moral, and aesthetic wasteland in its place—not only in society but also in the church.

Our challenge is not just to see the mistakes of a previous generation, obvious because not ours, but to see as well the problems of our own time, far closer and therefore harder to see.

Third, we must guard visionary faith by watching out for deceptive look-alikes. One modern example is the powerful stream of "self help" and "positive thinking." With sources far wider than the church, "possibility thinking" has different expressions such as Ralph Waldo Emerson's transcendentalism, Mary Baker Eddy's Christian Science, and William James's "religion of healthy-mindedness." And its popular Christian expressions commonly topple into heresy. Calling, instead of being an objective standard by which we are led, becomes a power to harness for the sake of gaining our own power—and thus the key to health, wealth, popularity, significance, and peace of mind. The result is heresy: Faith in God becomes faith in faith—for our own interests.

An older and deeper look-alike grows from the confusion of visionary faith with the ideal of chivalry. As with positive thinking, the overlap of calling and questing is important—for example, in Francis of Assisi's "troubadours for Christ" and Søren Kierkegaard's "knight of faith." But the timeless appeal of the warrior spirit also has its perils. Above all it serves to justify anything and everything through its ideal of soaring aspirations—including militarism, crusading, cults of violence, male chauvinism, the idolatry of love, or just plain empty-headed romanticism and posturing.

The martial ideal and the strenuous life are appealing to a generation feeling guilty about its comforts and worried about the effects of "overcivilization." But their ideals, their initiations, their testings, their brotherhoods, and their calls to sacrifice are often a counterfeit of the call of Jesus and a dangerous bypath for the pilgrim. As St. Francis cried out to a young knight offering to join him: "Long enough hast thou borne the belt, the sword, and the spurs! The time has now come for you to change the belt for a rope, the sword for the Cross of Jesus Christ, the spurs for the dust and dirt of the road! Follow me and I will make you a knight in the army of Christ!"

The most seductive look-alike today is the ideal of Faustian striving. Adam and Eve, Prometheus, Pandora, Icarus, Johann Faust, Frankenstein—follow the stories through history and literature and the warning is powerful for all to see. Those who transgress boundaries in their all-consuming life search for knowledge, riches, power, and sexual prowess will overreach themselves until their pact with the devil destroys them.

But we moderns have changed the script. Just as in Goethe's version Faust is not damned but saved through his pact with the devil, so we pretend that striving has no limits and no sting. Call it ambition, call it enterprise, call it the competitive spirit, call it the pursuit of excellence, call it the full expansion of human potentialities, call it the will to power—Faustian man bestrides the stage of modern life with a rage to transgress. Applauded and unchallenged, he leaps over barriers, flouts conventions, disarms moral judgments, and disdains prohibitions—blind to his own excesses, and oblivious to his fate.

In our modern giantism of the unbounded ego, what the Puritans called "Adam's disease" has become the modern condition. Nietzsche has promoted this spirit most brilliantly:

No one can construct for you the bridge upon which precisely you must cross the stream of life, no one but you yourself alone. There are, to be sure, countless paths and bridges and demi-gods which would bear you through this stream; but only at the cost of yourself: you would put yourself in pawn and lose yourself. There exists in the world a single path along which no one can go except you: whither does it lead? Do not ask, go along it. Who was it who said: 'a man never rises higher than when he does not know whither his path can still lead him'?

Who was it? Ironically, perhaps unbeknown to Nietzsche, the original speaker was Oliver Cromwell. In other words, the context was Christian and the theme Cromwell discusses is the truth that makes such striving both possible and yet modest—calling.

Put the claim back on its proper foundations and it is no longer dangerous. "A man never rises higher than when he does not know whither his path can still lead him"—so long as the one who calls him is God. As the writer of Hebrews says, "By faith, Abraham, when called to go to a place he would later receive as an inheritance, obeyed and went, even though he did not know where he was going."

"Every man is made to reach out beyond his grasp," Oswald Chambers writes. Or as he says about himself to his wife, "Hourly almost my sense of His call grows. It will have to be a rover life I am afraid, all over the world. There are grand days coming for you and me." Or again, "Oh what a grand strenuous life there lies out in front of us. The unbribed soul for His enterprises, that is my charge." Dreamers of the day come into their own and stay on course when they follow the calling of Christ.

Does your faith see only what is in front of your nose, or is it also "sure of what we hope for and certain of what we do not see"? Does the here and now, the present and the accepted,

form a prison cell for your thinking, or are you reaching for more than you have grasped? Has your vision suffered from leakage since you were young, or are you still paying its price and closing its gap with reality? Listen to Jesus of Nazareth; answer his call.

22

PATCHES OF GODLIGHT

I have heard of many reasons why people step back from the verge of suicide, but the one that has meant the most to my family is also the most unusual—the fascination of seeing work well done.

The young woman was eighteen years old, with two small children, and evidently vivacious, talented, and beautiful. But she was also orphaned, penniless, completely alone, away from home, and recently widowed in a duel that rocked her country and drove her into voluntary exile. So Jane Lucretia D'Esterre could be forgiven for her dark thoughts as she pondered the waters of the little river in Ecclefechan, Scotland. Pain ran through every fiber of her being. Despair filled her horizon. Death beckoned her with an offer of peace as alluring as the still depths of the water in front of her.

The year was 1815, the time of Wellington's victory over Napoleon at Waterloo. Dueling was still legal in England and Ireland, though increasingly frowned upon socially. But Jane Lucretia first heard of the duel that shattered her life when friends carried her dying husband into the house.

By all accounts, John Frederick D'Esterre, a candidate for the post of city sheriff, was an undistinguished member of the Dublin Corporation but a deadly shot with a pistol. Rashly, however, he had taken exception to Daniel O'Connell's attack on the corporation and challenged the great Irish liberator to a duel. O'Connell, almost twice D'Esterre's size and the people's champion, refused at first but was eventually goaded into accepting, although he was known as a poor shot.

The fateful rendezvous took place twelve miles west of Dublin on a snowy late afternoon in February before the assembled carriages of the Dublin Corporation and a crowd of watching peasants.

D'Esterre won the toss, fired first, and uncharacteristically missed—his shot ricocheting off the ground at O'Connell's feet. O'Connell then fired, deliberately aiming low, but hit D'Esterre in the groin. The corporation's champion fell writhing to the ground and was carried home. "Mr. D'Esterre's wound is considered dangerous," the *Dublin Journal* reported, "the ball has not been extracted." In fact, D'Esterre died the next day, having uttered words of forgiveness to O'Connell as a gentleman was expected to do.

O'Connell, however, could not forgive himself. Remorseful for the rest of his life, he is said to have taken communion from then on wearing a black glove on the hand that had fired the fatal shot. On visiting the young widow, O'Connell offered her a share of his income. She refused with a quiet dignity though for thirty years until his death he paid a small annuity to her daughter.

Jane Lucretia D'Esterre, née Cramer, was from a family of musicians, probably Jewish, who had come to England and then Ireland from southern Germany. Her father was leader of George III's Court Band and of the Handel festivals at Westminster Abbey. Her half-brother Johann was a pianist so admired by Handel that, as the great composer said, "All the rest went for nothing."

But none of that counted that day as Jane D'Esterre gazed into the dark depths of the river. For some reason, however, she looked up and saw a young plowman setting to work in a field on the other bank of the river. He was about her age but quite oblivious to her and to anything but his work. Meticulous, absorbed, skilled, he displayed such a pride in his work that the newly turned furrows looked as finely executed as the paint strokes on an artist's canvas.

Despite herself, Jane Lucretia was fascinated. Slowly she was drawn into the plowman's pride until admiration turned into wonder and wonder into rebuke. What was she doing collapsing into self-pity? How could she be so wrapped up in herself when two small children were dependent on her? Rebuked and braced, she got up, returned to Dublin and resumed life—saved from suicide and reinvigorated for life by the sight of work well done.

I said earlier that such a reason was unusual. I also said that of all the reasons I know, it meant the most to my family. The explanation is simple: Jane D'Esterre was my great-great-grandmother. A few weeks after this near brush with death, she came to faith. A few years later she met and married my great-great-grandfather, Captain John Grattan Guinness, youngest son of Arthur Guinness the Dublin brewer, and a former officer under a fellow Irishman, Arthur Wellesley, the Duke of Wellington.

If it had not been for the duel, our side of the family would not have come into being. If it had not been for the plowman, the tragedy of the dueling husband would have been followed by the tragedy of the duelist's widow. She had been arrested by work done in a special way.

My great-great-grandmother was unusual for several reasons—including the fact that she conscientiously prayed for her descendants down through a dozen generations. Ours is a heritage of faith for which I, for one, am deeply grateful. But the rarity of her reason for stepping back from suicide illustrates another vital dimension of calling. Nothing is known of the Scottish farmer's son except what was seen in his plowing and could be guessed from his whistling hymns as he worked. But knowing the common motivation of that most Christian of centuries in Scotland, it is not too much to say that the incident underscores how *calling transforms life so that even the commonplace and menial are invested with the splendor of the ordinary.*

THE SPLENDOR OF THE ORDINARY

The temptation at this point is to allow rhetoric to slip the leash of reality. But it is simply ludicrous to pretend that all our work is exciting, fulfilling, and profitable. Much work is drudgery, and there is no getting away from it. It simply has to be done. Floors have to be cleaned, diapers changed, drains cleared, trash collected, and criminals punished. "In politics," as Abraham Lincoln used to say, "every man must skin his own skunk." "Someone has to do it," we often say of the dirty work, doing our utmost to make sure it won't be us. Hence the burden that typically falls on the mother in the family and the poor in society.

Not only that, much of our modern world is geared to help us avoid such drudgery. Convenience has joined choice and change to form the holy trinity of the consumer lifestyle. With "instant" this and "user-friendly" that, all wrapped up in packaging free from sin, pain, dirt, and hassles, everyone reasonably well off can achieve a way of living that obscures drudgery. So a dangerous combination grows: Unpleasant realities recede while distaste for unpleasant realities grows. The result is our modern fastidiousness. We are too important to appreciate the commonplace and too refined to handle drudgery ourselves.

Turn the kaleidoscope of modern life again and a further feature emerges. Not only are we disdainful toward the menial, but we are also ceaselessly urged to do things for reasons that are modern, limited, and dissatisfying. Instead of doing things because of their intrinsic importance—their value in themselves—we do things for instrumental reasons—their value for our self-expression, our fulfillment, our profit, and our publicity. As a guide in Florida's Universal Studios told me, pointing to the false-fronted film set houses, "In Orlando, nothing is real that the camera does not see."

The truth of calling stands against all such attitudes by challenging us to see and treat life differently. An appreciation of the commonplace and an elevation of the menial are two different things. But calling helps us with both of them in significant ways.

First, calling transforms things by reminding us once again of our audience. Drudgery done for ourselves or for other human audiences will always be drudgery. But drudgery done for God is lifted and changed. Hudson Taylor, a great nineteenth-century pioneer missionary to China, used to teach: "A little thing is a little thing, but faithfulness in a little thing is a big thing." Similarly, Mother Teresa said, "I don't do big things. I do small things with big love."

This theme is also prominent in the seventeenth-century under-standing of calling. John Cotton stressed that calling encourages a person "to the most homeliest and difficultest and most dangerous things his calling can lead and expose himself to." Someone with a mind-set shaped by the world "knows not how to submit unto it." But "there is no work too hard or homely" for the follower of Christ, for "what drudgery can be too homely for me to do for God?"

The same era's most beautiful expression of this truth is the poem by George Herbert, often sung as a hymn:

> Teach me, my God and King,
>   In all things Thee to see,
> And what I do in anything
>   To do it as for Thee!
> A man that looks on glass,
>   On it may stay his eye;
> Or if he pleaseth, through it pass,
>   And then the heaven espy.
> All may of Thee partake;
>   Nothing can be so mean,
> Which, with this tincture "for Thy sake,"
>   Will not grow bright and clean.
> A servant with this clause
>   Makes drudgery divine:
> Who sweeps a room, as for Thy laws,
>   Makes that and the action fine.
> This is the famous stone
>   That turneth all to gold;
> For that which God doth touch and own
>   Cannot for less be told.

Is this just elegant piety? Anyone who doubts its practicality should consider how it was applied—for instance, in the later phi-losophy of Shaker furniture-making. "Make every product better than it's ever been done before. Make the parts you cannot see as well as the parts you can see. Use only the best of materials, even for the most everyday items. Give the same attention to the smallest detail as you do to the largest. Design every item you make to last forever." Each Shaker chair, it was said, was made fit for an angel to sit on.

At a very different level and on a global stage, the same awareness of audience has also touched statecraft. In 1885, for example, General Charles Gordon left Europe for the Congo in order to help King Leopold of Belgium. His friends were dismayed. One peer wrote, "You have had enough of liver-grilling climates, and the world does not seem bounded with the clear horizon that would warrant—if I may venture to say to an old friend—our very best man burying himself . . . on the Equator."

Gordon, however, would not be deterred. Flattery and pride were not considerations for him. If the assignment was part of his calling, its status and its probable outcome were irrelevant. Earlier he had written to another friend, "To be A, governing huge countries, or B, occupying the smallest place, are the same in reality, for Christ rules events as much with respect to A's government as He does in B's little affairs." So out he went. It was not what he was doing, but for whom he was doing it, that made the difference.

Second, calling transforms things by focusing our attention, under God, on things as they are. Many religions, such as Buddhism and Gnosticism, are world denying. As they see it, matter means decay, place means limitation, and time means death. The Christian faith, by contrast, has a bifocal vision—it is world affirming and world denying at the same time. Seen one way, the world is marred, broken by the ravages of evil. But seen another way, the world was made and pronounced good. Despite the ruin, the reality and goodness of God's creation are constant and inalienable.

Dorothy Sayers applied this vision of creation to work. The Christian view, she wrote in *Creed or Chaos*, directly opposes the modern tendency to identify work with gainful employment, and so to work to make money to do something else. In the modern view, "Doctors practice medicine not primarily to relieve suffering, but to make a living. . . . Lawyers accept briefs not because they have a passion for justice, but because the law is the profession that enables them to live." Or as John Ruskin had recognized earlier during the Industrial Age, "It is not that men are ill-fed, but that they have no pleasure in the work by which they make their bread, and therefore look to wealth as the only means of pleasure."

The result, Sayers observes, is a modern heresy and a modern fallacy. "The fallacy is that work is not the expression of man's creative energy in the service of society, but only something he does in order to obtain money and leisure." For the called person, by contrast, work should be as close as possible to the fulfillment of our natures and the expression of our God-given creativeness—"work shall be such as a man may do with his whole heart, and that he shall do it for the very work's sake."

C. S. Lewis applies the same doctrine of creation to nature. He is better known for his golden paragraph in "The Weight of Glory" expanding on the Christian view that "there are no *ordinary* people."

> You have never talked to a mere mortal. Nations, cultures, arts, civilization—these are mortal, and their life is to ours as the life of a gnat. But it is immortals whom we joke with, work with, marry, snub, and exploit—immortal horrors or everlasting splendors.

But Lewis also argues the companion point: There are no ordinary *things*. In *Letters to Malcolm* he talks of his experience of creation in all its ordinariness, everydayness, and homeliness. A row of cabbages, a farmyard cat, a wrinkled motherly face, a tiled roof, a single sentence in a book—each can be seen as a tiny revelation of God as Creator. Just as fragments of sunlight break through a dark wood, so parts of creation seen for what they are act as "patches of Godlight" in the world.

"I have tried," Lewis wrote, "to make every pleasure into a channel of adoration." "Glory be to God for dappled things," Gerard Manley Hopkins wrote, and in one sermon spoke similarly: "To lift up the hands in prayer gives God glory, but a man with a dungfork in his hand, a woman with a sloppail, give him glory too. He is so great that all things give him glory if you mean they should."

The chasm between this Christian view and the modern view is so vast that we need to appreciate its size before attempting to close it. The Christian view always comes back to the rootedness and intrinsic worth of things as they are; the modern view, by contrast, is rarely so contented. "No man makes a greater mistake," Edmund Burke warned, "than he who does nothing because he knows it is not everything." George Macdonald offered the same caution in *Phantastes:* "I learned that he that will be a hero, will barely be a man; that he that will be nothing but a doer of his work, is sure of his manhood." Or as he wrote in "The Shadows," the mark of a true vision of things is that "instead of making common things look commonplace, as a false vision would have done, it had made common things disclose the wonderful that was in them."

Does this sound dangerously like a celebration of amateurism? It is. To our shame we moderns have taken the word *amateur*, opposed it to professionalism and excellence, and turned it into a matter of tepid motives and shoddy results. But *amateur*, as G. K. Chesterton never tired of saying, means "lover." "A man must love a thing very much if he not only practices it without any hope of fame or money, but even practices it without any hope of doing it well." Which, of course, is the origin of Chesterton's famous subversion of the traditional proverb: "If a thing is worth doing, it is worth doing badly."

Third, calling transforms things by reminding us that drudgery is part of the cost of discipleship. No one has written on this more persistently and bluntly than Oswald Chambers. Repeatedly he hammers home the point that "drudgery is the touchstone of character." We look for the big things to do—Jesus took a towel and washed the disciples' feet. We presume the place to be is the mountaintop of vision—he sends us back into the valley. We like to speak and act out of the rare moments of inspiration—he requires our obedience in the routine, the unseen, and the thankless. Our idea for ourselves is the grand moment and the hushed crowd—his is ordinary things when the footlights are switched off.

After all, Chambers continued,

Walking on the water is easy to impulsive pluck, but walking on dry land as a disciple of Jesus Christ is a different thing. Peter walked on the water to go to Jesus, but he followed Him afar off on the land. We do not need the grace of God to stand crises, human nature and pride are sufficient, we can face the strain magnificently; but it does require the supernatural grace of God to live twenty-four hours in every day as a saint, to go through drudgery as a disciple, to live an ordinary, unobserved, ignored existence as a disciple of Jesus. It is inbred in us that we have to do exceptional things for God; but we have not. We have to be exceptional in the ordinary things, to be holy in mean streets, among mean people, and this is not learned in five minutes.

In the second century, Christian apologist Justin Martyr grew up over the hill from Galilee. Interestingly, he notes that the plows made by Joseph and Jesus were still being used widely in his day. How intriguing to think of Jesus' plow rather than his cross—to wonder what it was that made his plows and yokes last and stand out.

Not long ago a philosophy professor became so fabled for his lectures that his classes were standing room only at the back of the hall. Students flocked to hear his wisdom, but his class assignments always produced consternation.

"But sir," a chorus of voices typically rang out after he explained the topic in detail, "how long does the essay have to be? How many pages do you want?"

The question always seemed to make the professor wince, but then it was the students' turn. "Look," he would reply, "don't worry about the length. Forget your future careers for the moment. Remember that the grade is secondary. Just hand in something that you can *respect.*"

For those who answer the call, everything under God has its own importance, though the final respect is not ours to bestow. If it is ever to be ours, it will come from the "well done" of the Caller. But before the eventual "well done," our task today is to do well—by loving people, things, and work for their sake and his.

As Rudyard Kipling wrote in "L'Envoi" of the artists' heaven,

> And only the Master shall praise us,
>   and only the master shall blame;
> And no one shall work for money,
>   and no one shall work for fame;
> But each for the joy of the working,
>   and each in his separate star,
> Shall draw the Thing as he sees It
>   for the God of Things as They Are!

Are you blind to the splendor of the ordinary? Do you depend on the adrenaline of the impressive and the inspirational? Or do you long for a "philosopher's stone" to turn life into gold? Listen to Jesus of Nazareth; answer his call.

23

LET ALL YOUR THINKS
BE THANKS

Salvador Dali, the Spanish surrealist painter, was a flamboyant showman in real life as well as in his art. Impresario to his own public image, he produced paintings and orchestrated a lifestyle that flouted convention and loved to catch public expectations on the hop. This drive to defiance had its deepest roots in his own story.

Dali's relationship to his own father had been turbulent. Once, after a tempestuous scene between father and son, the young Dali stormed out of his father's home. Going to his own house, he masturbated, put his semen in an envelope, addressed the envelope to his father, and—as if paying a gas or electricity bill—wrote on the envelope: "Paid in full."

Which is worse, you might ask: the heartless ingratitude of the son toward his father? Or the enormity of the reductionism that considers the fruit of an angry ejaculation the repayment for life itself? Many people have used the story to ponder deeper questions: What does it mean to pay back in life? To discharge our deepest debts of all? To fulfill our obligations for simply being human? How do we pay back our fathers and mothers? Were our parents just "the luck of the womb" for us, or more? How do we pay back the one teacher who made all the difference in our school years? Or the youth director or team coach whose noticing us in a special way drew out a part of us that was crucial in our becoming who we are today?

Or, at another level, how do we repay the profound way we are moved by films such as David Lean's *Lawrence of Arabia*? Or by such dramas as Sophocles' *Oedipus Rex* and Shakespeare's *King Lear*? Or by listening to a Bach cantata or Mozart requiem? And most profoundly of all, what do we owe for the beauty of a sunset or a daisy? And to whom do we direct our gratitude simply for being alive?

The answer is easier for those with a sense of the "miraculous" in their story. Fyodor Dostoevsky was capriciously reprieved seconds before his execution by firing squad in 1849; he saw all his subsequent life with the sweetly lit intensity of a man come back from the dead. Aleksandr Solzhenitsyn was inexplicably healed from cancer in Tashkent in 1954 only weeks from death after being discharged from the hospital to die; he gained a new sense of mission from his gratitude. "I did not die, however. With a hopelessly neglected and acutely malignant tumor, this was a divine miracle; I could see no other explanation. Since then, all the life that has been given back to me has not been mine in the full sense: it is built around a purpose."

But for most of us the underlying debts of life are not so obvious or dramatic. Unless we are forced to think about them, we take them for granted. We can pick up a CD-ROM and a few presses of a finger conjures up an entire dictionary the likes of which Samuel Johnson labored years to assemble. A few more touches and the computer spews forth information that would have been the envy of Aristotle or Augustine, and that would have taken a monastery full of monks slaving several lifetimes to copy.

In a speech to the German League of Human Rights in 1932, Albert Einstein delivered "My Credo." "I am often worried," he said, "at the thought that my life is based to such a large extent on the work of my fellow human beings, and I am aware of my great indebtedness to them." But most of us forget all that, and ever deeper debts, because we are modern. All we have is our entitlement. The "luck of the womb" covers not only families but also centuries and generations. It can all be taken for granted. Ridiculously, it can even make us feel superior—as if there were moral achievement in being born the right side of Beethoven, Orville Wright, Thomas Edison, or Bill Gates.

Worse still, if we think about it at all, we moderns come perilously close to Salvador Dali's reductionism when we assume that paying the market price of an object means paying in full what we owe. A few minutes and a few dollars and the best editions of Beethoven's Ninth Symphony can be ours to enjoy when we like. But can we ever repay how we are touched by the fire of his "Ode to Joy"?

All sorts of curious twists arise when we pursue such questions. Isn't it hypocritical, for example, that when we convict people for doing wrong to society, we say they "owe" something and must "repay the debt"—yet when society has so obviously showered so much good on the rest of us, we take it as our right and live as if we owe nothing in return?

But in the end we come back to the same basic question. What does it mean to repay in life? For our heritage? Our schooling? Our language? Our freedom? Our physique? Our looks? Our health? Our life? At that point a deep divide opens up. By its very character the modern world answers: You owe nothing. By its very character, the Christian gospel answers: You owe everything.

Thus a further dimension of calling appears—*calling is a reminder for followers of Christ that nothing in life should be taken for granted; everything in life must be received with gratitude.*

THE UNGRATEFUL BIPED

In his *Notes from Underground* in 1864, Dostoevsky wrote of humanity, "If he is not stupid, he is monstrously ungrateful! Phenomenally ungrateful. In fact, I believe that the best definition of man is the ungrateful biped." Albert Camus wrote similarly, "Man's first faculty is forgetting." More recently novelist Milan Kundera attacked the Marxist censorship of history as "organized forgetting." Ingratitude and forgetfulness are ultimately moral rather than mental; they are the direct expression of sin. No culture has nourished such tendencies as consistently as ours. We pride ourselves on being autonomous, self-created, and freestanding. A modern world with no need of God produces modern people with no sense of gratitude.

Needless to say, sin's drive to forgetfulness was also at work in the traditional world. But the traditional world never quite succeeded in drowning out two things vital to gratitude. One was a sense of our total dependency in life. With lifespans short, disease rampant, and such disasters as storm, famine, drought, flood, and earthquake ever threatening, the fragility and precariousness of life was never far from the mind.

The other thing vital to gratitude was a sense of moral debt. Doubtless a Puritan's conscience in the American colonies was pricked more often and more deeply than a French courtier's conscience in the reign of Louis XIV or a Mongol footsoldier's in the army of Genghis Khan. But all lived in a world of moral convictions and conventions. There were clear sanctions for crossing the lines and breaking the taboos, whether they were caught stealing a loaf of bread or failing to kiss the emperor's toe.

The modern world has decisively subverted what was left of both these things. On the one hand, it has transformed a sense of dependency into a sense of autonomy. "Man does not live on bread alone," said Jesus. "But that was yesterday," says our modern world. "Today man can live extremely well on bread alone—or at least on reason alone, on technology alone, on sex alone, or on shopping alone." Formerly the philosopher atheist would shout defiantly, "There is no God!" Now the practical atheist who is the modern manager, marketer, expert, or consultant says with quiet professional authority, "There is no need of God—and, frankly, this is not the time or the place for such questions."

On the other hand, the modern world has transformed a sense of debt into a sense of rights and entitlement. Gradually wrong has been debased from being "sin," defined before God, to "crime," defined before law, to "sickness," once defined carefully by psychiatry but now subject to the shifting breezes of pop-cultural fashion. Freud once worried that patients' "claim to exceptionalism" provided an "insurance dole" of victimhood off which the emotionally wounded could live. What he feared has become an industry of rights and a way of life. Ours is "the golden age of exoneration."

Thus at the very heart of the modern world is the almost complete absence of dependency and indebtedness and a corresponding reinforcement of forgetfulness and ingratitude. Abraham Lincoln warned his fellow countrymen against this tendency early in the modern world. In 1863 he declared, "We have grown in numbers, wealth, and power, as no other nation has ever grown. But we have forgotten God." Now the problem is universal. "If I were called upon to identify the principal trait of the entire twentieth century," Solzhenitsyn declared, "men have forgotten God." Or as Bart Simpson, America's favorite cartoon kid, put it baldly when asked to say grace at supper time, "Dear God, we pay for all this ourselves. So thanks for nothing."

WHAT DO YOU HAVE THAT
YOU DID NOT RECEIVE?

What has gratitude to do with calling? It is surely easier and more correct to see gratitude as a response to the cross of Christ. Around 1546 Michelangelo did a pencil drawing of the Pietà for Vittoria Colonna, his saintly aristocratic friend. With the dead body of Jesus supported by angels at her feet, Mary does not cradle her son as in his other renderings of the Pietà but raises her eyes and her hands to heaven in speechless wonder. On the upright beam of the cross Michelangelo inscribed a line from Dante's *Paradise*, which is the focus of the drawing's meditation: "No one thinks of how much blood it costs."

Certainly anyone thinking of how much blood it cost, and whose and why, can only stop and adore. So the adulterous woman, forgiven, bathes Jesus' feet with her kisses, her perfume, and her tears—her extravagant giving is the response to his even more extravagant forgiving. As Simone Weil expressed it eloquently, "our country is the Cross."

But although secondary to the cross, calling contributes to faith its own sense of wonder and gratitude because of its insistence on God's sovereign initiative and grace in the call.

"What do you have that you did not receive?" Many of the greatest

Christians of the centuries, including St. Augustine and St. Francis, have been influenced decisively by meditating on Paul's question to the church in Corinth. It admits only one answer: Nothing, for everything of God and good in our lives without a single exception is all of grace. That covers calling too. There is nothing fatalistic or arbitrary here. The motive, the initiative, and the action of calling are entirely God's and all of grace. Christ does not choose us because we are worth choosing, but simply because in his grace he loves us and chooses us—he calls us, in fact, despite all that he had to do to seal that choice in blood.

Without a due sense of gratitude, the "chosen people" would be insufferable. As Moses reminded the Jewish people, "The Lord did not set his affection on you and choose you because you were more numerous than other peoples, for you were the fewest of all peoples. But it was because the Lord loved you." Similarly, King David was overwhelmed by the same wonder at his own calling as an individual, "Who am I, Lord God, and what is my family, that you have brought me this far? . . . There is no one like you, O Lord, and there is no God but you."

The grace that constitutes the cross also constitutes calling. Seen one way, calling initiates in our lives what the cross completes. Seen another, what the cross concludes beyond question as its final verdict, calling declares as its opening statement. Here is one relationship whose secret does not lie with us; self-conceit is absurd because our call to God is all of God and all of grace. Hilaire Belloc's famous short poem about the Jews applies to all who have been called:

> How odd
> of God
> to choose
> the Jews.

The link between calling and gratitude, chosenness and wonder touches our lives practically in two main places. First, it reminds us that with so much grace given to us, we should be givers of grace to others. Indeed, Jesus warns us in the parable of the unforgiving debtor, not to give grace to others after God has been so gracious to us is literally to double-deal God—and God will not stand for it.

We saw earlier how calling can be demonically twisted into conceit. An even fouler distortion can happen with talk about the grace of calling. People who start out in wonder at their own calling can slowly, through conceit, slip into speculation about God's calling them and not calling others, and end in making calling a thing of horror, not wonder, and God a monster.

A week after Andrew Carnegie was born on a stormy day in November 1835 in Dunfermline, Scotland, his father William went as usual to the local Presbyterian Church. The minister had chosen for his sermon the subject of infant damnation and he warmed to his topic with both eloquence and the vivid imagery of the torture of infants typical of certain hyper-Calvinists.

William Carnegie, naturally hearing the sermon through the ears of the fiercely proud father of a newborn son, felt a fury rising within him he had never felt before—against the preacher, against the congregation who would accept such teaching, and against God as the minister portrayed him. Getting up from his seat, to the astonishment of the congregation, and with a voice choking with emotion, William Carnegie declared : "If that be your religion and that your God, I shall seek a better religion and a nobler God."

With those words Andrew Carnegie's father left the church and never returned, committed to bringing up his young son as a skeptic. The "nobler God" his father had in mind, Andrew Carnegie said later, was "a forgiving God"—whom neither father nor son ever found.

Do we have to pit grace and judgment, heaven and hell against each other as alternatives? Of course not. Jesus clearly believes and teaches both. But, strikingly, his many warnings about hell are not delivered to those whom most people in his day thought were going there. To the so-called publicans and sinners he spoke of grace. He usually directed his warnings about hell against those who were complacent about their places in heaven. Full of themselves and their sense of "chosenness" and "purity," the Pharisees had forgotten grace and felt no sense of gratitude.

The most common equivalent to Pharisaism today is moralism, the curse of Christian witness in the public square. Moralism operates in a characteristic way. First, it removes grace from the discussion in question. Then it reduces the whole issue to the moral dimension. Next it rationalizes its own sense of superiority by using moral judgment as a weapon to attack others. In the end it reinforces both sin and hostility to God, who—alas—is blamed for the moralism dispensed in his name.

As readers of the New Testament should know well, attempts to establish a moral standard by prescription alone is futile—even when the prescription, or law, comes from God himself. Put differently, sin *is* wrong and unnatural, as moralists say. But what they forget is that it is also so unnatural *not to sin* that God treats us with grace—not as our sins deserve. So followers of Christ must follow Christ in standing for grace as well as truth. G. K. Chesterton wrote of the little troubadour from Assisi what should be true of all Christ's followers: "St. Francis walked the world like the Pardon of God." After all, as Oswald Chambers wrote, "I have never met the man I could despair of after discerning what lies in me apart from the grace of God."

Second, the link between calling and grace reminds us that gratitude must be our first and constant response to God. The great Czech composer Anton'n Dvorak began writing his new music with the words, "with God" and ended "God be thanked." Similarly Johann Sebastian Bach wrote in the margins of his music "SDG" (*Soli Deo Gloria*) and "Glory to the Lamb."

Augustine described the Christian as an "alleluia from head to foot." George Herbert, a seventeenth-century Anglican poet, wrote a prayer in one of his poems, "You have given so much to me. Give me one thing more—a grateful heart." G. K. Chesterton stated as "the chief idea of my life" the practice of "taking things with gratitude and not taking things for granted." He passionately agreed with the artist Dante Gabriel Rossetti, "The worst moment for an atheist is when he is genuinely thankful, but has nobody to thank." And Chesterton remarked, typically, "If my children wake up on Christmas morning and have somebody to thank for putting candy into their stocking, have I no one to thank for putting two feet into mine?" W. H. Auden wrote simply, "Let your last thinks be all thanks."

Dostoevsky was so aware of the deep importance of gratitude in his own life that he was troubled for humankind if God were not there to be thanked: "Who is man going to love then?" he asks in *The Brothers Karamazov.* "To whom will he be thankful? To whom will he sing his hymn?" Only an idiot, he believed, could love and be grateful to humanity instead of God.

But whatever false turns secular culture may take, followers of Christ should know where they stand on this point—amazed and humbled ever to be chosen and called. Adapting G. K. Chesterton, we may state the motto of every follower of Christ moved to wonder by the mystery and grace of God's calling: "Nothing taken for granted; everything received with gratitude; everything passed on with grace."

Do you wear your chosenness like a badge of honor? Do you take it as a compliment to the general decency of your life? Or does the unfathomable wonder of calling grip you like a grand compelling you can never satisfy or shake off? Have you ever been carried away beyond yourself by love for Christ who called you? Would Jesus ever be able to say of you what he said of the woman who bathed his feet in her tears? Listen to Jesus of Nazareth; answer his call.

24

Everybody's Fools

According to one account, his real name was John, not Francis. Twenty-two years old and the oldest son of Pietro de Bernardone, Assisi's richest cloth merchant, he was given the name Francesco as a nickname. Francesco means "the little Frenchman," and he was famed for his passion for France, especially the ideal and tradition of courtly love. Throughout his life, it was said later, whenever Francis spoke French, those who knew him knew he was happy.

But on this particular day in the spring of A.D. 1207 Francesco de Bernardone was not the carefree troubadour he had been. Riding alone through the beautiful Umbrian countryside, he was deep in a reverie that both attracted and challenged him. Earlier he had been calling on God as usual, and he had heard this answer: "Francis, everything you have loved and desired in the flesh it is your duty to despise and hate, if you wish to know my will. And when you have begun this, all that which now seems to you sweet and lovely will become intolerable and bitter, but all which you used to abhor will turn itself to great sweetness and exceeding joy."

Lost in thought over these words, Francis was suddenly jerked back to reality. His horse had started and the sudden movement woke him up. Looking up, he saw on the road a few steps ahead of him a leper in the advanced stages of the disease.

His first impulse was to wheel the horse and ride away. If there was anything he "used to abhor," it was leprosy. Based on a passage in Isaiah 53, lepers were looked on in the thirteenth century as an image of the suffering Messiah, more than all other sufferers. There was a special order of knights to care for them—the knights of Lazarus—and remarkably there were 19,000 special houses for their care—the houses of St. George. But in spite of everything, most people still found leprosy repulsive and Francis was no exception. The mere sight of leprosy always filled him with horror. He would only give alms to the lepers if someone else took it for him. He hated the nauseating odor of the disease, and when the wind wafted it into town from the leprosarium he put his fingers in his nostrils.

Yet this time, meditating on the Great Reversal in Christ's words, he knew what he must do. Springing from his horse, he went to the leper, put alms in his wasted outstretched hand and kissed the fingers that stank from the awful disease. Then, remounting his horse, he rode home overcome with emotion. God had kept his word. Joy streamed into his heart.

The next day he returned and went into the leprosarium. Momentarily holding his nose to block out the stench, he steadied himself and went around the sad, ghastly crowd, distributing alms and kissing every one of the disease-ridden hands, as he had done the day before.

Francis of Assisi, one biographer writes, had "won the greatest victory a man can win—the victory over oneself." More accurately, Francis himself would probably have said, the Lord had won the greatest victory over him. He was no longer simply the troubadour singing to his love or the knight of faith riding forth on his quest. Learning to despise what he had loved and to love what he had despised, Francis of Assisi had been turned upside down and become God's jester, God's juggler, God's fool.

As G. K. Chesterton said in his brilliant biography, this self-awareness that he was Christ's fool is the key to understanding St. Francis. For after his frustrated military campaigns, his hapless quarrels with his father, and the shame of the bishop's public rebuke, he knew he had made a fool of himself. But as he mused bitterly on the word *fool*, the word itself changed. So it was that as "Francis came forth from his cave of vision, he was wearing the same word 'fool' as a feather in his cap; as a crest or even a crown. He would go on being a fool; he would ever become more and more of a fool; he would be the court fool of the King of Paradise."

In this way, St. Francis wrote later, "the Lord granted me to begin my conversion." His calling was to be the rebuilder of the ruined church (and churches); his plan was to comply literally with the words of the gospel and forsake everything to take up his cross and follow Jesus; his style was always to be God's humble fool (*le jongleur de Dieu*).

When Francis's idea for the order of "The Little Brothers" was opposed in the College of Cardinals, one of the cardinals in support said simply: "These men only want us to allow them to live after the gospel. If we now declare that this is impossible, then we declare that the gospel cannot be followed, and thus insult Christ, who is the origin of the gospel." So began one of history's most simple, radical, and powerful attempts to put the gospel of Jesus into practice. And it was accompanied by the theme of holy folly that is one of the oldest and most distinctive badges of followers of Christ.

This awareness of St. Francis, and the actions it spurred him to take, reinforce a further dimension of calling without which no account of the subject would be complete—*calling entails the cost of discipleship. The deepest challenge is to renounce self and identify with Jesus in his sufferings and rejection.*

WEARING THE LIVERY OF THE MOCK KING

Many Christians today are so opposed to the extremes of relativism that they reject relativism altogether and insist that everything is absolute. But in a fallen world, relativism is a reality and the deepest root of relativism is not social or philosophical but theological. Sin is "the claim to the right to myself"—and therefore "the claim to my right to my view of things"—and therefore the root of a profound and inescapable relativism.

What this point means is that "folly" and "heroism" are always relative. Someone is seen or treated as foolish from the perspective of some group or another. But people with their wits about them should never accept such descriptions at face value. They should always ask, "Says who?" The "fool proper" is the person whom God says is a fool—who, lacking a fear of the Lord, lacks wisdom and is truly a fool. But a "foolbearer" is different. They are foolish in the eyes of the world, not God.

This relativity of sin is the springboard from which "holy folly" gains its characteristic resilience. "Fools for Christ" are not actually, or literally, or objectively fools but those who are prepared to be seen and treated as fools *for Christ's sake.* Since the world in its pretended wisdom foolishly thinks itself wise, it sees God's true wisdom as foolishness. Those faithful to God must therefore break with the world and bear its folly. They are what I call "foolbearers," acting out of love for Christ and wearing the world's shame as a badge of allegiance and honor.

The term *fool for Christ* comes from Paul's letter to Corinth—where the apostle is writing to fellow-Christians and with a deep irony. But the idea is much older. King David danced with such joy before the Lord that his own wife dismissed him as an idiot. And many of the prophets were called on to act in ways that appeared insane from one perspective or another. Isaiah was to walk around naked and barefoot for three years, Jeremiah was to put a wooden yoke around his neck and be a laughing stock for a generation, Ezekiel was to eat excrement in public, and Hosea was to marry a whore.

Paul's word for "fool" is the word from which we get our word "moron." Used by Sophocles of Antigone's insanity, it is strong and insulting. Clearly the Apostle himself was used to being accused of being mad—by the Athens intellectuals and by the Roman Governor Festus in the presence of King Agrippa.

But all these examples pale beside the supreme foolbearer in Scripture—Jesus himself. Dismissed by his own family as insane, Jesus finally stands before the Roman Praetorian Guard and is made an object of derision. He who is about to bear the sin of the world first bears the folly of the world. Dressed up derisively with a purple robe, a crown of thorns, and a reed scepter, Jesus becomes the mock king with deliberately ludicrous regalia. Little wonder that countless followers of Jesus have echoed the later words of Ignatius of Loyola: "Out of gratitude and love for him, we should desire to be reckoned fools and glory in wearing his livery."

Holy folly has unquestionably gained a bad name in some Christian circles and for solid reasons. Sometimes it inspired what looks like plain weirdness, for example, some of the wild men of Byzantium and Ireland. Sometimes it has been used to justify flagrant anti-intellectualism, such as the persistent strains of *Credo quia absurdum* ("I believe because it is absurd") that have flourished from Tertullian in the second century to certain fundamentalists in the twentieth.

But holy folly is central to the call to discipleship. Throughout the centuries it has inspired many of the greatest examples of faithfulness to Jesus Christ—Francis of Assisi being only one of many. *Children, fool, jester, clown, idiot, joker*—many words have been used but all in service of men and women prepared to be both "merry and mad" in the service of God who in his own "foolishness" was prepared to lie "defenseless in a crib" and hang "derelict on a cross."

In a controlling, calculating age, the world's ideal is always to be in charge, never to be caught out—in short, to be "nobody's fool." On the contrary, say the fools for Christ, in a world gone mad through its own worldly wisdom, true wisdom is to "go mad for God" even at the price of being hopelessly vulnerable—to be "everybody's fools."

Talk of jesting and clowning sounds purely fun. Indeed, fool-bearing might be fun for followers of Christ if it were not deadly real and did not begin with a cross. Genuine freedom is always close to frivolity, but frivolity—like grace—can be either costly or cheap. We therefore need to be practical about why holy folly is so important for calling and discipleship.

First, foolbearing is essential to calling because it is the true way to count the cost of identifying with Jesus. It is the price of obeying his call, renouncing self, and taking up the cross to follow him. "When Christ calls a man, he bids him come and die." Dietrich Bonhoeffer's words in *The Cost of Discipleship* in 1937 are probably the most famous theological sentence of the twentieth century. In his stand against Hitler, he underwrote them with his own blood.

But Bonhoeffer who taught that "the cross is laid on every Christian" also taught that there are different kinds of dying. Or as the church traditionally put it, there are three kinds of martyrdom—red martyrdom, by blood; green martyrdom, by the exercise of the spiritual disciplines of abstinence, such as fasting; and white martyrdom, by abandoning everything for the love of God. Discipleship therefore means a "white funeral," the funeral of our own independence.

But make no mistake. No fancy words must ever disguise the fact that choosing suffering is not normal. Human beings avoid suffering and prefer not to think about death. Given a choice, we prefer better weather. We take aspirin. We appreciate a cushion. We come in out of the cold. We don't go down dark alleys. We don't drive cars without brakes. Anyone who chooses pain is odd, if not a masochist, in the eyes of most of us.

The Gospels, however, are unambiguously clear about the cost of discipleship—and also that Jesus' call to discipleship is the echo of his father's call to him. Called to be the Messiah, Jesus knew he must suffer and be what appeared a contradiction in terms—a rejected Messiah. But he lays this necessity on the disciples too. Just as Jesus is the Messiah, the Christ, only insofar as he suffers and is rejected, so the disciples of Jesus are obedient to the call of Jesus only insofar as they are prepared to pay the cost.

Here is where the Gospel of Jesus is most subversive. It is not only revolutionary, but—compared with all other revolutions and revolutionaries—it is a revolutionary way of being revolutionary. Jesus fights and defeats evil by letting evil do its worst to him. And then, wonder of wonders, he calls us to do the same. Those who seek to save their lives, lose them; only those who lose their lives, save them.

In easy times the external cost of calling may be minimal, in hard times—as they were for Bonhoeffer—the cost may be supreme. All followers of Christ are called to be fools for Christ, but some are made to be more foolish than others. Regardless, the internal cost is always the same: death to self. After all, as C. S. Lewis wrote in *The Great Divorce*, "There are only two kinds of people in the end: those who say to God, 'Thy will be done,' and those to whom God says, in the end, '*Thy* will be done.'" That is the difference between heaven and hell.

The call of Jesus brooks neither refusal nor rivals; it costs us every allegiance that competes with him and every practice that contradicts his lordship. As always, the call is all. But also, as always, the choice to have no choice is underscored as a choice. "*If* anyone would come after me . . ." Jesus says although the disciples to whom he speaks were already following him. Once more he sets them free to choose or reject him. Bonhoeffer commented suggestively, "The disciple must say to himself the same words Peter said of Christ when he denied him: 'I know not this man.'"

Bonhoeffer knew well ahead what he was choosing. He was lecturing in the United States when World War II broke out. Friends on all sides urged him to stay, but his allegiance was clear. He had to be back in his homeland serving Christ above Germany:

> I have had time to think and pray about my situation and that of my nation and to have God's will for me clarified. I have come to the conclusion that I have made a mistake in coming to America. I shall have no right to participate in the reconstruction of Christian life in Germany after the war if I do not share in the trials of this time with my people. Christians in Germany face the terrible alternatives of willing the defeat of their nation in order that civilization may survive or willing the victory of their nation and thereby destroying civilization. I know which of these alternatives I must choose, but I cannot make that decision in security.

To renounce oneself is ridiculous, to renounce self-interest is foolhardy, to renounce self-protection is absurd. But it is precisely this patent folly that disciples choose in order to wear the uniform of the derided Messiah who is the crucified God-Man. Such folly, however, is not the outcome of a joyless, grim-faced asceticism. History inspires us with stories of thousands who have died with joy on their faces or lived with singing hearts even as they suffered—because our suffering is as nothing compared with his, and his was all for us.

"We are like jesters and tumblers," Bernard of Clairvaux wrote in the twelfth century, deliberately picking words that were then pejorative and a trade that was then forbidden to the clergy. But the extreme Cistercian devotion was not just a way of highlighting corruption or shocking people out of the mediocrity of worthy respectability. It was above all a response to the cross. Bernard declared in a sermon:

> Brethren, the tears of Christ overwhelm me with shame and fear and sorrow. I was playing out of doors in the street, while sentence of death was being passed upon me in the privacy of the royal council-chamber. But the King's only-begotten Son heard of it. And what did he do? He went forth from the palace, put off his diadem, covered himself with sackcloth, strewed ashes on his head, bared his feet, and wept and lamented because his poor slave was condemned to death. I meet him unexpectedly in this sad condition. I am astonished at the woeful change in him and inquire the cause. He tells me the whole story. What am I to do now? Shall I continue to play and make a mockery of his tears? Surely I am insane and devoid of reason if I do not follow him and unite my tears with his.

Second, foolbearing is essential to calling because it positions us unmistakably before the world as a counterculture, antithetical to the world's very being. The church has always maintained a necessary tension between a world-affirming stance and a world-denying stance. Due to its extraordinary power, the modern world has swung the balance heavily toward the former. Hardly any Christians are world-denying these days. There are few deserts to retreat to and ghettoes are out of fashion. On every side we see Christians pursuing the rage for relevance, whether seeking the respect of the "cultured despisers" of the gospel, reaching out to the contemporary "unchurched" with a "user friendly" gospel, or just enjoying the comforts of the age.

For many believers the Christian life is now the good life: It simply "goes better with Jesus" even if there is no God and no Resurrection. The result is a series of adaptations of the Christian faith to modern man that are a capitulation with few rivals in two thousand years.

Against all such attempts the holy fools stand as a weeping road block. In the gospel there is an antithesis to the world that we dare not relax, a cost to discipleship that we cannot waive, a challenge to obedience that we must not conceal, and a scandal to faith that we should never airbrush away. If loyalty to those truths puts us beyond the pale, so be it. Today's worldly wisdom that pronounces us mad will soon be tomorrow's outmoded theory. So long as our folly is truly the gospel and not our own delusion as simpletons, we will not be "ignorantly ignorant" or "unwisely unwise" but humble students in the school of Christ. As theologian Helmut Thielicke wrote of Don Quixote, "The fool is always right; *only* the fool is right in this world."

For followers of Jesus, he decides the canons of rationality, normality, and sanity, not professors, pundits, and polls. To the world, we may be "impossible people" and our ideas "insane." But for anyone who ponders the lunacies and ironies of the modern world, it should be comforting to be regarded as foolish where we differ from it and discomforting that the world does not regard us as more foolish because we are largely conformed to it. Holy folly is a countercultural stance. We are "fools of love" in relationship to Jesus, but in relation to the powers that be, we are radical insurrectionists.

Engulfed by the worldliness of the nineteenth-century church in Denmark, Kierkegaard wrote in his journal,

When a man has a toothache the world says, "Poor man"; when a man's wife is unfaithful to him the world says, "Poor man"; when

a man is in financial embarrassment the world says, "Poor man"—
when it pleased God in the form of a lowly servant to suffer in this
world the world says, "Poor man"; when an Apostle with a divine
commission has the honor to suffer for the truth the world says,
"Poor man"—poor world!

Third, foolbearing is essential to calling because it is Christ's way
of responding to injury. Nothing in the Gospels is more revolutionary than Jesus' call to respond to injury in a new way. ("But I tell you
who hear me: Love your enemies, do good to those who hate you,
bless those who curse you, pray for those who mistreat you.") Equally,
nothing in the modern church is more anti-Christian than those
Christians and Christian leaders in public life who play the politics
of resentment and pass their followers off as "a small, persecuted
minority" when they are not.

Gaspard de Coligny, the French admiral and Huguenot leader
assassinated for his Protestant beliefs in 1572, declared: "I will freely
forget all things, whether evil weal or injury, done unto me alone, provided that the glory of God and the public [welfare] be safe." Yet prominent parts of the Western church today, in pursuit of public influence,
have abandoned Christ's response to injury and shamelessly promoted
a contemporary secular strategy—redress through blaming or playing
the victim. Suddenly such Christians have gone from portraying themselves as "the sleeping giant" of public life to "the poor little whipping
boy" of hostile secular forces arrayed against them.

Shame on such a deliberately chosen strategy! The merciless persecution of Christians in many parts of the non-Western world, simply for confessing Christ, is a crime. And, there is unquestionably a
good deal of anti-Christian bias and prejudice in parts of Western
society today; examples are easy to find. But a strategy of victim playing to defend the latter should be unthinkable for followers of Christ.
Put simply, it is factually misleading, morally hypocritical, politically
ineffective, and psychologically dangerous. Worst of all, it is unfaithful, a deliberate and outright denial of Jesus' teaching and call to suffering and rejection.

Have these Christian leaders no shame? Let them scour the New Testament from beginning to end. They will not find one single line to justify the politics of anxiety and resentment that has character-ized parts of their stand in public life recently.

The foolbearer must go another way. Followers of Christ will be called many names, but our identity comes only from the One whose call reveals our names and natures. Followers of Christ may no more like shouldering the cost of their commitments than followers of other ways, but no one who knows what our Master bore can bear to shrug off the blame on others. In reality, today's brotherhood of the victimized ones is a twisted counterfeit of the fellowship of the crucified one. All of us as followers of Christ will flinch at times from the pain of wounds and the smart of slights, but that cost is in the contract of calling and the way of the cross.

This theme of holy folly, or foolbearing, is fertile with implica-tions. It carries extraordinary potential for Christian witness. It sug-gests possibilities for a new reforming order in the church. It even demonstrates the centrality of the evangelical tradition to the church of Christ (to be evangelical, as St. Francis expressed it, to "live after the gospel of Jesus" and thus to define ourselves and our lives by the first things of the evangel itself).

But when all is said and done, foolbearing is simply faithfulness. Or better still, it is what Bernard of Clairvaux called "the serious game" and Gregory of Nyssa "the sober inebriation" of those transported by the heart of the good news of Jesus—the wonder of a crucified God. As Austin Farrer, the Oxford philosopher, once stated: "If Jesus is willing to be in us, and to let us show him to the world, it's a small thing that we should endure being fools for Christ's sake, and be shown up by the part we have to play."

❦

Have you had your "white funeral"? Or is your faith respectable,
sober, moderate, calculated, and comfortable, with as little
tension with the world as possible? Are you prepared, in the

223

words of the Little Flower of Lisieux, to "have no other desire than to love Jesus unto folly"? Do you, in your own way, "live after the gospel"? Listen to Jesus of Nazareth; answer his call.

25

THE HOUR HAS COME

Gaius Julius Caesar was famous for his decisive swiftness (the *celeritas Caesaris*). More famously still, he summarily carved up Rome's greatest province, Gaul, in three simple parts. Most famous of all, his brilliant generalship was so stunning that after one characteristically brief victory—at the battle of Zela in Asia Minor—he made the immortal comment to a friend, "Veni, vidi, vici." ("I came, I saw, I conquered.") It was later said that he fought more than fifty victorious battles and killed well over a million enemies. Julius Caesar, needless to say, never became Great Caesar by being a doubting Thomas or a hesitating Hamlet.

But on one chilly mid-January night in 49 B.C., when he was fifty-one, Caesar was slowed to a standstill. None of his unquestioned abilities and assets seemed to count. Or rather, they threw into sharp relief the momentous decision he faced. At his feet rushed the dark waters of a narrow river swollen with heavy rains. This river marked the southern boundary of the province of Cisalpine Gaul over which he had authority as governor. On the other side lay Italy proper, where the authority of Rome and the Roman Senate held sway.

Was Caesar to cross the river with a few friends but no soldiers and so lay down his command and proceed to Rome to press his grievances as a private citizen? Or was he to cross with his legionaries, flout the authority of the Senate, and march on Rome as an act of defiance and civil war? "To refrain from crossing," he said to his friends, "will bring me misfortune; but to cross will bring misfortune to all men."

Since January 1 that year, the consuls in Rome had done everything in their power to remove Julius Caesar from his governorship, even passing "the extreme decree" amounting to a state of emergency. Caesar's term as governor had expired after ten years, and they anticipated he would now re-enter Rome and stand as a candidate for Proconsul. Once in that position, he would be beyond their power, so they were eager to curb his ambitions by prosecuting him for breaches of the Constitution when he had been consul ten years earlier.

The issue between Caesar and the Senate was personal but far, far more. Behind the power and the prominence of the old republic of Rome was the Senate, an extraordinary body of the "fathers" (*patres*) who were the will and voice and executive arm of Rome itself. But as time had gone by, the strains in the republic had mounted, especially the social problems caused by the growing number of the poor, the veterans of Rome's wars, and the influx of people from Rome's expanding empire.

In short, the Senate was caught: It could no longer master the challenges of governing a burgeoning world empire, yet it was not flexible enough to reform itself, and it did not like the periodic military leaders who threatened to take reform—and supreme power—into their own hands.

Julius Caesar was the latest and greatest of these military leaders and therefore a deadly threat to the authority of the Senate. Captured by pirates when he was twenty-six years old, Caesar refused their offer to ransom him for twenty talents, saying he was worth at least fifty. When he was thirty-one and in Cadiz, Spain, he came across the monument to Alexander the Great at the temple of Hercules. Suetonius reports that Caesar was overcome by emotion to think that he had not yet achieved anything remarkable, whereas Alexander by that age had conquered the world.

Certainly by the time Caesar stood by the little river, he had carved out a name as a conqueror. Without orders and without permission he had succeeded in a conquest greater than any Roman general before him. The number of his legions had swelled from four to ten and the world lay at his feet. Cicero wrote that Caesar was favored with a good following wind. Plutarch reported that the night before he halted at the river, Caesar had dreamed about raping his mother—his mother supposedly representing the earth that lay subdued before him.

Perhaps, then, there could be only one outcome of Caesar's riverside review. But for a moment he paused in genuine indecision. For a while, one friend reported, Caesar was silent, lost in his own thoughts. Then gravely he reviewed the consequences aloud before them. In one scale lay the universal misfortune brought by a civil war. In the other lay his own misfortune—the slights and grievances he had suffered in his dealings with the Senate.

Finally, the reports say, Caesar roused himself from his pondering. Announcing his gambler's verdict that "the die must be cast," he gave the orders to cross the river—the Rubicon—and led his soldiers into the nearby town before dawn. In effect he had declared war on the Senate. Five years, many battles, and a river of blood later, Julius Caesar bestrode the narrow world like a Colossus. Not long afterward he would pay for his hubris with his own blood, dying in a hail of dagger blows led by his friend Marcus Brutus. But the old republic had been brought to its knees and the Imperial Rome of the Caesars was about to be born in his image.

Earlier in 63 B.C. Cicero had declared that there were no limits on earth to Roman rule; the only limits were those determined by heaven. Now he wrote of Caesar's action in causing civil war, "This cause lacks nothing but a cause." Julius Caesar was simply his own cause. And if the auspices of heaven were also needed to assure the general public, he would help them along by his own daring and decisiveness.

Subsequent tributes to Julius Caesar have been lavish—"The First Emperor," "the second most influential man who ever lived," the executive arm of "the world spirit" (Hegel), "perhaps the most gifted of mortals" (Jacob Burckhardt). "You should write about the death of Caesar in a fully worthy manner, greater than Voltaire's," Napoleon told Goethe (probably thinking also of himself). "It could be the greatest task of your life."

But while Julius Caesar's stock has mostly ridden high and remained high, my concern here is not with his greatness or his genius but with the sense of timing that was a key part of his achievement. His gamer's words ("the die must be cast") are now part and parcel of decision making. His action ("crossing the Rubicon") now stands for any fateful decision. And Shakespeare's equally famous lines by Caesar's murderer, Marcus Brutus, apply also to Caesar and describe the vital place of timing in human destiny.

> There is a tide in the affairs of men
> Which, taken at the flood, leads on to fortune;
> Omitted, all the voyage of their life
> Is bound in shallows and in miseries.
> On such a full sea are we now afloat;
> And we must take the current when it serves
> Or lose our ventures.

The extraordinary career of Julius Caesar and the manner of his seizing his moment and taking his destiny into his own hands highlights a further feature of the truth of calling—*calling is an essential part of the sense of timing that characterizes a successful life.*

GOD'S GOOD TIME

Julius Caesar's extraordinary sense of timing can be found in modern leaders too. For example, Benjamin Disraeli, British statesman and author, wrote in his journal, "Spirit of the Times, to know it and oneself the secret of success." Similarly Count von Bismarck, the creator of modern Germany, was a ruthless power broker, but he recognized his need to be in tune with forces vaster than he could engineer. He liked to say that a statesman's main task was "to listen until he hears the rustle of God's robe, then leap up and grasp the hem of the garment."

Winston Churchill had a similar sense of timing. In his case it was allied with a da Vinci-like sense of the shortness of human life and the immensity of possible human accomplishment. "Curse ruth-less time!" he once said to a friend. "How cruelly short is the allot-ted span for all we must cram into it!" Timing was therefore a key to Churchill's sense of urgency and personal mission. "Chance, Fortune, Luck, Destiny, Fate, Providence," he wrote, "seem to me only dif-ferent ways of expressing the same thing, to wit, that a man's own contribution to his life story is continually dominated by an exter-nal superior power."

Needless to say, a sense of timing does not mean that someone is omnipotent. On the contrary, the significance of timing is that it makes up in intuition for what a person lacks in brute power—as is shown constantly by the best batters in baseball, the best generals in war, or the best leaders in national affairs. Great leaders make a dif-ference even when forces and obstacles are truly daunting because of the "fit" between themselves and the moment in which they live and act. Obviously, not every leader fits every hour. Some come too early; most linger on until too late; only a few have that sense of timing that is a secret of success.

Nor does a sense of timing mean that someone is omniscient, or even prescient. As General George Marshall, U.S. Secretary of State, insisted, leaders mostly make decisions in "chronic obscurity." Hindsight may have the benefit of 20/20 vision, but in real life the capacity to act is often greatest when the clarity to see is worst. Conversely, by the time everything is crystal clear, freedom to act may be heavily constrained. Adolph Hitler, for example, could easily have been stopped in his tracks early in his career; it was not until he could only be stopped at enormous cost that people knew beyond doubt why he needed to be stopped at any cost.

Oddly, a sense of timing is harder in the modern world because of our modern obsession with timing. We define ourselves by our generations, we count on generational conflict as a staple expecta-tion, we label our decades cutely, and we simultaneously celebrate progress and indulge in nostalgia for a lost past. The result is a dra-matic shortening of historical attention, the creation of new group-ings of identity and style, and an acceleration of the turnover between generations, decades, and styles. A sense of timing is now subject to the fashions and frustrations of the market just as much as Paris's fashions and Detroit's new models in cars.

Thus a pinch of salt is in order. We should handle all claims about timing with a dose of caution. Every age senses itself falling in morals. The rhetoric of pundits is dotted with claims of "watersheds" and "great divides." "Crisis" is both a constant and a cliché under the conditions of modern change. All that trembles does not fall and many a "tidal wave of the future" proves to be only a minor eddy. Most trumpeted "turning points" barely register on the scales of history, and pitfalls in turning point talk are legion.

Worst of all, timing is now confused with trend spotting, which itself is now a highly profitable trend. Trend spotters are the fortune-tellers of the modern world; they tell our futures and make theirs. As Winston Churchill quipped about quack prophets in politics, "The main qualification for political office is the ability to foretell what is going to happen tomorrow, next week, next month, and next year— and to have the ability afterward to explain why it didn't happen."

Yet, for all that, only a fool would ignore the importance of timing. Doing the right thing at the right moment multiplies its effect incalculably. For followers of Christ, timing is not only part and parcel of life and a vital component for understanding history under God. It is also essential for understanding someone far greater than Julius Caesar—Jesus Christ. Concepts such as "day," "time," "age," "hour," "moment," and "generation" are critical to understanding Jesus and his gospel.

There is no Hebrew word for chronological time in the abstract. Instead the stress is on the providence and purpose of time rather than its passage; on the significance of a day rather than the succession of days; on the meaning of a moment rather than how it is measured; and on time as linear and purposeful rather than the pagan view of time as cyclical. Shakespeare's notion of a flood tide or a "full sea" is very close to the New Testament's "fullness of time" and the later Christian phrase, "God's good time."

The Bible contains many examples of good timing—for instance, in the Old Testament celebration of David's men who were "skilled in reading the signs of the times to discover what course Israel should follow." It also contains striking examples of bad timing and missed moments, as in Jeremiah's stinging dismissal of Pharaoh Neco: "Give Pharaoh of Egypt the title King Bombast, the man who missed his moment."

Unquestionably the strongest biblical awareness of timing is in Jesus. Eleven times in a single chapter (Luke 11) Jesus referred to "generation," six of them to "this generation." Each time, he underscored his generation's responsibility to answer for all the crucial events going on in its day. When Jesus wept over Jerusalem because it missed his "way of peace" and brought down on itself the siege of Rome in A.D. 70, it was "because you did not recognize the time of God's coming to you."

But all the biblical examples pale beside Jesus' awareness of timing in his own calling. Many followers of Christ today seek to understand Jesus solely through his claims. Jesus' claims are vital, but they lose much of their power if they are isolated rather than understood through his sense of calling. Jesus did not stride around Galilee as a "claim maker." In pursuit of his calling, he made and implied claims that opened a window into his self-understanding and threw down the ultimate gauntlet to human response.

Jesus' sense of calling is especially critical in a world awash with conflicting portraits of him. Recent years have offered us Jesus the great moral teacher and example, Jesus the nationalistic firebrand and failed Jewish revolutionary, Jesus the wild-eyed apocalyptic prophet announcing the end of the world, Jesus the wandering Cynic preacher or shrewd Galilean holy man, and Jesus the family man—divorced and remarried with three children. Skeptics and opponents of the church have made hay with such confusion.

How are seekers and believers to assess these vastly different portraits? How do we know the wilder versions are not true rather than the church's belief that Jesus is Lord and God? Four principles are helpful in sorting out the confusion. First, Christians ask for no special pleading or protection for their faith; it has to be investigated and checked out like any other. Second, the best way to investigate is to examine the evidence of history; the problem with the false views is not that they offend us but that they are fiction. Third, the way to examine history is through a double approach: working forward from the expectations of Judaism and working backward from the evidence of the Gospels. Fourth, conclusions that claim to answer the question, "Who was Jesus?" must deal satisfactorily with the evidence surrounding a trio of core issues: How did Jesus understand himself? Why did Jesus die? What explains the rise of the Christian church?

The first of these core issues—Jesus' self-understanding—is pivotal to resolving the other two. And it emerges most clearly in Jesus' understanding of his calling. It is simply not true that a sense of life-purpose is a uniquely modern thing. Like John the Baptist, Paul of Tarsus, and many ancient leaders such as Pericles, Socrates, Cicero, and Augustus Caesar, Jesus of Nazareth was undeniably motivated by a long-held, overarching purpose that he followed consistently. Like John and Paul but not the others, Jesus clearly viewed his life-purpose as a calling from God—announced at his baptism and recorded plainly by all four Gospels. Yet unlike anyone before or since, Jesus' awareness of his calling from God burst the bounds of human thinking.

First, Jesus spoke and acted as a prophet announcing the end of Israel's exile, the arrival of God's Kingdom, and imminent catastrophe for all who miss his "way of peace."

Second, and more shocking, Jesus spoke and acted as the Messiah representing Israel in himself, a new Israel-in-person around whom the old Israel was being forgiven, healed, redefined, and reconstituted.

Third, and most offensive of all to his generation, Jesus spoke and acted as if he actually embodied *Israel's God, YHWH, come down in person and in power.* In Jesus, God has arrived, Israel's king has returned to his people. Jesus saw himself as coming to do for Israel and the world that which the Scriptures teach only God can do and be. To worship Jesus as Lord and God is therefore natural and entirely appropriate. God spoke through him. God acted in him. God spoke and acted *as him.*

This awesome, category-shattering calling of Jesus runs powerfully through his entire life. It was glimpsed in his boyhood, confirmed and announced at his baptism, nourished through his prayer and spiritual discipline, tested in his confrontation with the powers of evil, demonstrated in his public words and deeds, acted out in such symbolic acts as riding into Jerusalem on a donkey, agonized over in his doubts in Gethsemane, climaxed in his death on the cross, and vindicated at his Resurrection from the grave.

A sense of timing was central to Jesus' sense of calling. "My hour has not yet come," he said to his mother at the wedding in Cana when she attempted to thrust him into the limelight prematurely. "My time is not yet at hand," he said to his brothers when they urged him to go up to Jerusalem to establish himself prematurely. "The hour has come," he later prayed to his Father in the Garden of Gethsemane, which was his own crossing of the Rubicon on the road to the cross. Clearly, Jesus, who expected his hearers to be able to read "the signs of the times," showed that he read his own times perfectly.

But what of us? How can we ordinary followers of Christ be "unriddlers of our time" when we have neither his knowledge nor his power and we cannot influence history like Caesar and Bismarck? There are those who teach that Christian obedience is simply a matter of seeing what God is doing and joining in. But is it really as simple as that? God often moves in a mysterious way. So the advice that we wait until we understand him often proves a recipe for passivity and paralysis. Four themes in Jesus' teaching bear closely on a sense of timing in our own callings.

First, calling is a matter of *relying on God.* "Have faith in God. . . . Do not fear. . . . Do not be anxious. . . . Your heavenly Father knows what you need." No example of Jesus is clearer, no exhortation of Jesus is more insistent, than that we his disciples should place our whole reliance on God, at this point as well as elsewhere. After all, "our times are in his hands."

Here is where other expressions of timing fall short and the best intuition falters. We humans simply do not have the knowledge or power to stay in tune with our times. The desire for timing in our lives is as difficult as it is natural. But for those called, it is not all left to us. We do not have to pretend to escape the chronic obscurity of human decisions. Nor do we need to resort to trend spotters or palm readers. He whose eye is on the sparrow can be trusted with the timing of our lives if our eyes are upon him. As King Jehoshaphat prayed to God when facing daunting enemies: "We do not know what to do, but our eyes are upon you." God's timing is rarely our timing. But far better than we do, he numbers our days and knows our moments and our hours. Our task is to trust.

Second, calling is a matter of *renouncing inadequate methods for achieving timeliness.* "If anyone wishes to come after me, let him deny himself. . . . If your right hand makes you stumble, cut it off. . . . If your right eye makes your stumble, tear it out. . . . You cannot serve God and Mammon." The same drastic repudiation of other points of reliance applies to timing in calling. There are, of course, many ways of pursuing timeliness apart from following Christ—clairvoyance, fortune-telling, futurism, public relations, and marketing, to name a few.

Jesus sharpened this contrast when he rejected his brothers' urging that he promote himself by going up to Jerusalem. "My hour has not yet come," he said, and then pointedly added: "but your time is always opportune." Whereas God's way depends on God's initiative in God's time, our human way is to promote ourselves by any means at any time. We have to; everything is up to us. The problem with the outcome is not that human promotions and public relations cannot match providence for strength; they cannot match providence for timing. In a day when many Christians confuse punditry for prophecy, we need to choose our authorities carefully and be clear about what we are turning from as well as to whom we are turning.

Third, calling is a matter of *readiness.* "Be on your guard. . . . Remember Lot's wife. . . . When the Son of Man comes, will he find faith on the earth? . . . Be on your alert at all times." From his stories about the wise and foolish bridesmaids to his references to "the days of Noah" and his coming "like a thief in the night" to his real-life rebuke of his sleeping disciples, Jesus repeatedly urged his followers to be on the alert, waiting, watching, ready.

When Hamlet's friend Horatio wondered if he was avoiding a duel with Laertes because he was afraid of death, Hamlet replied: "Not a whit, we defy augury. There's a special providence in the fall of a sparrow. If it be now, 'tis not to come; if it be not to come, it will be now; if it be not now, yet it will come; the readiness is all."

Readiness for followers of Christ is obedience honed to the highest level of responsiveness. Like a symphony orchestra well rehearsed, perfectly tuned, and with all eyes on the conductor's baton, followers of Christ should be poised to respond to his slightest word or sign. The Book of Numbers describes Israel's responsiveness to the pillar of cloud and fire with a revealing string of adverbs: Israel moved or rested "whenever . . . at the place where . . . as long as . . . as soon as . . . only when" God guided. The very words conjure up Israel's readiness in responding to the conductor.

Fourth, calling is a matter of *resolution.* "No one, after putting his hand to the plow and looking back, is fit for the kingdom of God. . . . For which one of you, when he wants to build a tower, does not first sit down and calculate the cost, to see if he has enough to complete it? Otherwise, when he has laid a foundation, and is not able to finish, all who observe it begin to ridicule him."

God calls men and women who will be committed to their life tasks with no reservations, no retreats, no regrets. Like Søren Kierkegaard's "knight of faith" mentioned earlier, followers of Christ have staked the meaning and outcome of their lives on the Royal Majesty by whom they were dubbed. They are therefore free to turn from their own affairs and to center their lives on the priorities of their questing. In pursuit of this quest, no pettiness is so petty that it disturbs their meaning. No task is so immense that it daunts the courage of their calling. They engage in the world on the world's terms, yet they are never diverted from their quest because they always have an eye to interests and ideals that are invisible to the eyes of others.

Such are the people who will always be found in "the gap." They are the ones prepared "for such a time as this." People after God's own heart, they are ready to read the signs of the times and serve his purpose in their generation.

Do you try to march to your own drum? Unriddle the puzzle of your own life? Bring in your own chorus of prophets to interpret your omens? Or do you live with your eye upon God and the assurance that your times are in his hands? Listen to Jesus of Nazareth; answer his call.

26

LAST CALL

The name Moltke had resounded proudly through two centuries of Prussian and German history. Count Helmuth Carl Bernhard von Moltke had been Chancellor Bismarck's field marshal and the terrible, swift sword wielded in his crushing German victories over the Danes, the Austrians, and the French. The field marshal's greatest triumph, the destruction of the French Imperial Army at Sedan in 1871, had led to the capture of Paris and the creation of the German Empire.

So Helmuth James von Moltke, great-great nephew to the field marshal, was the scion of a famous Teuton clan and privileged to live at Kreisau, the grand Silesian estate given to his illustrious forebear by a grateful nation. But though brave and like his forebear a man of deep faith in Christ, his calling and future fame lay in a very different direction. His great-great uncle had been nineteenth-century Germany's greatest military strategist. Despite his illustrious name, the younger Moltke was to be one of twentieth-century Germany's most famous martyrs—under Hitler.

The gathering political storm clouds of the 1930s confronted the best Germans with a painful decision—to flee or to stay. Many like scientist Albert Einstein, novelist Thomas Mann, and architect Mies van der Rohe took refuge abroad. Others stayed and wondered how much tyranny they would accept and how much they would resist. Like Dietrich Bonhoeffer, James von Moltke, who was twenty-six when Hitler came to power, could easily have gone abroad. He nearly did. ("I even picked out the curtains" in London, his wife Freya said.)

But when war broke out in September 1939, he knew, like Bonhoeffer, that his place was in his homeland. His name and character made him a natural rallying point for resisters to the regime.

Trained in international law, Moltke was drafted into the Abwehr or German military intelligence, little realizing that it was to be the center of anti-Nazi resistance. He used his job overtly to try and curb the Nazis with the restraints of international law. Covertly, he dedicated himself to two main tasks: countering the deportation and murder of Jews and the execution of captured soldiers (his alert in 1943 helped save the lives of thousands of Jews in Denmark), and bringing the most brilliant resisters to his estate at Kreisau to plan the shape of a democratic Germany that would follow the collapse of the Third Reich. In his *Memoirs,* American diplomat George F. Kennan called Moltke "the greatest person, morally, and the largest and most enlightened in his concepts that I met on either side of the battle-lines in the Second World War."

But not even Moltke's famous name could hold the Nazis at bay forever. Inevitably, he was betrayed and on January 19, 1944, he was arrested. He had refused to join Bonhoeffer in the conspiracy to assassinate Hitler and had been in prison six months when the attempt on July 20, 1944, failed. In spite of six attempts on his life in the last quarter of that year, the "Lord of all Vermin" seemed to have a charmed life and escaped. Admiral Canaris and Dietrich Bonhoeffer were among the 4,500 slaughtered after the July attempt, and the circle of revenge slowly broadened to all known opponents of the regime, including Moltke.

Moltke and seven friends from his Kreisau Circle went on trial in January 1945 in the notorious "People's Court," presided over by the vicious prosecutor Roland Freisler. Moltke described the travesty of the secret trial in a profoundly moving letter to his wife Freya. It was the last of 1,600 letters written to her between their courtship in 1929 and his death in 1945, all hidden in beehives on the family estate until the war was over and published in 1990 as *Letters to Freya.*

The presence of God is very close in Moltke's last letter to his wife. The letter is partly a love letter, beautiful because of his final message to her. "You are not a means God employed to make me who I am, rather you are myself. You are my 13th chapter of the First Letter to the Corinthians. Without this chapter no human being is human."

The letter is also Moltke's testament as a resister. He was braced by a reminder in the Nazi prosecutor's tirade that "only in one respect are we and Christianity alike: We demand the whole man!" He was therefore proud to stand before the prosecutor "not as a Protestant, not as a big landowner, not as a nobleman, not as a Prussian, not as a German . . . but as a Christian and nothing else."

But Moltke's letter is also the final word of a human being in the departure lounge for eternity. "I always imagined that one would only feel shock," he wrote, "that one would say to oneself: now the sun sets for the last time for you, now the clock only goes to twelve twice more, now you go to bed for the last time. None of that is the case. I wonder if I am a bit high for I can't deny that my mood is positively elated. I only beg the Lord in Heaven that he will keep me in it, for it is surely easier for the flesh to die like that."

Facing death at the age of thirty-seven, Moltke does acknowledge, "Now there is still a hard bit of the road ahead of me." But from the beginning to end the letter's theme is gratitude and its tone is trusting. "For what a mighty task your husband was chosen: all the trouble the Lord took with him, the infinite detours, the intricate zigzag curves, all suddenly find their explanation in one hour. . . . Everything acquires its meaning in retrospect, which was hidden. Mami and Papi, the brothers and sisters, the little sons, Kreisau and its troubles . . . it has all at last become comprehensible in a single hour."

"Dear heart, my life is finished . . ." Moltke concluded. "This doesn't alter the fact that I would gladly go on living and that I would gladly accompany you a bit further on this earth. But then I would need a new task for God. The task for which God made me is done."

One of ten executed at Plötenzee prison just months before the end of the war, Count Helmuth James von Moltke died unshadowed. "Right to the end," a fellow conspirator recorded, "he was completely free in soul, friendly, helpful, considerate, a truly free and noble man amid all the trappings of horror." His wife Freya later said from her home in Vermont, "It was much more bitter, in my opinion, to lose one's husband as a soldier *for* Hitler than losing him as a soldier *against* Hitler."

FINISHING WELL

The bright but poignant courage of Helmuth James von Moltke's dying underscores one last aspect of the many-splendored truth of calling: *Calling is central to the challenge and privilege of finishing well in life.*

There have been different times and different societies where "dying well" was a high ideal. For example, when Michelangelo was eighty-eight, a medal was struck in his honor. On one side was his profile. On the other was a blind pilgrim with a staff, led by a dog, and an inscription from Psalm 51: "Then will I teach transgressors thy ways; and sinners shall be converted unto thee." The artist himself had chosen the psalm, wishing to picture himself as old and frail but submissive to the will of God. In one of his famous last "Sonnets of Renunciation" Michelangelo the sculptor-painter-architect-turned-poet had written with deep devotion:

> The voyage of my life at last has reached,
> across tempestuous sea, in fragile boat
> the common port all must pass through to give
> cause and account of every evil, every pious deed.

Such an attitude is rare today and not simply because of our modern denial of death. For such obvious reasons as greater life expectancy, the larger number of older people in our families, and the greatly expanded opportunities and services offered to senior citizens, our modern stress is on finishing well rather than dying well. The trouble is that for many people the "golden years" are not all they are cracked up to be.

The truth of calling is as vital to our ending as to our beginning. It is an important key to finishing well because it helps us with three of the greatest challenges of our last years of life.

First, calling is the spur that keeps us journeying purposefully—and thus growing and maturing—to the very end of our lives. People make two equal but opposite errors about life as a journey and faith as the Way. On one side, usually at the less educated level, are those who prematurely speak as if they have arrived. Such people properly emphasize the certainties and triumphs of faith but minimize the uncertainties, tragedies, and incompletenesses. Having come to faith, they speak and live as if they have nothing more to learn. All truths are clear-cut, all mysteries solved, all hopes materialized, all conclusion foregone—and all sense of journeying is reduced to the vanishing point. There are seemingly no risks, trials, dangers, setbacks, or disasters on the horizon. Or so they seem to talk.

On the other side, usually at the more educated level, are those who are so conscious of the journey that journey without end becomes their passion and their way of life. To such people it is unthinkable ever to arrive, and the ultimate gaffe is the claim of finding a way or reaching a conclusion. Like the perennial seekers we met earlier, for them the journey itself is all. Questions, inquiry, searching, and conquering become an end in themselves. Ambiguity is everything.

Yet the Christian faith has an extraordinary balance between these extremes. As those responding to God's call, we are followers of Christ and followers of the Way. So we are on a journey and we are truly travelers, with all the attendant costs, risks, and dangers of the journey. Never in this life can we say we have arrived. But we know why we have lost our original home and, more importantly, we know the home to which we are going.

So we who are followers of Christ are wayfarers, and though we have found the Way, we have not yet come to our destination. We may retire from our jobs, but there is no retiring from our individual callings. We may cut back from our public responsibilities, but there is no cutting back from our corporate calling as the people of God. Above all, we may reach the place where we can see the end of the road, but our eyes are then to be fixed more closely on the one at the end of the road who is Father and home. As Henri Nouwen wrote, "He who thinks that he has finished is finished. Those who think they have arrived have lost their way."

Second, calling helps us to finish well because it prevents us from confusing the termination of our occupations with the termination of our vocations. This is where the "Protestant distortion" of equating calling with jobs rears its ugly head for the last time. If we ever limit our calling to what we do, and that task is taken away from us—we suddenly find ourselves unemployed, fired, retired, or pronounced terminally ill—then we are tempted to depression or doubt. What has happened? We have let our occupation become so intertwined with our vocation that losing the occupation means losing the sense of vocation too.

"When a man knows how to do something," Pablo Picasso told a friend, "he ceases being a man when he stops doing it." The result was drivenness. Picasso's gift, once idolized, held him in thrall. Every empty canvas was an affront to his creativity. Like an addict, he made work his source of satisfaction only to find himself dissatisfied. "I have only one thought: work," Picasso said toward the end of his life, when neither his family nor his friends could help him to relax. "I paint just as I breathe. When I work, I relax; not doing anything or entertaining visitors makes me tired."

William Wilberforce, by contrast, was called, not driven. He was on his deathbed in June 1833 in Cadogan Place, London, when he heard news of the great victory in abolishing slavery throughout the British Empire. Three days later he died. "It is a singular fact," said Thomas Fowell Buxton, his chosen successor in leading the cause, "that on the very night on which we were successfully engaged in the House of Commons, in passing the clause of the Act of Emancipation—one of the most important clauses ever enacted . . . the spirit of our friend left the world. The day which was the termination of his labours was the termination of his life."

Such symmetry is very rare. Very few people have the privilege of ending their "labors" and their "life" at the same time. In a world marred and broken by sin, our lives are often terminated before our tasks or our tasks are taken away from us long before the ending of our lives. This means we must be sure that our sense of calling is deeper, wider, higher, and longer than the best and highest of the tasks we undertake.

Put differently, most human lives are an incomplete story if not a story of incompletion. As Reinhold Niebuhr wrote, "Nothing that is worth doing can be achieved in our lifetime; therefore we must be saved by hope. Nothing which is true or beautiful or good makes complete sense in any immediate context of history; therefore we must be saved by faith. Nothing we do, however virtuous, can be accomplished alone; therefore we are saved by love. No virtuous act is quite as virtuous from the standpoint of our friend or foe as it is from our standpoint. Therefore we must be saved by the final form of love which is forgiveness."

John Cotton's famous sermon rises magnificently to a central consequence of calling in the face of death. "The last work which faith puts forth about a man's calling is this: faith with boldness resigns up his calling into the hands of God or man; whenever God calls a man to lay down his calling when his work is finished, herein the sons of God far exceed the sons of men. Another man when his calling comes to be removed from him, he is much ashamed and much afraid; but if a Christian man is to forego his calling, he lays it down with comfort and boldness in the sight of God."

A friend once said to Winston Churchill that there was something to be said for being a *retired* Roman Emperor. "Why retired?" Churchill growled. "There's nothing to be said for retiring from anything." As followers of Christ we are called to be before we are called to do and our calling both to be and do is fulfilled only in being called to him. So calling should not only precede career but outlast it too. Vocations never end, even when occupations do. We may retire from our jobs but never from our calling. We may at times be unemployed, but no one ever becomes uncalled.

Most important of all, the Last Call of death is a termination from the secular perspective, but from the spiritual perspective it is the culmination of life. After a lifetime of journeying, we are arriving home. After all the years of hearing only the voice, we are about to see the face and feel the arms. The Caller is our Father and the Last Call is the call home.

Until that day comes, our task is to keep on and to keep on keeping on. In the words of the famous Anglican prayer adapted from the writings of the great Elizabethan sailor and adventurer Sir Francis Drake, "O Lord God, when thou givest to thy servants to endeavour any great matter, grant us also to know that it is not the beginning, but the continuing of the same to the end, until it be thoroughly finished, which yieldeth the true glory; through him who for the finishing of thy work laid down his life, our Redeemer, Jesus Christ."

Third, calling helps us finish well because it encourages us to leave the entire outcome of our lives to God. In his masterwork *Orthodoxy,* G. K. Chesterton wrote: "To the question, 'What are you?' I could only answer, 'God knows.'" But such reticence is rare today. Blithely, glibly, with no sense of the ridiculousness of our arrogance, we modern people talk of "discovering our identities," specifying our callings in a single sentence, and pronouncing about our life accomplishments as if they were things we could pile on a little red wagon and trundle in to God to solicit his approval and add to our pride of achievement.

Other people, bearing the entire burden of sustaining their own significance, go to the other extreme—weariness and despair. In his autobiography, nineteenth-century writer Van Wyck Brooks surveyed his life and concluded that his efforts had been sown in an environment where they could not grow and not even the furrow would remain. He had "ploughed the sea." The great Irish poet W. B. Yeats wrote similarly in his memoir *Reveries:* "All life weighed in the scale of my own life seems a preparation for something that never happens."

Both the arrogant and the despairing overlook what God alone must do. They forget the mystery at the heart of calling as well as identity. God calls and, just as we hear him but don't see him on this earth, so we grow to become what he calls, even though we don't see until heaven what he is calling us to become.

No one has captured this more profoundly than George Macdonald in his sermon "The New Name" from *Unspoken Sermons.* In his message in Revelation to the Church in Pergamum, Jesus promised "a white stone with a new name written on it, known only to him who receives it." Macdonald pointed out in good biblical fashion that "the true name is one which expresses the character, the nature, the *meaning* of the person who bears it. It is the man's own symbol—his soul's picture, in a word—the sign which belongs to him and no one else. Who can give a man this, his own nature? God alone. For no one but God sees what a man is."

But then, in a hauntingly suggestive passage, Macdonald went further and gave the lie to all who think that "discovering our giftedness and calling" and "fulfilling the real you" is a simple and straightforward matter.

It is only when the man has become his name that God gives him the stone with the name upon it, for then first can he understand what his name signifies. It is the blossom, the perfection, the completeness, that determines the name: and God foresees that from the first because He made it so: but the tree of the soul, before its blossom comes, cannot understand what blossom it is to bear and could not know what the word meant, which, in representing its own unarrived completeness, named itself.

Such a name cannot be given until the man is the name. God's name for the man must be the expression of His own idea of the man, that being whom He had in his thought when he began to make the child, and whom He keeps in His thought through the long process of creation that went to realize the idea. To tell the name is to seal the success—to say "In thee also I am well pleased."

Perhaps you are frustrated by the gap that still remains between your vision and your accomplishment. Or you may be depressed by the pages of your life that are blotched with compromises, failures, betrayals, and sin. You have had your say. Other may have had their say. But make no judgments and draw no conclusions until the scaffolding of history is stripped away and you see what it means for God to have had his say—and made you what you are called to be.

We are "called to be." Who dares set against this sublime vision the crude insult of being "constrained to be," the puny audacity of "the courage to be" or the pedestrian fatalism of being "constituted to be"? From its awesome beginning, when a voice was heard but no figure seen, to its soaring climax, when God will unveil his design for all his children at our Last Call, the character and purpose of calling beggar the imagination and thrill the heart and soul of all but the most deaf and unresponsive.

Ponder these things well. When the Last Call comes to each of us, may it be found that we have all answered the call, followed the way, and finished well—and are able to respond to the final summons like Mr. Valiant-for-Truth in John Bunyan's *Pilgrim's Progress*:

> After this, it was noised abroad, that Mr. *Valiant-for-Truth* was taken with a summons by the same post as the other; and had this for a token that the summons was true, *That his pitcher was broken at the fountain.* When he understood it, he called for his friends, and told them of it. Then, said he, I am going to my Father's, and tho' with great difficulty I am got hither, yet now I do not repent me of all the trouble I have been at to arrive where I am. My *Sword* I give to him that shall succeed me in my Pilgrimage, and my *Courage* and *Skill* to him that can get it. My *marks* and *scars* I carry with me, to be a witness for me, that I have fought His battles, who now will be my Rewarder. When the day that he must go

hence was come, many accompany'd him to the River-side, into which as he went, he said *Death, where is thy Sting?* And as he went down deeper, he said, *Grave, where is thy Victory?* So he passed over, and all the Trumpets sounded for him on the other side.

GRATEFUL ACKNOWLEDGMENTS

H aving wrestled with the idea and issues of calling for more than thirty years, I owe a debt to more people than I could possibly mention. But I am specially grateful to the following:

To William Perkins, whose *Treatise of the Vocations or Callings of Men* (1603) first introduced me to the theme.

To Francis and Edith Schaeffer, whose example, love, and guidance was critical in the period I was discovering my calling.

To Gary Wilburn, at that time of Bel Air Presbyterian Church, who first invited me to speak on the subject.

To Al McDonald and the board of Trinity Forum, who encouraged me to take the time finally to get these ideas down on paper.

To Dick Ohman, Peter Edman, Margaret Gardner, Kyle Loveless, Amy Pye, and Debi Siler, my Trinity Forum colleagues, whose encouragement and support in the writing was practical and unflagging.

To Debi Siler, whose help in typing the manuscript was cheerful, flawless, and indefatigable.

To Robert Wolgemuth, the late Kip Jordon, Joey Paul, Lela Gilbert, Laura Kendall, and Janet Reed whose superb gifts and professionalism made the publishing and editing as pleasurable and painless as it could possibly be.

To Margaret Gardner, David Melvin, David Powlison, and David Wells, whose careful and critical response to the first draft of the book was invaluable in saving me from errors and improving the final version.

To Doug and Ann Holladay, Bob and Diane Kramer, Skip and Barbara Ryan, Bud and Jane Smith, and Ralph and Lynne Veerman, whose friendship, especially in the most difficult days of my journey, is beyond description and beyond repayment.

To Jenny and C.J., my family and closest partners in the journey.

And to the one before whom I simply stand, *Seulement, toujours, partout, malgré tous et malgré tout, et pour toujours. Soli Deo Gloria.*